GUS

W

AND LAUREY K.

Gustave Flaubert (1821–1880) is universally acknowledged to be among the greatest theorists and practitioners of the novel in the history of world literature. He has left an indelible stamp on the development of the genre with his masterpiece *Madame Bovary* (1857) and his later diverse works. Recognized as a master, both by his direct disciples Emile Zola, Alphonse Daudet, and Guy de Maupassant in France, and by novelists as disparate as Ivan Turgenev, Henry James, and James Joyce, Flaubert has received more critical attention than any other French novelist.

In this latest addition to Twayne's World Authors Series, William J. Berg and Laurey K. Martin offer a complete overview of Flaubert's fiction, from the early pieces to the major works: *Madame Bovary, Salammbô, Sentimental Education, The Temptation of Saint Anthony, Three Tales,* and *Bouvard and Pécuchet*. Through detailed readings based on stylistic and thematic analyses, the authors show how in each work Flaubert develops new literary forms and techniques that enable him to explore problems that plague humankind in a world devoid of sense and structure.

In their thorough study, Berg and Martin consider many of the critical approaches applied to Flaubert's works in order to add new perspectives. Their cogent examination of the novelist's own innovative theories about literature demonstrates how Flaubert inaugurated new ways of reading the novel. In answer to the question "Why Read Flaubert?" underlying this study, Berg and Martin contend that Flaubert's writings present an uncannily modern painting of the human condition and confirm the redemptive power of art in dealing with the problems that beset humankind.

Gustave Flaubert

Twayne's World Authors Series
French Literature

David O'Connell, Editor

Georgia State University

TWAS 866

GUSTAVE FLAUBERT (1821–1880)
Photograph by Mulnier.

Gustave Flaubert

William J. Berg and Laurey K. Martin

University of Wisconsin–Madison

Twayne Publishers
An Imprint of Simon & Schuster Macmillan
New York

Prentice Hall International
London • Mexico City • New Delhi • Singapore • Sydney • Toronto

Twayne's World Authors Series No. 866

Gustave Flaubert
William J. Berg and Laurey K. Martin

Twayne Publishers
An Imprint of Simon & Schuster Macmillan
1633 Broadway
New York, NY 10019

Library of Congress Cataloging-in-Publication Data

Berg, William J.
Gustave Flaubert / William J. Berg and Laurey K. Martin.
p. cm. — (English world authors series ; TWAS 866. French literature)
Includes bibliographical references and index.
ISBN 0-8057-8295-8 (alk. paper)
1. Flaubert, Gustave, 1821–1880—Criticism and interpretation. I. Martin, Laurey Kramer. II. Title. III. Series: Twayne's world authors series ; TWAS 866. IV. Series: Twayne's world authors series. French literature.
PQ2249.B43 1997
843'.8—dc21 96-39866
CIP

The paper used in this publication meets the minimum requirements of American National Standard for Information Sciences—Permanence of Paper for Printed Library Materials. ANSI Z39.48-1984. ∞ ™

10 9 8 7 6 5 4 3 2 1

Printed in the United States of America

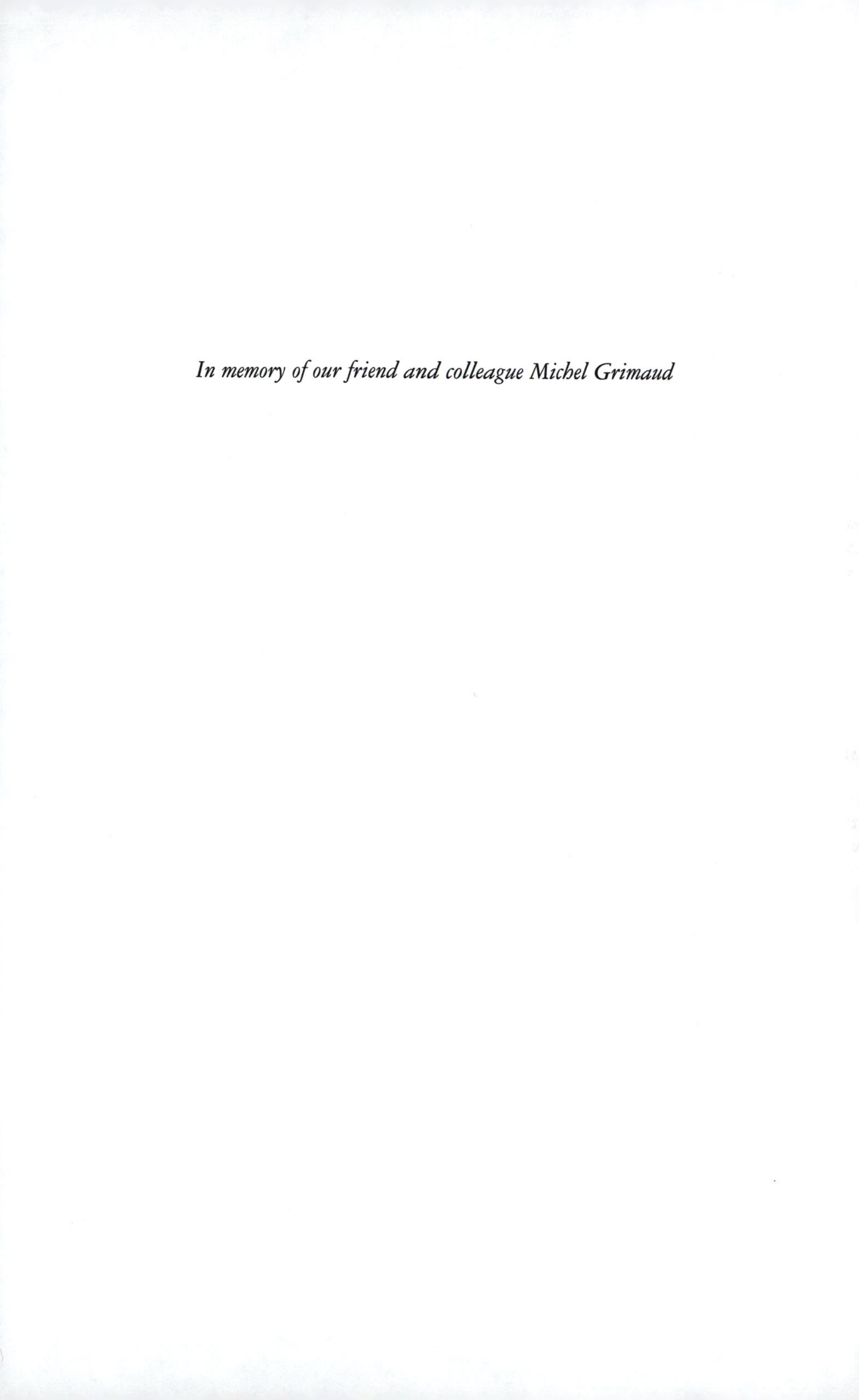

In memory of our friend and colleague Michel Grimaud

Contents

Publisher's Note

More than three decades have passed since the publication of *Gustave Flaubert* by Stratton Buck, the third volume in Twayne's World Authors series. In recognition of the many advances that have occurred in Flaubert scholarship in the interim, we are pleased to offer this new critical study of Gustave Flaubert, one of the acknowledged masters of the European novel.

Preface

Gustave Flaubert is universally acknowledged to be among the greatest theorists and practitioners of the novel in the history of world literature. Recognized as a master not only by his direct disciples Emile Zola, Alphonse Daudet, and Guy de Maupassant in France but by novelists as disparate as Ivan Turgenev, Henry James, and James Joyce, Flaubert left an indelible stamp on the development of the genre.

More critical attention has been focused on Flaubert than on any other French novelist, and since the publication of Stratton Buck's *Gustave Flaubert* in 1966 (TWAS #3), there has been an explosion of publications that represent a dizzying variety of approaches.[1] In our book, we take account of many of these approaches in order to add new perspectives to the reading of Flaubert's novels. Whereas Buck relates Flaubert's works primarily to the author, we expand this approach by relating his works to the reader, as does much of modern criticism.

In his voluminous correspondence, Flaubert expressed numerous innovative theories about literature.[2] In particular, three of his theoretical concepts foster new ways of reading, which we explore throughout our study:

1. "Style is, in and of itself, an absolute manner of seeing things."[3] Flaubert brought to the novel a stylistic density, an attention to sound patterns, rhythm, rhetorical figures, polyvalent meaning, grammar, and sentence structure previously reserved for poetry. We attempt to bring out these techniques and the ways in which they reinforce, even produce meaning in concrete textual analyses of selected passages from each of his works.[4] Flaubert's famous concept of *le mot juste,* or "the right word," has led critics to comment on the "accuracy" and "evocative power" of his descriptions, but we see Flaubert's use of words less in terms of their denotative function than in relation to the connotations they engender and the connections they establish within the text.

2. "The artist should be in his work like God in creation, invisible but all-powerful; one should never see him but sense him everywhere."[5] This oft-quoted dictum, paraphrased by Joyce in his *Portrait of the Artist,* is usually seen by novelists and critics in terms of the doctrine of narrative impartiality, the techniques by which the author distances himself from events and characters. We take the opposite tact and stress techniques by which the author asserts his power (albeit invisibly) in the fictive world and thus guides interpretation (however subtly). In short, in Flaubert's novels, the reader must assume a position alongside the narrator as well as with the characters.

3. "What seems beautiful to me, what I'd like to do, is a book about nothing, a book without external relationships, which would hold together by the internal force of its style, as the earth, without being supported, maintains itself in the air . . . a book that would have almost no subject or at least where the subject would be nearly invisible."[6] Again, whereas novelists and critics have focused on the possibility of an invisible or nonexistent subject in Flaubert's novels, we concentrate on the notion of internal force, of internal relationships. Individual textual elements (words, metaphors, objects, characters, scenes) must be read less as mirrors of the referential universe or repositories of meaning than as reflections of each other, as parts of patterns, configurations, networks of associations that run throughout the work and lend it its self-sufficient solidity. In short, Flaubert's works should be read in terms of their structure as well as their themes and plot.

Discovering all three of these principles as they operate in Flaubert's novels reminds us of the debt the modern reader, for whom such reading strategies have now become commonplace, owes to this master craftsman. In emphasizing his artistic techniques, however, we by no means see Flaubert as a sterile artisan—style is not an end but a means of expressing and indeed attaining meaning in the modern universe threatened by absurdity. Fortunately Flaubert did not write "a book about nothing," but he did write books about "nothingness," as well as excess, alienation, lack of communication, and other problems that plague human experience. Flaubert's novels are well wrought but nonetheless compellingly human.

The organization of our study of Flaubert's works and the ways of reading they inaugurated is as follows:

Chapter 1: Flaubert's Life

An initial chapter deals with the major events in Flaubert's life. On a personal level, it explores his temperament and his interactions with family, friends, and the various women in his life. On a literary level, it examines his early works (especially as they relate to the novels published during his lifetime, which are highlighted in the subsequent chapters of our book) along with his contacts and correspondence with other writers and critics of the time, notably Louis Bouilhet, Louise Colet, Maxime Du Camp, Ivan Turgenev, George Sand, and Guy de Maupassant.

Chapter 2: *Three Tales* (1877)

Our only violation of chronological order in presenting Flaubert's major works is to begin with *Three Tales,* his last complete work. These three short stories provide a concise introduction to the three distinct temporal spheres that dominate Flaubert's works: "A Simple Heart" depicts the contemporary bourgeois reality that also provides the setting for *Madame Bovary, Sentimental Education,* and *Bouvard and Pécuchet;* "The Legend of Saint Julian the Hospitaler" presents a medieval saint subject to hallucination and supernatural occurrences, much as does *The Temptation of Saint Anthony;* and "Herodias" involves the same detailed archaeological resurrection of ancient history that we find in *Salammbô*. Moreover, because of the reduced length of the three tales, the reader is able to follow easily Flaubert's creation of networks of associations—between parrot and Holy Ghost in "A Simple Heart," among father, stag, and leper in "Saint Julian," between Saint John's voice (spirituality) and Salome's body (sensuality) in "Herodias," a coupling that defines the very dualism of human existence for Herod and, indeed, for all of humankind as portrayed in Flaubert's universe.

Chapter 3: *Madame Bovary* (1857)

In addition to describing the novel's plot and themes (many of which have emerged from recent studies), we examine the operation of the three artistic principles and corresponding reading modes mentioned above. By positioning ourselves with the narrator in such scenes as the opening one showing Charles's first day in school, the famous country fair, and Léon's seduction of Emma in a coach, we witness Flaubert's process of controlled distancing, which leads to the sense of irony that permeates the novel. We also examine Flaubert's language (in describing Emma's wedding bouquet, her mealtime, her madness) in several short passages to illustrate the impact of style on the production of meaning. Finally, we trace patterns of internal associations surrounding objects (the plaster statue), scenes (the ball), and characters (the blind beggar) to capture the organizing principles that structure *Madame Bovary*'s fictional universe.

Chapter 4: *Salammbô* (1862)

Like "Herodias," *Salammbô* is structured according to a binary opposition that encompasses human traits, history, religion, and nature. On the one hand, Flaubert constructs a chain of feminine associations that link Salammbô, the goddess Tanit, the moon, water, and Carthage; on the other hand, he creates a parallel masculine series that involves Mâtho, Moloch, the sun, the desert, and the Barbarians. The novel's architecture seems so solid that any element reveals what is happening to the other elements in its network (by similarity) and in the other network (by opposition). Furthermore, the interaction of the two systems constitutes a dialectical relationship that evolves toward its inevitable conclusion, the death of both male and female, unable to coexist harmoniously or to exist independently without the other. At the same time, the characters' failure to comprehend events and each other mirrors the reader's struggle to grasp the text's elusive meanings, for which Tanit's veil is emblematic. It is, however, through art—through the narrator's dispassionate stance and the palpable power of Flaubert's style—that the fundamental oppositions of human experience are resolved, that certain forms of meaning are restored, fixed immutably on the page in this Parnassian poem of plasticity.

Chapter 5: *Sentimental Education* (1869)

In *Sentimental Education,* more than in any of the above works, Flaubert entrusts the viewpoint to his main character, Frédéric Moreau. The scope of the novel is thus more personal than panoramic and plastic, although the story is set against the broad backdrop of Paris and depicts historical events during the Revolution of 1848. Yet history, however magnificently it is represented, is but one more screen on which Frédéric projects his inner visions and longings, one more example of the failure of idealism. The novel is structured less by the kind of overwhelming networks that characterize *Salammbô* than by subtle patterns (the voyage between Paris and Nogent, the quest for Madame Arnoux), fluid pulsations (between immobility and movement, dream and reality, the present and the past), and clusters of characters that form rather obvious arrays of categorization (each of the four women in Frédéric's life embodies a type—Madame Arnoux, the ideal, Rosanette, the mundane, Madame Dambreuse, the sophisticated, Louise Roque, the naive—and Flaubert does the same for political positions and artistic theories). The structuring principles are more than architectural; they capture the very essence of Frédéric Moreau—the passive spectator embarked on a futile voyage, suspended between points, and paralyzed by equally plausible yet mutually exclusive alternatives in which the ideal falls before reality. Indeed, if there is an "education" it appears to involve *unlearning* one's ideals, a solution neither Frédéric (who nostalgically reminisces in the memorable final scene, the language and themes of which are analyzed in detail) nor Flaubert (the author in his quest for beauty) seems prepared to accept.

Chapter 6: *The Temptation of Saint Anthony* (1874)

Conceived as early as 1845, a first version of *The Temptation of Saint Anthony* was read in 1849 to Flaubert's friends Du Camp and Bouilhet, who advised him to burn it. The length of gestation suggests both the importance of the story to its author and the difficulty he had controlling the material. In fact, *The Temptation* is no doubt the strangest of Flaubert's complete works. It is less a novel than a dramatic monologue, interwoven with dialogues between the saint and various mythological characters, through which we glimpse his cascading visions, philosophies, prophecies, and temptations. Without the controlling presence of the third-person narrator and the reassuring organization of a plot, the work threatens to dissolve into nothingness, the author's ultimate temptation. As in "Saint Julian," however, Flaubert is successful in transposing the medieval content into a psychological context in which the structuring mechanisms of dream and desire—displacement, substitution, and symbolism—rescue the work from meaningless chaos. As Michel Foucault has noted, the Bible the saint is reading engenders a certain number of the fantasies that beset him; it is our contention that others stem from the visual elements of the initial setting (the tree, the cross, the abyss). Together, these sources illustrate Flaubert's principles of self-engendering and transmuting forms and also lend the work a compelling organic unity despite the twin temptations of profusion and nothingness.

Chapter 7: *Bouvard and Pécuchet* (1881)

Published posthumously and never completed, *Bouvard and Pécuchet* has nonetheless drawn a great deal of critical attention, especially in recent years. As the two former copyists attempt to master all of human knowledge, their excursions into archaeology, chemistry, geology, and medicine meet with the same resounding failure as their explorations of politics, literature, religion, and education. Theory fails not only in the light of other, equally plausible theories but especially before reality, whose amorphous forms fail to comply with the sharp lines of systematic thought. On the surface the work's irony seems directed at the former clerks, whose naive inflexibility creates a great deal of humor, and more generally at humanity itself, whose knowledge and culture is clearly inadequate to deal with the complexities of human experience. On yet another level, in guiding the copyists through the very areas of study that characterize his own works, Flaubert clearly burlesques his encyclopedic propensity for research, cataloguing, and learning (indeed, he could not help but confront the irony that, in order to make fun of the clerks' excessive pedantry, he himself had to skim through some 1,500 volumes). Finally, readers who have wrestled with the multifaceted rigors of a liberal arts education and struggled to resurrect enough of freshman philosophy to understand chapter 8 must recognize themselves in the futile efforts of the copyists. Indeed, the novel is particularly poignant in an era that has seen an explosion of human knowledge and no concomitant reduction in human problems and suffering. Although the copyists' final decision to return to copying can be read as a rejection of the possibility of original endeavor, it might also be seen as a celebration of the value of work itself, regardless of goal or success, of writing as its own reward, of reading for the pleasure of the text.

Chapter 8: Why Read Flaubert?

In the conclusion we attempt to answer the rather inevitable question that underlies this study, focused as it is on reading tactics and the reader: why do we read Flaubert today? Exploring this question affords us the opportunity to draw all of Flaubert's works together and to reiterate our main contention that his writings present an uncannily modern painting of the human condition while suggesting the redemptive power of art in dealing with the problems that beset humankind.

Acknowledgments

Coincidentally, as we were putting the finishing touches on this book, our former colleague and longtime friend Alfred Glauser, professor emeritus of the University of Wisconsin, was cleaning out his Madison apartment. In doing so, he gave us many books—dictionaries, encyclopedias, critical editions, and cookbooks!—that we had long admired and will continue to cherish. This tangible gift is itself symbolic of Alfred Glauser's intellectual legacy, as evidenced in his contention, reiterated in some 10 books and a lifetime of brilliant lectures, that a great literary work is, among other things, about literature itself. Alfred Glauser's ideas permeate the pages of this study, which we are proud to dedicate to him.

We would also like to thank Impressions Book and Journal Services for their conscientious editing of the manuscript and Associate Editor Margaret Dornfeld of Twayne Publishers for shepherding the book through the various stages of production. We are especially grateful to our general editor, David O'Connell, for asking us to do a second book in the Twayne's World Authors Series, a collection whose goal is the highest to which scholarship can aspire: the universal sharing of ideas.

Acknowledgments

Chronology

1812 Marriage of Dr. Achille-Cléophas Flaubert and Anne-Justine-Caroline Fleuriot, Gustave Flaubert's parents.

1813 Birth of the Flauberts' first child, Achille. They would eventually have six children, three of whom would die in infancy.

1821 Gustave Flaubert born in Rouen 12 December.

1824 Birth of Caroline Flaubert, Gustave's younger sister.

1830 Flaubert begins to write plays that are staged for family and servants in collaboration with his sister and childhood friends Ernest Chevalier and Alfred Le Poittevin.

1832 Flaubert enters the Collège Royal in Rouen. Reads voraciously and continues writing.

1836 Meets Elisa Schlésinger during a summer trip to Trouville and is immediately and lastingly infatuated. Begins writing *Memories of a Madman*.

1838 Completes *Memories of a Madman.*

1839 Composes *Smarh*.

1840 Passes his baccalaureate exams and travels to Corsica and the Pyrenees. In Marseilles, has an affair with Eulalie Foucaud.

1841 Registers for legal studies in Paris in November.

1842 Meets the Colliers, with their daughters Harriet and Gertrude, during a September visit to Trouville. Writes *November*. Passes his first-year law exam in December.

1843 Begins friendship with Maxime Du Camp. Fails his second-year law exam in August. Begins writing the first *Sentimental Education*. Meets Victor Hugo.

1844 In January has a seizure while riding in a carriage with his brother Achille. Withdraws from legal studies and retreats to Croisset.

1845 Completes the first *Sentimental Education*. Caroline Flaubert marries Emile Hamard. Flaubert and his parents accompany them on their wedding trip. In Genoa Flaubert sees the Breughel painting that later inspires *The Temptation of Saint Anthony.*

1846 Dr. Flaubert dies in January. Caroline Hamard gives birth to a daughter, Caroline, a few days later and succumbs to puerperal fever in March. Marriage of Alfred Le Poittevin. Beginning of Flaubert's friendship with Louis Bouilhet. Beginning of amorous liaison with Louise Colet.

1847 Flaubert and Du Camp travel through Normandy, Brittany, and Touraine. They jointly write *Across Field and Strand* on their return.

1848 Flaubert and Bouilhet travel to Paris to observe the events of the revolution. Death of Alfred Le Poittevin. Emile Hamard begins to lose his sanity; Madame Flaubert is awarded custody of Caroline. Flaubert begins writing the first version of *The Temptation of Saint Anthony*. Frequent quarrels with Louise Colet.

1849 Completes the first *Saint Anthony*. Reads it to Bouilhet and Du Camp, who suggest he abandon it. In November departs for the Middle East with Du Camp.

1850 Continues travels in Middle East.

1851 Returns to Croisset and begins writing *Madame Bovary*.

1852 Quarrels with Du Camp, who has become codirector of the *Revue de Paris*. Meets Louise Colet in Paris or Mantes every few months.

1853 Begins a correspondence with Victor Hugo. Learns that the Schlésingers have moved to Baden after encountering financial problems.

1854 Final rupture with Louise Colet.

1856 Reconciliation with Du Camp. *Madame Bovary* is published in installments in the *Revue de Paris*. Flaubert begins working on a second version of *The Temptation of Saint Anthony*.

1857 Trial in January of Flaubert and the editors of the *Revue de Paris* for offending religion and public morals in *Madame Bovary*. They are acquitted in February. In April *Madame Bovary* is published in book form by Michel Lévy. Flaubert decides not to pursue publication of *Saint Anthony* and begins a new project on ancient Carthage that will become *Salammbô*. Begins his correspondence with Marie-Sophie Leroyer de Chantepie.

1858 Spends the winter in Paris socializing with other writers (especially Sainte-Beuve, Théophile Gautier, Ernest Feydeau) and various actresses (particularly Jeanne de Tourbey). In April travels to Tunisia to visit the ruins of Carthage.

1859 Louise Colet publishes *Him,* a vengeful roman à clef that portrays Flaubert as insensitive and overly glum.

1860 Becomes friends with Edmond and Jules de Goncourt.

1862 Completes *Salammbô,* which is published in November.

1863 Begins correspondence with George Sand. Socializes with Princess Mathilde, who introduces him to the emperor, Napoleon III. Attends the Magny dinners, where he meets the Russian writer Ivan Turgenev. Begins to receive visitors every Sunday afternoon in his Paris apartment.

1864 Flaubert's niece Caroline marries Ernest Commanville in April. In May he begins to outline the second *Sentimental Education*. In the fall is invited to Compiègne by the emperor.

1865 Begins composing the definitive version of *Sentimental Education.*

1866 Named knight in the Legion of Honor.

1869 Completes *Sentimental Education* in May; it is published in November. Begins a third version of *The Temptation of Saint Anthony*. Bouilhet dies in July; Flaubert takes on the sad and time-consuming task of literary executor. Sainte-Beuve dies in October.

1870 Jules de Goncourt dies in June. The Franco-Prussian War breaks out; Flaubert becomes a lieutenant in the National Guard. The Flauberts are forced to billet Prussian soldiers at Croisset.

1871 Experiences bitterness and depression as a reaction to the war and the events of the Paris Commune. Returns to work on *Saint Anthony.*

1872 Flaubert's mother dies in April, leaving the property in Croisset to her granddaughter Caroline; Flaubert is accorded life tenancy. Rupture with Michel Lévy over the publication of Bouilhet's posthumous *Last Songs.* Begins friendship with Edmond Laporte. Starts to outline *Bouvard and Pécuchet.*

1873 Georges Charpentier agrees to become Flaubert's new publisher. Flaubert composes a theatrical comedy, *The Candidate*.

1874 *The Candidate* closes after its fourth performance. *The Temptation of Saint Anthony* is published in April.

1875 Works on *Bouvard and Pécuchet* early in the year, then puts it aside to write "The Legend of Saint Julian," the first of his *Three Tales*. Sells his property in Deauville to help the Commanvilles save their failing lumber business, impoverishing himself in the process.

1876 Composes "A Simple Heart" and begins "Herodias."

1877 Completes "Herodias"; Charpentier publishes *Three Tales* in April. Returns to work on *Bouvard and Pécuchet.*

1878 Suffers poor health and continued financial worries.

1879 In January slips on the ice and breaks his leg; remains bedridden for several months. After concerted lobbying efforts by his friends, is appointed deputy director of the Mazarine Library, with a small income.

1880 Begins the final chapter of the first part of *Bouvard and Pécuchet*. Suffers a cerebral hemorrhage and dies 8 May.

1881 Posthumous publication of *Bouvard and Pécuchet*.

Chapter One

Flaubert's Life

The Formative Years: From Malaise to Malady

Gustave Flaubert was born on 12 December 1821 in Rouen, a city he came to scorn as the epitome of self-satisfied bourgeois provincialism.[1] His family resided in the Hôtel Dieu, a hospital where his father was chief surgeon, and it has been often claimed that this gloomy medical milieu influenced the young Gustave's inherent pessimism as well as his penchant for meticulous, "scientific" observation. His early family life was far from happy: Gustave differed dramatically in temperament from his energetic and practical father, and their personality conflicts led to frequent disputes.[2] Madame Flaubert doted on her children but manipulated them throughout their lives through her moodiness and emotional dependence. The family's eldest child, Achille, was nine years older than Gustave and determined to follow his father into the practice of medicine. He played virtually no role in Gustave's young life except as a rival for their father's approval and affection. Only Caroline, three years younger than Gustave and the baby of the family, provided him with undemanding friendship and affection. He was devoted to her, and she became his first "disciple," as he shared with her his knowledge and ideas. Gustave also benefited from the companionship of Julie, the faithful family servant who continued in his service until the time of his death (and who many feel served as the model for Félicité in his tale "A Simple Heart").

Flaubert had only two close childhood friends: Ernest Chevalier, who shared his passionate interest in literature, and Alfred Le Poittevin, who shared his introspective, melancholy temperament, his insecure ambition, and his disgust with life. His earliest writings (1830) were plays staged before servants and relatives in the billiard room at the Hôtel Dieu in collaboration with Caroline, Ernest, Alfred, and Alfred's sister Laure (who later became the mother of the short-story writer Guy de Maupassant). Gustave never distinguished himself in school but nonetheless read voraciously, preferring Shakespeare, Goethe, Byron, Hugo, and Montaigne. Like many adolescents of his generation, he was swept up in the romantic exaltation and despair of such writers as Chateaubriand, Lamartine, and Vigny. Much of his early writing displays this romantic bent, including the pessimistic *Passion and Virtue* (*Passion et vertu,* 1837), the grotesque *Drunk and Dead* (*Ivre et mort,* 1838), the metaphysical *Smarh* (1839), and various autobiographical confessions, including *Memories of a Madman* (*Mémoires d'un fou,* 1838) and *November* (*Novembre*, 1842).

During a family vacation to Trouville in 1836 Flaubert met Maurice Schlésinger, the director of a music-publishing house, and his wife, Elisa. Eleven years Gustave's senior, Madame Schlésinger provoked in the young man an infatuation that became a lasting passion. Unattainable, she symbolized for him the incarnation of all that was worth seeking in earthly love. He continued to adore her throughout his life, yet although she was undoubtedly aware of his devotion to her, it is not clear to what extent she was aware of or acknowledged the passion that underlay it. What Flaubert did not know (and perhaps never knew) was that at the time of their first meeting Elisa was not, in fact, Maurice Schlésinger's wife. Elisa, née Foucault, had married Emile Judée, an army officer, when she was 19, then left him for reasons that remain unknown. Divorce was not possible in France at the time, and thus, although she and Maurice posed as husband and wife and had a six-month-old daughter at the time of their introduction to Flaubert, they did not actually marry until after Judée's death in 1839. Her irregular civil status notwithstanding, Elisa Schlésinger had a profound effect not just on Flaubert's emotional development (he never seemed to associate love and fulfillment) but on his creative output, serving as the inspiration for Maria in *Memories of a Madman,* for Marie in *November,* for Madame Renaud in the first *Sentimental Education,* and finally for Madame Arnoux in the definitive *Sentimental Education*.

In 1840 Flaubert passed his baccalaureate exams and was rewarded by his family with a trip to the Pyrenees and Corsica. While in Marseilles he engaged in a brief but torrid affair with Eulalie Foucaud, whom he met in the street on his way back from the beach and who, like Elisa Schlésinger, surpassed him in age enough to exert a maternal as well as a physical attraction. On his return he was pressured by his family to choose a respectable career and after much hesitation finally agreed to study law. His enthusiasm for the law was strictly limited, and his studies were sporadic at best. In November of 1841 he went to Paris and registered for classes but almost immediately returned to Rouen, ostensibly to read the law but in fact to pursue his true interest, literature. After a short period of intensive study, he passed the first-year law exam in December of 1842, but his pattern of neglect followed by frantic preparation could not sustain him for long and, much to his humiliation, he failed the second-year exam in August of 1843.

During the time of his studies in Paris he renewed acquaintance with the Schlésingers, frequented the studio of the sculptor Pradier (where he met Victor Hugo), and became a regular visitor at the home of the Colliers, an English family with two eligible daughters he had met at Trouville. Both Gertrude and Harriet Collier fell in love with the handsome young Frenchman. Gertrude pursued him quite openly, but Flaubert preferred her sister. Harriet shared Flaubert's love of literature, and because she had a spine ailment that made her more or less an invalid, he read to her for hours on end. He briefly considered marrying her, but the relationship cooled, perhaps because of her father's concern regarding Flaubert's struggles with his legal studies, perhaps because of Flaubert's own disgust and despair at this stage of his life, perhaps, ironically, given what was to develop, because Flaubert found her invalid status too limiting.

During this period Flaubert also made the acquaintance of Maxime Du Camp, whom he immediately recognized as a kindred spirit. Du Camp shared his vague, unfocused desires and sorrows along with his disdain for contemporary society. They held common literary ambitions and tastes and remained close friends, confidants, and traveling companions for many years. A gulf developed between them in the early 1850s because of a difference of opinion about the proper way to achieve artistic success, but their friendship survived until Flaubert's death.

In January 1844, while riding in a carriage with his brother, Flaubert was suddenly struck by a seizure that he later described as causing him to feel as though he were being carried off in a cascade of flames. Although Flaubert himself referred to his disease with such euphemisms as "a nervous ailment," it is generally believed today that he suffered from a form of epilepsy, which at the time was a feared and mysterious illness considered by many as a sort of divine curse. The precise diagnosis notwithstanding, he was subject to seizures for the rest of his life, and his illness greatly influenced the course of his existence. He withdrew from his legal studies and retreated to an estate his father purchased at Croisset. There he devoted himself entirely to literature, renouncing participation in the active life of society for meditation, observation, and artistic creation, which led to his becoming known as "the hermit of Croisset."

The Early Works: Traces of Autobiography

Before the onset of his illness, the most notable of Flaubert's literary efforts were primarily autobiographical.[3] *Memories of a Madman* (begun in 1836 and completed in 1838) is essentially formless, consisting of the random flow of the author's ideas, many of which parallel those of his favorite writers at the time. Thus the text resounds with echoes of Rousseau's self-pity, the ennui of Chateaubriand's René, and Montaigne's skepticism.

The central theme of *Memories* is one of loss. A telling example is the dream the narrator recalls in which he is strolling along a riverbank with his mother when she suddenly disappears into the water. Looking into the river, he sees only his own reflection and is either unwilling or unable to go to her rescue. In another episode he begins to recount his memory of visiting an old lady in a castle, but just after introducing her to the reader he breaks off the story, bemoaning the fact that the woman is now dead and her castle a factory. In another episode he meets a handsome, dark-haired woman named Maria (a projection of Elisa Schlésinger) at the seashore. He rescues her coat from the water but is unable to stop the waves from continuously washing away her footprints. He loves her but, realizing he cannot have her, comes to despise love, all the while knowing his passion for her will never disappear.

Another important theme of *Memories of a Madman* is that of doubt. It is not an easily read text because the temporal relationship between the various episodes the narrator recounts is often ambiguous and the boundary between reminiscing and imagining remains generally hazy. The "I" in *Memories* is not only narrator and character but also reader, who in the dedication introducing the work declares he is not sure that he recognizes himself in the self-portrait he has produced. At this early stage, Flaubert was already struggling with the imperfection of language as a means of communication and with the profound differences between representation and reality.

In *Smarh* (1839), the title character, who desires knowledge to set himself apart from the common man, is tempted by Satan, who promises to dispel his ignorance but, in doing so, introduces him to despair in the face of the inexorable fatality that governs the universe. (This notion of fatality recurs in *Madame Bovary*.) Smarh, reflecting his creator's mind-set in the late 1830s, combines the egotistical desire of Goethe's Faust and the ennui of Chateaubriand's René. Thematically and structurally (much of the first half of the work takes the form of a dramatic dialogue) *Smarh* foreshadows Flaubert's various versions of *The Temptation of Saint Anthony,* while its scenes of carnage point toward the violence and bloodshed in *Salammbô.*

November (1842) is the story of a young romantic who is unable to adapt to the human condition and who eventually dies under the weight of his own pessimism: "Finally, last December, he died, but slowly, little by little, by the force of thought alone, without any organ having been ill, just as one dies of sadness." This hero, another incarnation of the author, also owes much to Chateaubriand's René, especially the ennui from which he suffers yet in which he revels.

November, like *Memories of a Madman,* is filled with musings and reminiscences, but the tone of the later work differs in being markedly bitter. Also, whereas *Memories of a Madman* is characterized by platonic love and vague desires, *November* examines sensuality and carnal love. Elisa Schlésinger, still the object of the young Flaubert's desire, appears this time as the figure of Marie, the hero's prostitute mistress. (Evidently, since the overwhelmingly emotional first meeting with Madame Schlésinger, Flaubert's obsession with her had grown increasingly erotic.) Like *Memories of a Madman, November* is narrated primarily in the first person, although near the end of the tale there is a narrative shift: a friend of the hero finds the uncompleted manuscript, which he proceeds to elaborate and comment on.

The first *Sentimental Education,* begun in 1843 and completed in 1845, was the first novel-like work that Flaubert wrote entirely in the third person, although it was still autobiographical in nature. It is marked by a complicated plot, an inconsistent chronology, and a resulting sense of disjointedness. Although it shares a title and some elements with the later-published and definitive *Sentimental Education,* it also foreshadows many of the themes and situations that appear in *Madame Bovary.*

There are two protagonists in the original *Sentimental Education,* each of whom represents a certain aspect of Flaubert. Henry is a young student who falls in love and has an affair with Madame Renaud, the wife of the director of his rooming house (and yet another incarnation of Elisa Schlésinger). When their passion begins to wane they conclude that their surroundings are to blame. They flee to America, where they soon run out of money without having rekindled the flames of their attraction. They come back to France; Madame Renaud returns to her husband, and Henry goes on to become a success in the world, desired for his beauty, envied for his spirit, sought after for his talent. Jules, Henry's childhood friend, is a would-be writer who learns that romantic ideals cannot be reconciled with life. Duped and then abandoned by Lucinde, the woman he loves, he contemplates suicide but decides instead to dedicate himself to his art. He adopts the attitude of a spectator rather than that of a participant in life: "Existence provides him with the accidental, he renders it immutable; what life offers him, he gives to art."

By 1845 it was clear that Flaubert was maturing, both emotionally and artistically. While these early autobiographical works are imperfect, especially in comparison with the carefully crafted works he later published, they offer—at a time that antedates his voluminous correspondence—a valuable archaeology of his intellectual and creative development and provide useful insights into his feelings and ideas during his adolescence and early adulthood.

The Hermit of Croisset

After the onset of Flaubert's illness, his life was basically defined by his work, punctuated by his travels, and enlivened by a few close friendships. By March of 1845 he was well enough to accompany his family on his sister Caroline's honeymoon. They went first to Paris (where Gustave visited the Colliers and renewed acquaintance with Louise Pradier, who had left her husband to live with a younger man), then to Nogent-sur-Seine, then to Marseille (where he futilely attempted to locate Eulalie Foucaud). In Genoa he saw Breughel's painting *The Temptation of Saint Anthony* and wrote to his friend Alfred Le Poittevin that it had provoked his interest in writing a play on the same subject. In general, however, Flaubert found the trip frustrating and confining, and he did not regret that it was cut short.

The following year, 1846, was one of loss for Flaubert. His father died in January as the result of an abscess on his leg, and in March his beloved sister, Caroline, finally succumbed to a puerperal fever incurred when she gave birth to a daughter a few days after her father's death. After Caroline's funeral Gustave and his mother retreated to Croisset with Caroline's daughter, also named Caroline, whom they were determined to raise. The Flauberts had never liked Emile Hamard, Caroline's choice of husband—Gustave considered him pitiable in his stupidity and the incarnation of vulgarity—and did not consider him a suitable parent or role model for her child. An additional loss occurred in June when Alfred Le Poittevin got married. Flaubert felt abandoned by his fellow artist and worried that his friend would slip from the role of poet into that of mere bourgeois. Although he maintained that his concerns were only for Alfred and his art, at bottom he undoubtedly worried that, once married, his friend would not be there for him in times of need.

Eighteen forty-six was also a time of new beginnings. Not only was Caroline Hamard born, but in May Flaubert renewed acquaintance with a schoolmate, Louis Bouilhet, who would become his faithful friend and trusted critic, and in July he met Louise Colet. "La Muse," as she was called, was a beautiful and successful poetess. She and Flaubert became lovers, but almost from the start theirs was a troubled relationship, detailed in the lengthy and numerous letters they exchanged. (Their correspondence continued for eight years and informs us today not only of their affections but of the progress of Flaubert's works and his ideas on art and literature.) Louise longed for Flaubert's constant attention and sought continual proof of his devotion; he was constrained by his mother's demands and by his own personality: his fear of attachments that would upset the calm necessary for his nerves and his work and his reluctance to put anything ahead of art. He refused to declare his eternal love and make her the defining point in his life; the more she pushed, pleaded, and cajoled, the more determined he became in his course. He offered not to see her so as not to make her suffer but declined to take the initiative of breaking off definitively, a rupture that did not occur until 1854.

In the spring and early summer of 1847 Flaubert and Maxime Du Camp traveled together in Brittany, Normandy, and Touraine, then in the fall collaborated on a joint work entitled *Across Field and Strand* (*Par les champs et par les grèves*), which they decided not to publish. Early the next year when the Revolution of 1848 broke out, Flaubert was in Paris with Bouilhet and Du Camp, hoping to observe the events from an artist's point of view. All in all 1848 was a sad and stressful year for Flaubert. In April Alfred Le Poittevin died, and although they had been estranged after Le Poittevin's marriage, Flaubert rallied to his friend's sickbed, providing companionship and solace until the end. Family life for Flaubert was stressful; Madame Flaubert did little to disguise her continuing sadness at the loss of her husband and daughter; Emile Hamard had begun to lose his sanity and was causing legal troubles (that summer Madame Flaubert finally obtained a court order awarding her temporary custody of Caroline); little Caroline reacted to her uncle's ill-concealed anxieties and frustration with tears and what he feared to be hallucinations like his own. Meanwhile, frequent quarrels marred his relationship with Louise Colet.

It was in the spring of 1848 that Flaubert began writing the first version (of three) of *The Temptation of Saint Anthony*. When it was completed in the early fall of the following year, he read the work aloud to Bouilhet and Du Camp to get their reaction. It was not favorable: finding it too vague, too personal, too lyrical and romantic, they suggested that he throw the manuscript into the fire and never mention it again.

In November of 1849 Flaubert and Du Camp embarked on a trip to the Middle East and southern Europe: Alexandria, Cairo, Beirut, Jerusalem, Tripoli, Rhodes, Constantinople, and Athens. The voyage was traumatic for Flaubert because it revealed to him the extent of his attachment to his mother; he had long railed against the tyranny of her affection but now realized that he as much as she was responsible for his inability to love and marry a woman his own age. Other women—various prostitutes, Louise Colet, the actresses who would follow her as objects of his desire—were fine to satisfy his (considerable) sexual appetite, but in the realm of love and devotion his mother could know no rival. Nonetheless, Flaubert ended up enjoying the trip, soaking up local color and customs and admiring the proud vestiges of antiquity. Artistically, his observation of the frequent juxtaposition of the beautiful and the squalid reinforced his sense of the grotesque, while philosophically, his observation of social interactions convinced him that human stupidity, selfishness, and maliciousness were universal.

Fame and Notoriety: *Madame Bovary*

On his return to France in 1851 he began writing *Madame Bovary,* a task that was to occupy him until 1856. The rhythm of his days was fixed: in the morning he instructed his niece; then he worked alone in his study from early afternoon until the middle of the night, taking only a short break for the evening meal. During the weekend, Bouilhet frequently visited; during these visits they passed their time reading and critiquing each other's work. Occasionally, Flaubert would rendezvous with Louise Colet in Paris or in Mantes for a brief respite from the strain of writing. During this five-year period Flaubert quarreled with Du Camp, who had become the codirector of the *Revue de Paris* (1852), began to correspond with Victor Hugo (1853), learned that the Schlésingers, bankrupt, had moved to Baden (1853), ended definitively his liaison with Louise Colet (1854), took up with the actress Béatrix Person (1854), and reconciled with Du Camp (1856).

The process of writing *Madame Bovary* was arduous. Anxious to avoid the pitfalls of personal commentary and excessive lyricism that had provoked his friends' negative reactions to *Saint Anthony,* he focused his attention on matters of structure and style to a degree unknown in his previous writing. Word choice, sound, rhythm, tone, coherence, and connections between parts of the work became obsessions. Every sentence was written, modified, corrected, read aloud, rewritten until he found the exact expression to capture his idea. Often he produced no more than three pages in a week, and occasionally he spent five or six days working on a single page. When the novel was complete, he agreed to let Du Camp's *Revue de Paris* publish it in six installments.

During publication problems arose. Flaubert was adamant that the *Revue de Paris* editors not make any changes or cuts in his carefully crafted manuscript—cuts that the editors felt compelled to make so as not to offend their readers and particularly in order to avoid condemnation by the government. *The Revue* had already been warned twice by the conservative government of the Second Empire (which considered the publication excessively liberal) and feared being shut down if accused of another transgression. Flaubert, on the other hand, for whom artistic considerations outweighed all others, declared that he cared nothing about irritating the magazine's bourgeois readers and even less about being taken to court, but in spite of his protests, certain "offensive" scenes (Emma and Léon's carriage ride in Rouen, part of the scene depicting Emma's death) were, in fact, deleted from the published installments. Despite these omissions, after the publication of the last installment, Flaubert and the magazine were indicted for transgressions against religion and morality. The trial was held on 29 January 1857, and a verdict of acquittal was rendered nine days later; Flaubert's defense had been based on the notion that *Madame Bovary* was actually eminently moral, inciting virtuous behavior by inspiring horror at the results of vice. The complete novel was then published by Michel Lévy at the end of April and enjoyed immediate success, due in part to the notoriety the trial had provided its author.

Maturity

After the publication of *Madame Bovary,* Flaubert decided not to pursue publication of the second version of *Saint Anthony* that he had been working on (perhaps to avoid potential new charges of immorality and disrespect for religion) and instead undertook a new project, a novel dealing with ancient Carthage. He began writing the first chapter of what would ultimately become *Salammbô* in the fall of 1857 and did not complete the book until early 1862. In the intervening years, he spent much time in Paris, hobnobbing with other writers (Sainte-Beuve, Théophile Gautier, Ernest Feydeau, the Goncourt brothers, George Sand) and frequenting *les lionnes* ("the lionesses"), an assortment of fashionable actresses and *demi-mondaines,* including Auguste Sabatier, Suzanne Lagier, and Jeanne de Tourbey. He entered into a lasting correspondence with Marie-Sophie Leroyer de Chantepie, a spinster some 20 years his senior who initially contacted him to compliment him on the "truth" of *Madame Bovary*. Although they never met, she became a confidante and sounding board, and he paid her the ultimate compliment by saying that they could talk together like two men. He reacted with detachment to Louise Colet's publication of her vengeful novel *Him* (*Lui*), a thinly disguised roman à clef about her affairs with Flaubert and Alfred de Musset. He also made a short trip to Tunisia to experience firsthand the landscape that would frame his Carthaginian novel, a trip that caused him to discard all he had written to date on the project and begin afresh.

Salammbô was completed in April of 1862 and published by Lévy in November of that year (although it was dated 1863). It sold well, but critical reaction was mixed at best. Sainte-Beuve found it overly classic and virtually unreadable, but Baudelaire felt its scope and grandeur more than overcame its flaws. In 1863 Flaubert continued his social activities in Paris, visiting more and more frequently Princess Mathilde, who became a close friend and who introduced him to her cousin, Emperor Napoleon III, and the empress. As his social contacts with the imperial court increased, he could not really hide his pride and pleasure, although he maintained a good-natured self-knowledge about his vanity in this area. He began receiving visitors regularly at his Paris apartment on Sunday afternoons. Eighteen sixty-three also marked the beginning of his long correspondence with George Sand and his friendship with the Russian author Ivan Turgenev.

In 1864 Flaubert's niece Caroline married Ernest Commanville, a timber dealer. Flaubert knew that he would miss her liveliness and cheerfulness at Croisset. He believed that no spouse could ever match her wit and intelligence, but he consoled himself with the notion that Commanville could at least offer her financial security. Often alone at Croisset after Caroline's marriage, Flaubert set to work on a new novel, the second *Sentimental Education,* the composition of which would occupy him until 1869. He maintained his literary and imperial social contacts and in 1866 was named to the Legion of Honor. During this period he also reestablished contact with Elisa Schlésinger, who had been hospitalized with depression earlier in the decade. His dear friend Bouilhet died of kidney disease in the summer of 1869, having bequeathed to Flaubert, his literary executor, the tasks of arranging for the staging of his just-completed play *Mademoiselle Aïssé* and of determining which of his unpublished works should appear posthumously. Sainte-Beuve's death followed shortly thereafter the same year, and these two deaths marked the beginning of a progressive shrinking of the circle of Flaubert's intimate friends. In fact, in the next four years he would lose his mother, Maurice Schlésinger, and his writer friends Jules de Goncourt, Théophile Gautier, and Ernest Feydeau.

When the definitive *Sentimental Education* appeared in print in November 1869 (dated 1870) it was neither a popular nor a critical success. Flaubert was disappointed but soon reconciled himself to the critics' judgment and began to acknowledge some of the book's shortcomings. In 1870 the Franco-Prussian War interrupted Flaubert's creative work. He served as a lieutenant in the National Guard and after the defeat of the imperial forces at Sédan was forced to billet Prussian soldiers at Croisset. Fortunately, none of his carefully preserved manuscripts were lost or damaged during this occupation. He was appalled by the events of the Commune and expressed disgust with the rebellious Parisian workers who took to the barricades.

In 1871 he took up again the reworking of *Saint Anthony,* a task he had undertaken in 1869 just before Bouilhet's death. He completed the definitive version of this work, which had followed, even haunted, him throughout his writing career, during the summer of 1872, and it was finally published in 1874. (Having quarreled with Michel Lévy over the publication of Bouilhet's *Last Songs,* Flaubert needed a new publisher and in 1873 made a deal with Georges Charpentier.) *Saint Anthony* sold fairly well, but critical reaction was lukewarm. During the early 1870s Flaubert suffered from bouts of depression provoked by loneliness after the deaths of so many close friends and distress at approaching old age. When his mother died in the spring of 1872 he was struck once again by the strength of his emotional attachment to her and proclaimed that losing her was like having part of his own body ripped away. During this time he did, however, make a new friend, Edmond Laporte, a factory manager who lived a few miles from Croisset. Laporte had no connections to the literary or Parisian social circles inhabited by Flaubert's other intimates but would provide the writer with loyal companionship in his later years. Meanwhile, George Sand continued to be his closest confidante, bolstering his spirits and encouraging him to be less misanthropic. In addition to addressing personal issues, their correspondence constituted a compelling dialogue on literary aesthetics.

The Last Years: Toward Immortality

In the summer of 1872 Flaubert started work on *Bouvard and Pécuchet,* a project that was to be interrupted by the composition of a theatrical comedy, *The Candidate* (1873), a flop that closed after four performances, and *Three Tales* (begun in 1875 and published in 1877). In 1875 financial disaster struck when Commanville's lumber business failed. Flaubert, who was devoted to his niece, sold his farm at Deauville (which amounted to the majority of his remaining capital—some of which had already been invested with and eaten up by Commanville) and gave the money to Caroline and her husband, but it was too little to save the business from liquidation. Having thus impoverished himself, Flaubert was to live the rest of his life in difficult financial straits, dependent on the Commanvilles—who were not always prompt in advancing the small sums he needed to meet his obligations. Happily, Caroline was able to hold on to the property at Croisset, which Madame Flaubert had bequeathed to her on the condition that Gustave be allowed to live there until his death, provided he did not marry. In 1876 Flaubert suffered another loss with the death of his dear friend George Sand.

After the publication of *Three Tales* in the spring of 1877, Flaubert returned to work on *Bouvard and Pécuchet*. He worked steadily through 1878 and 1879 although his health had begun to fail, and in early 1879 he was bedridden for months after slipping on the ice and fracturing his leg. He was estranged from his friend Laporte out of loyalty to Caroline, who was bitter that Laporte would not do more to help with their continuing business woes. (He had, nonetheless, guaranteed a certain number of notes that had helped the Commanvilles to avoid total bankruptcy.) Worry over the Commanvilles' ongoing money problems and embarrassment about his own financial distress plagued Flaubert also. In Paris, various friends and admirers (especially the writers Turgenev, Zola, and Maupassant, who had become a devoted disciple) worked behind the scenes to secure for him a post as a library curator so as to provide him a small income; in May 1879 he was appointed deputy curator of the Mazarine Library with no official duties and an income of three thousand francs. It was hard for Flaubert to swallow his pride and accept the post, but his desperate financial situation gave him little choice.

In the spring of 1880 Flaubert was at work on the final chapter of the first part of *Bouvard and Pécuchet*. He was planning to go to Paris to visit friends, but on May 8, the eve of his departure, he suffered a stroke and died. He was 58 years old. His funeral in Rouen was attended by the Commanvilles (his brother, Achille, was too infirm to attend), Maupassant, Zola, Edmond de Goncourt, Alphonse Daudet, Charpentier, numerous local officials, friends from his inner circle, and influential Parisians he had not known well personally—more than three hundred people in all. He was buried in the Rouen cemetery with his parents and sister. A few months later the incomplete *Bouvard and Pécuchet* began appearing in the *Nouvelle Revue* and was published as a single volume in May of 1881. This publication marked the end of Flaubert's career, but his death could not diminish the impact of his work and its influence on French letters throughout the rest of the nineteenth and all of the twentieth centuries.

Chapter Two

Three Tales: Three Trails

Published in 1877, *Three Tales* (*Trois contes*) constitutes Flaubert's final complete work. Befitting such a culminating point, each story represents one of the three historical periods that serve as settings for his major novels: "A Simple Heart" ("*Un Coeur simple*") depicts contemporary bourgeois life in the French provinces, as do *Madame Bovary, Sentimental Education,* and *Bouvard and Pécuchet*. "The Legend of Saint Julian the Hospitaler" ("*La Légende de Saint-Julien l'hospitalier*"), like *The Temptation of Saint Anthony* (*La Tentation de Saint Antoine*), is set in the Middle Ages. "Herodias" ("*Hérodias*") is a historical reconstruction of life in ancient times, as is *Salammbô*.

The stories' main characters—the servant Félicité, the saint Julian, and the Roman governor Herod—reflect this same diversity. Although none of the protagonists is portrayed as introspective and although the respective narrators of their stories, in keeping with Flaubert's principle of impartiality, do not analyze them, all three of their portraits are richly drawn, due to the author's deft use of associational patterns, which at once structure the stories and chart the inner geography of their main characters. Thus, despite the diversity of the paths the three tales pursue, their mapping mechanisms remain the same and serve, like the historical periods they paint, as a (p)review of the novels.[1]

"A Simple Heart": The Bird's the Word

Among the most famous of French short stories, "A Simple Heart" is noted for its poignant yet impersonal portrait of a simple servant woman, the striking hallucinatory image of a hovering parrot that terminates the tale, and the careful craftsmanship of the author.[2] Unlike most modern short stories, including those of Flaubert's disciple Maupassant, which focus on a slice of life or a salient scene representing an emblematic moment in the character's existence, "A Simple Heart" depicts the entire life of Félicité, whose name, denoting happiness, strikes an ironic note when set against the bleak melody of her fate.

"For a half-century," the opening sentence tells the reader, "the bourgeois women of Pont-L'Évêque envied Madame Aubain her servant Félicité"; the sentence's very structure suggests the immutable hierarchy of classes that governs the provincial village of Pont-L'Évêque (in Flaubert's beloved Normandy) and Félicité's subordinate position in it. Indeed, Flaubert's style is consistently striking in its suggestive simplicity. In drawing Félicité's portrait, for example, the narrator tells us that "she would get up at dawn, so as not to miss mass." Rather than state the conclusion that she is religious or devoted, as such earlier novelists as Honoré de Balzac, Stendhal, or George Sand might have done (adding perhaps a generalization about provincial servants), Flaubert lets the reader draw the conclusion from the spare details. Moreover, the subtle use of the negative construction, "so as not to miss mass," instead of "in order to go to mass," captures the blind devotion to a duty-imposed role that characterizes Félicité's behavior throughout the tale. Here, as usual, the power of Flaubert's *mot juste* lies less in the capacity of words to denote a particular place or event than in the connotations they conjure for the alert reader. After a short introductory section, the narrator then uses flashbacks to reconstruct the servant's life, beginning with her first and only love affair, with Théodore, a country lad who jilts her for an older woman. Grief stricken, Félicité leaves home and finds employment with Madame Aubain and her children Paul and Virginie (whose names are borrowed from the preromantic novel of exoticism and escape *Paul et Virginie* by Bernardin de Saint-Pierre). Félicité soon becomes noted (and her mistress envied) for her devotion to the family, especially her heroic defense of them during an attack by a bull.

During a family trip to the seaside, while passing through the little village of Toucques, Félicité overhears part of a conversation about "Madame Lehoussais, who, instead of marrying a younger man . . . " Félicité never hears the rest of the story. This seemingly insignificant detail acquires its full force of meaning when the reader recalls that the woman for whom Théodore left Félicité was a certain Madame Lehoussais and that she was, in fact, from Toucques. The obliqueness of the presentation, in which the character is deprived of significant news, thereby emphasizing the narrator's control over the story, is typical of Flaubert's style. Although one can well argue, as does Jean-Paul Sartre, that information essential to the plot is withheld also from the reader, at the same time the vigilant reader is invited to seize the allusion, to pursue the clues, to unravel the web of associations Flaubert has woven.

Thus the initiated reader, thwarted on the level of plot, is rewarded on the loftier levels of structure and meaning. With Flaubert, the literary text rises above the trivial and elevates the reader, in collusion with the narrator, into the domain of art. Indeed, in this compelling story, Félicité herself can be said to rise above the mundane through the not-so-simple associative mechanisms that constitute her vivid imagination.

During the course of her life, Félicité becomes attached to her young nephew Victor, who later dies at sea, and especially to Virginie, through whom she vicariously experiences the mystic joys of religion. At Virginie's first communion, for example:

> Félicité leaned forward to see her; and, with an imagination born of true affection, it seemed to her that she herself was that child; her face became her own, her robe clothed her, her heart beat in her chest; at the moment she opened her mouth, closing her eyes, she almost fainted.[3]

Here the confusion of the repeated personal pronouns and adjectives "she" and "her" suggests the extent to which Félicité's personality is projected in and absorbed by Virginie. When the young girl dies of tuberculosis, Félicité then turns her devotion to Mme. Aubain, cholera victims, Polish refugees, and a cancer-stricken old man, all of whom disappear or die in turn. In the meantime, she has acquired a parrot, Loulou; the bird is described lavishly by Flaubert, who kept a stuffed parrot, borrowed from the Museum at Rouen, before him while writing "A Simple Heart." Loulou keeps Félicité company as she grows older, becoming "almost a son, a lover" and thereby playing the roles formerly filled by Victor and Théodore respectively. Overcome by grief when the bird dies, she has it stuffed and puts it in the place of honor in her souvenir-laden bedroom, where it joins other remnants of her deteriorating physical world. Finally, deaf, blind, and near death, she gives the stuffed bird, her most prized possession, to the church for a series of outdoor services to be performed in the area. As the sounds and scents of a religious ceremony rise from the courtyard below her bedroom, Félicité, in her dying breath, sees the gigantic parrot hovering above her in the awaiting heavens:

> A blue vapor rose up into Félicité's bedroom. She opened her nostrils wide, inhaling it with mystical sensuousness; then closed her eyes. Her lips were smiling. The movements of her heart slowed down one by one, more faint each time, more soft, like a fountain running dry, like an echo

> fading out; and, as she exhaled her last breath, she thought she saw, in the half-opened skies, a gigantic parrot, hovering above her head.[4]

The passage is structured by Félicité's breathing in and out and by her heartbeat, whose waning rhythm is mirrored by the repeated words "one," "more," and "like," placed at ever-greater intervals. The reader may remember that Félicité's heartbeat figured prominently in Virginie's communion scene, as did the closing eyes; in effect, by dint of its inner beauty and its resonance with the earlier scene, this final scene becomes one of ultimate communion for Félicité.[5]

Although seemingly grotesque and, for some, blasphemous, the climactic appearance of the bird is a tour de force that seems perfectly natural in terms of the logic created by the story's ordering principles. On the one hand, the plot is strictly governed by a recurrent pattern of love and loss, continued but also transcended by the parrot, who is loved, lost, and then resurrected, through taxidermy. Most significant, however, is the series of mental associations between the parrot and the other meaningful components of Félicité's life, the reconstruction of which constitutes both the tale's structure and the mapping of its main character's inner world.

Because the parrot comes from America, it is clearly associated with Victor, who died there: "It had occupied Félicité's imagination for a long time, for it came from America, and this word reminded her of Victor." This association between Victor and the parrot is reinforced through a series of exotic images, whose ultimate origin is an illustrated geography book that was Félicité's "entire literary education." At the same time, by virtue of being at once bird, flame, and breath, the parrot, for Félicité, is the living embodiment of the Holy Ghost. Even more, the parrot, unlike other birds but in keeping with the Holy Ghost, can talk and, as Félicité's hearing diminishes, becomes the only voice that can reach her. When the stuffed bird is returned from the taxidermist, she places it beside a portrait of the Holy Ghost, and the two images together create both religious ecstasy ("Sometimes, the sun coming through the little window would strike its glass eye, and shoot out a great ray of light that would send her into ecstasy") and personal memories, along with a sense of fulfillment whose message is unmistakably (and uncharacteristically for Flaubert) positive: "Each day, while waking up, she would see it in the light of dawn, and remember bygone days, and insignificant actions in the most minute detail, without sorrow, full of tranquillity."

The typical French reader, steeped in Roman Catholicism, can readily accept the image of the Holy Ghost as a dove, but he or she would (and did and does) decry the appearance of the parrot in this role. For Flaubert, however, the parrot is the more logical symbol in terms of the network of associations that is woven within the story and that constitutes the fabric of Félicité's inner tapestry. Flaubert has pitted a contextual image (the parrot), that is, an image generated from within the context of the work, against a conventional one (the dove). And in this epic struggle fought with *plume* (the French word denotes both pen and feather!) on the fields of literature, art prevails over religion or, rather, becomes religion for this author who seeks to be like God in his fictional universe.

Félicité, by virtue of her generosity to others and her personal revitalizing of a traditional religious symbol, becomes a saintly figure; indeed, through her creation of a meaningful image from the chaotic debris of earthly existence, she may be said to be an artist figure as well. The parrot is the ultimate souvenir for Félicité, an icon signifying salvation for the world-weary Christian, and a synthesizing symbol marking the triumph of art over reality for the ascetic artist.

"The Legend of Saint Julian the Hospitaler": A Stag Party

Although Flaubert placed it second in the volume of *Three Tales* to create, no doubt, an antichronological order, "Saint Julian" was the first written.[6] Moreover, its conception goes back as far as 1835, when Flaubert was only 14. To determine the reasons for this long-standing fascination with the legend, the reader must again assemble a multitude of internal associations, which in turn reveal a striking pattern that characterizes what might be called in modern terms the hero's "unconscious."

According to the legend, which Flaubert encountered both through a medieval collection of saints' lives called *The Golden Legend* and through familiarity with a stained-glass window depicting Saint Julian's life,[7] Julian was a nobleman who turned to a life of self-denial after unwittingly fulfilling a stag's prophecy that he would kill his parents. In Flaubert's hands the legend takes on profound psychological dimensions: scenes appear like dreams, projections of Julian's inner desires and complexes.[8] Such is the case with the extended scene that terminates part 1 of the tale, in which Julian massacres improbably large numbers of animals at will "with the ease that one experiences in dreams."

In this inner landscape Julian mortally wounds a stag, which recalls the hunter's father in several ways: the most evident of these is its "white beard," which figures prominently in the description of Julian's father on several occasions. Flaubert goes so far as to call the stag a "patriarch" (a male leader of a family or tribe) and to compare it to a "justice giver," among the first qualities associated with Julian's father, who, furthermore, is often garbed in animal skins: "Always wrapped in a foxskin cape, he strolled about his estate, rendered justice among his vassals." The stag's death is directly linked with that of Julian's parents by the dying stag's prediction ("—'Accursed! accursed! accursed! One day, ferocious heart, thou shalt murder thy father and thy mother!' "). This link is solidified years later when, despite self-imposed exile, Julian returns from another night's hunt to find a bearded man with a woman (whom he takes to be his wife) in his wife's bed. Having slayed them in a fit of jealousy, Julian again hears the stag's voice as he holds a lantern before the bodies, which, of course, turn out to be those of his own parents, who had arrived in the interim and had been given the conjugal bed by Julian's wife. The beard common to Julian's father and the stag appears twice in the parricide scene, and his father's burning eye—"a lifeless eye that scorched him like fire"—directly recalls the "eyes aflame" of the stag just before its death, which leads the reader down yet another trail of associations.

At the tale's end, Julian, having become a hermit in the service of others, encounters a mysterious leper whose eyes, like those of Julian's father and the stag, are described as "redder than coals." The leper is garbed in "coarse linen rags," as were Julian's parents at the moment of death; his rotting flesh strongly suggests that of a cadaver, as does his "shroudlike garment"; his body resembles a "skeleton" and his face a "plaster mask." Finally, the "quickening death rattle" of the agonizing leper directly recalls the "almost equal death rattles" of Julian's dying parents.

What is the significance of this rather startling and somewhat disquieting connection between the stag, the leper, and Julian's parents, particularly his father? This short but striking trail opens onto two major avenues of interpretation: a rather traditional religious one and a more modern psychological one.

In a religious sense, God punishes Julian's "ferocious heart" and his arrogance in killing animals, God's creations, by placing Julian's parents in his path. By Julian's service to others, however, and by embracing the leper, the lowest of the low, he exhibits the self-denial, penance, mortification, and subordination to God's will that can finally lead to salvation, which then occurs in the story's final words: "Julian ascended toward the blue expanses, face to face with Our Lord Jesus [formerly the leper], who was carrying him into the heavens."

In a psychological sense, the stag's prediction can be said to merely uncover a hidden desire on Julian's part to do away with his parents, especially his father. In the days following the episode, in a tellingly modern passage, Julian is haunted by the great black animal's prediction and struggles against it: " 'No! no! no! I cannot murder them!' next he would reflect: 'Still, supposing I wanted to?' " Indeed, the father of modern psychoanalysis, Sigmund Freud, defined dreams (and by extension legends and texts) as "the disguised fulfillment of a repressed wish."[9] Freud added later that such wishes often reflect the desire to do away with the father (albeit symbolically) in order to take one's place with the mother. This universal pattern is the backbone of what Freud terms the Oedipus complex.[10] In this vein, the stag can be seen as a socially acceptable substitute for the father on which Julian can unleash sanctioned violence. In announcing that Julian will kill his parents, the stag is not so much pointing to a real future event as it is pointing out the symbolic content of the scene that is playing itself out before the reader, a scene that has been cast as a dreamlike scenario and that reads like a projection of Julian's inner fantasies.

From this perspective, the leper, who also appears at night in a dreamlike landscape, can himself be read as a disguised figure representing Julian's father and fulfilling his wish to be absolved of his father's death. By saving, nourishing, and embracing the leper, who has the form of his father's cadaver, Julian appears to assuage his guilt and effect a reconciliation with the father. Even more, as Julian embraces the leper, abandons his body and identity to the leper, the psychoanalytically inclined reader may detect a deeper desire: to identify with the leper, to become the leper and, by extension, the father. In short, Julian now resembles the father, is identified with the father, has become the father. The transformation of the leper into Christ might also be explored and explained from this perspective, since Christ, the very archetype of the exiled son, ascends to sit with the Father, to become the Father, in the mystery of the Trinity.

By a series of subtle markings, Flaubert has mapped out two trails, both of which descend to the very depths of the character's psyche.

Whatever the path ultimately pursued by the reader, whatever the interpretation, it is clear that Flaubert's mapping mechanisms allow him to present a complex conception of a literary character without having recourse to direct analysis or commentary by the narrator.

Given this narrative silence, it is all the more surprising that the tale should end with a startling postscript: "So there is the story of Saint Julian the Hospitaler, about as it is found on the stained-glass window of a church, in my birthplace."[11] Here the narrator marks the tale as belonging to his space ("my birthplace") and his time ("there is"). He identifies it as an artifact ("stained-glass window"), a work of fiction ("the story") in which he is free to exercise his own license ("about"). The interruption of the third-person narration by a first-person singular pronoun ("my"), a rare occurrence in all of Flaubert's later works and in direct contravention of his narrative principles, invites us to take another look at the entire story, again from the twin perspectives of religion and psychoanalysis but this time from the narrator's, not the character's, standpoint.

Although Flaubert's narration is highly impartial—one of his trademarks—the narrator's position remains clearly superior to that of the characters. This superiority is guaranteed from the outset by the type of narration, third person and past tense, which places the narrator above and beyond the character, whose fate is already sealed. Except for those infrequent (and thus highly noticeable) moments when the reader shares Julian's point of view, the tale is dominated by the narrator's transcendent perspective, mirroring that of God or the father, not that of the son. By making the associations between father, stag, and leper, the narrator and attentive reader transcend the chronological line of the story and impose a higher order on it. Through this network of intersecting connections that crisscross the entire text, the narrator creates his own space, superimposed on the character's world, which in turn becomes as static and immobile as the stained-glass window to which the narrator compares it in the final words of the tale. We know that this is precisely how Flaubert saw the literary work, not from the character's limited standpoint but from that of the narrator, transcendent and omnipotent, "like God in Creation, invisible and all-powerful." If Julian is carried off by Christ, the son, the narrator can be said to hold the position of God, the father.

Indeed, from a psychological perspective, given the narrator's position as creator and purveyor of order, his role is more analogous to the father's than to that of Julian, the would-be destroyer of order. In sharing the narrator's point of view, we approach the Oedipal configuration from a different direction, from that of the father, who seems to delight in the demise of the upstart son. In this way, we can read the narration not only as a defense against a fantasy represented by the character, to do away with the father, but as a separate, even opposite fantasy, to reaffirm the father's power, a fantasy doubtless more in tune with Flaubert's age and status when he wrote "Saint Julian."

The reader who makes the shift from character to narrator can join the author in accomplishing the ultimate reversal, from son to father, from creature to creator.

"Herodias": Horseplay

From the outset of Flaubert's final tale, "Hérodias," the citadel of Machaeros, looming large over the Judean landscape some 30 years after the birth of Christ, is configured in political and psychological terms.[12] Although its geometric forms lend it a semblance of reason and order, its proximity to the Dead Sea casts a foreboding pall over the entire story, which is replete with predictions of imminent doom and death. Moreover, the final words of the opening paragraph, a simile comparing the fortress towers to the ornaments of "a crown of stones, suspended over the abyss," suggest a monarch threatened by subterranean forces. Whereas the imposing citadel reflects a powerful ruler, its precarious perch prefigures his or her vulnerability. When, two sentences later, the tetrarch Herod steps forward to assume the viewpoint, staring "into the very depths of the abyss," Flaubert makes it clear by the verbal link effected by the repetition of "abyss" to whom the simile alludes. Furthermore, the psychological value of this spatial configuration and its application to Herod are reinforced several pages later when the reader is told in nearly identical terms that "the depth of the abysses was troubling him; and a sense of despair was invading him." Indeed, it soon becomes clear that, despite the story's title, which bears his wife's name, it is Herod who is the central character, the one on whom all forces—familial, political, and psychological—will be brought to bear, through the agency, to be sure, of Herodias.

On the one hand, Herod finds himself entangled in the twisted branches of his family tree: the son of Herod the Great, Herod married Herodias, who was both his sister's daughter and his brother's wife; that is, she was both Herod's niece and sister-in-law! Moreover, Herodias, for whom Herod no longer feels any passion, has been long engaged in a bitter struggle with her brother Agrippa, the outcome of which will determine Herod's political standing.

On the other hand, Herod is at the eye of a brewing desert storm, stirred by the perpetual clash of Romans (whose inspection visit is imminent), Arabs (currently camped outside the fortress, indignant that Herod jilted the king's daughter in favor of Herodias), and Jews (distrustful of Herod and themselves riddled with tribal feuding).

Do these formidable forces of family and politics form the vortex that threatens to pull Herod "into the very depths of the abyss"? As is so often the case with Flaubert, the answer lies less in the conventional meanings we might read into the word *depths* than in those associations created by the recurrence of the word in the text, associations that produce a deeper meaning through the "internal force" of style. For Flaubert the *mot juste* is not the word that best denotes a referent but the one that best serves as a nodal point in a web of intratextual connections.

A mere five paragraphs after its first link to Herod, the word "depths" occurs again: "Suddenly, a distant voice, as if escaping from the depths of the earth, made the Tetrarch go pale." This disembodied voice turns out to be that of Iaokanann, whom the Romans call John the Baptist and whom Herod has imprisoned in an underground cell, from which only his voice emerges. This "voice," detached from its body and thereby signaling its spirituality and prophetic mission to announce the coming birth of the Messiah, recurs no fewer than six times throughout the story. The recurrence, along with the reduction of the future saint to his voice, is a striking technique, highlighting a thematic thread that must be woven into any interpretation of the true nature of Herod's plight, particularly since the tetrarch admits of his captive, shortly before the end of part 1 of the tale, that "His power is strong! . . . Despite myself, I love him!"

There is, however, another presence "within the depths" that must also be accounted for. Shortly after the Roman party arrives in part 2, these imperial watchdogs begin an inspection tour and insist on visiting "the underground chambers of the fortress," whose layers of rooms "ever deeper" contain hidden stockpiles of weapons and munitions, suggesting both Herod's military might and his paranoia. Finally, in the farthest reaches of the cavern the party comes across a hidden door, which reveals "an arcade {that} opened out onto the depths of the precipice." The visitors are struck by the spectacle of a hundred white horses, "marvelous beasts, supple like serpents, light like birds," capable of leaping "over and above the abysses" and thus of great military value. The Romans make an inventory of this ultimate symbol of Herod's potential power with the implicit threat of taking the horses for themselves.

Meanwhile, the plot further thickens with Iaokanann's prophecies of impending doom, the Essenian Phanual's prediction of the death of an important person that very night in the citadel, the arrival of numerous guests of various ethnic backgrounds for the evening's festival in honor of Herod's birthday and the Romans' visit, and an ominous red evening sky, all of which propel us toward the final festival scene, depicted in part 3.

As the revelers gorge themselves with fine delicacies in the sumptuous setting of Herod's hall, talk turns to the prophet Elijah, who is supposed to announce the Messiah's coming. When one of the guests screams that Elijah is none other than Iaokanann, Herod "recoils, as if struck full in the chest." Shortly after the arrival of the regally garbed Herodias, there is a stir of surprise and admiration as a young girl, bearing an uncanny resemblance to a youthful Herodias, appears and begins to dance. Her exotic garments and graceful movements remind the reader of two earlier descriptions of a young woman who, in stark contrast with Iaokanann, has been seen but not heard. In both scenes, first on the balcony of a nearby house and later in Herodias's chambers, the tetrarch was transfixed by glimpses of parts of her body and futilely inquired of Herodias who she was. As the reader discovers during the dance scene, the body belongs to Salome, Herodias's daughter, whom she raised afar and secretly brought to Machaeros. Herodias planned to spring her on the unsuspecting Herod in the hopes of awakening his dormant desires and thereby manipulating him (thus warranting her role as the story's titular character). Indeed, Salome's nimble, provocative dance, performed with complete detachment, leads all the men to "quiver with desire" and draws "sobs of passion" from Herod, who promises her anything. Salome, barely able to articulate the words, demands the head of Iaokanann on a platter, and Herod, bound by his promise, is compelled despite himself to have the prophet beheaded. This famous scene from the Bible figures in numerous works of art during Flaubert's time,[13] including the epic poem *Hérodiade* by Stéphane Mallarmé, the paintings "The Dance of Salome" and "The Apparition" by Gustave Moreau, described by Joris-Karl Huysmans in his novel *A Rebours* (*Against the Grain*), the play *Salome* by Oscar Wilde, lavishly illustrated by Aubrey Beardsley, and the opera *Salome* by Richard Strauss. The image of the seductive yet dangerous young woman no doubt struck a resonant chord that resounded on the very fibers of masculine fantasies and fears of the period. In reading Flaubert, however, we must turn once again to the clues echoing within the text to grasp the meaning of the penultimate scene of "Herodias."

By her provocative dance and her appearance in body alone, Salome clearly represents sensuality. By her effect on Herod, she obviously appeals to and resurrects dormant desires, a latent aspect of his character, his sensual side. On the other hand, the appearance of Iaokanann's head, severed from its body, can be said to represent Herod's spiritual side, equally inactive and submerged in the depths of his being. The encounter of Salome and Iaokanann in the final scene raises both of these subterranean aspects of Herod's psyche to the surface, thus dramatizing a hidden conflict that remains unresolved: he neither obtains Salome nor retains Iaokanann. The extent of Iaokanann's significance for Herod can be measured by the tears flowing down the tetrarch's cheeks and by the fact that, after all guests have left, Herod remains, "his hands on his temples . . . still staring at the severed head." But if Iaokanann's voice from the depths symbolizes the submerged spiritual side of Herod's psyche, then what of the other depth dwellers, the magic horses, able to leap deep abysses in a single bound? We have already noted that the horses represent Herod's military and physical prowess, and as such they can be linked to his dormant virility and animal nature. Indeed, the horse has long symbolized passion, as in Plato's image of the psyche as a charioteer, reason, holding in check the bridled horses, passion. In "Herodias," the subterranean horses, with their "frenetic gallop . . . hungry for space, asking to run" yet kept in check, can be seen as symbolizing Herod's pool of repressed libidinal energy, released by Salome's dance and destroying the last remnant of his spirituality, represented by Iaokanann.[14] For the reader, however, Iaokanann's image persists, and his significance is revealed in the final paragraphs of the tale, as the three believers in the Messiah carry to Galilee the dead saint's head and his cryptic message: "If He is to wax, then I must wane."[15] In effect, for Christ to rise, Iaokanann must die; for spiritual salvation to happen, sacrifice must occur, a lesson that sheds light on all three of the tales as well as on the concept of creativity for Flaubert.

Trilogy and Triptych

By reading the first two tales in the light of the third, we come to confirm that it is Julian's suffering, sacrifice, and self-denial that lead to his ascent with Christ, just as Félicité's devotion to others and gift of the parrot account for the apotheosis that ends the tale. Similarly, the ascetic artist, devoted to art, must sacrifice himself for the growth of the work in order to achieve his own measure of redemption beyond the barren landscape of earthbound life.

In effect, by applying the principle of inner associations that we have just practiced for each tale individually to the collection of tales taken together, we come to grasp their interrelationships. Apart from the undeniable pleasure, inherent to great art but notably absent in reality, of things well constructed, these associations impart additional layers of meaning to each story and thus enrich our interpretations of them. Thus, the three tales should be read as a trilogy or, perhaps more appropriately given their religious context, as a triptych or a tripartite stained-glass window, the panels or panes of which, when superimposed, reflect each other, producing further dimensions and greater depth.

In all three tales, for example, the protagonist is a solitary figure, beset by trials and entrapped by his or her situation or surroundings; Iaokanann's solitary confinement is emblematic of the human condition that plagues Herod, Julian, and Félicité as well. All three main characters are further cut off from others by a lack of communication. In "A Simple Heart" and "Saint Julian" there is little dialogue, and in "Herodias," speech, though plentiful, is meaningless due to language differences and cross-purposes among the characters. The conflict between sensuality and spirituality that we found to govern Herod can also be readily applied to the other main characters: Julian's double nature and destiny are foreseen shortly after his birth by the predictions by a hermit that Julian will be a saint and by a traveler that he will be covered in blood and glory. Félicité's actions in the final scene are described by the narrator as reflecting "a mystical sensuality," while elsewhere her relationship to her mistress is characterized as "a bestial devotion and a religious veneration." Similarly, her room "seemed at once like a chapel and a bazaar, so much did it contain religious objects and miscellaneous things." Of the three protagonists, Félicité alone appears to resolve the conflict between sensuality and spirituality, through the all-encompassing presence of the parrot.

In all three tales the landscape is both mysterious and menacing, as suggested by the fog that appears in each, the abyss that recurs throughout "Herodias" and "Saint Julian," and the disappearance of worldly objects that characterizes "Saint Julian" and "A Simple Heart." Indeed, human experience is a state of perpetual fragmentation and gradual disintegration, culminating, in each tale, with a grotesque reminder of our mortality: the parrot's worm-eaten corpse, the leper's rotting flesh, and Iaokanann's severed head. Yet if each tale ends with death, it also suggests redemption, often heralded by a prophetic "voice," whether marking the coming of the Messiah, the ascension of Julian with Christ, the flight of the parrot/Holy Ghost, or, on another plane, the transformation and elevation of the events described by the power of Flaubert's artistry.

Ultimately, the similarity of the final scenes and the saintliness of Julian and Iaokanann lead us to read Félicité as a saint as well, in many ways the purest and most complete of the three protagonists, the central panel of the triptych, whose artisan is Flaubert. For Flaubert, of course, the artist's lot is itself one of saintliness, in which salvation stems from sacrifice to the highest form that God takes among us, that of art.

Chapter Three

Madame Bovary: Style as Strategy

Toward the end of September 1849, Flaubert invited his friends Maxime Du Camp and Louis Bouilhet to Croisset to read an early version of *The Temptation of Saint Anthony* (*La Tentation de Saint Antoine*). The two readers were so appalled at the work's unbridled visions and lyricism that they advised him to abandon the project forever and take up a more controlled subject, perhaps one based on a real, contemporary occurrence. When Bouilhet suggested the story of Delamare, an *officier de santé* (a medical practitioner less qualified than a full-fledged doctor) who had been a pupil of Flaubert's father, the author responded enthusiastically, "What an idea!" and began work immediately.

Delamare, whose first wife died unexpectedly, subsequently married a younger woman whom he adored and spoiled. She, however, had utter disdain for him and embarked on adulterous affairs that she fed by lavish expenditures. Heavily in debt and spurned by her lovers, she poisoned herself, leaving behind a daughter and a despondent, bankrupt husband, who soon followed her in death. In essence that story is the backbone of the plot of *Madame Bovary,* a novel so highly crafted that it took Flaubert 56 months of painstaking labor to complete it.

After its publication in serial form by the *Revue de Paris* in 1856, *Madame Bovary* was greeted with a lawsuit from the *Ministère Publique* (Ministry of Public Affairs), which cited the depiction of adulterous affairs and antireligious sentiments as dangerous to public morality—contrary to "family values," as we might say today. Flaubert was acquitted, and the novel, published as a single volume in 1857 and propelled by the publicity surrounding the trial, enjoyed a considerable success based largely on the scandal (*un succès de scandale,* as the French term it). But what is the secret of its enduring success and reputation as one of the greatest masterpieces of world literature? Why has it engendered no fewer than seven film versions, the most recent of which, starring Isabelle Huppert and directed by Claude Chabrol in 1991, had tremendous success both with the critics and at the box office?[1]

On the broadest level of appeal, *Madame Bovary* is a profound depiction of the modern human condition. Albert Camus's definition of the absurd, "the divorce between what man wants and what the world offers him,"[2] certainly applies to Emma Bovary's situation, however vague her desires and however confining the society that surrounds her. Flaubert unerringly draws out the themes that inevitably accompany such a view of existence: alienation, boredom, disintegration, lack of communication.

Flaubert's masterpiece is also a finely drawn, if negative, portrait of the condition and socialization of the modern woman. In a recent cartoon that appeared in *The New Yorker,* a woman shown reading *Madame Bovary* to her young daughter tells her that "the surprising thing is that Flaubert, who was a man, actually got it." Indeed, Flaubert is able to penetrate to the very roots of the roles that constrain and entrap human beings, male and female, according to the stereotypes affixed to their gender.

Finally, *Madame Bovary* has persisted as the ultimate example of the well-constructed work of art; in fact, it is often referred to as the first modern novel in the sense that the narrator effaces himself behind a web of associations that the reader must reconstruct to derive the work's meaning, not from didactic commentary but through the vehicle of style itself. *Madame Bovary* is perhaps the first work of prose fiction in which the narrator is at once invisible yet all-powerful, silent yet omniscient. Style is the means by which Flaubert achieves these seemingly incompatible aims. Indeed, Flaubert uses style as a strategy to manipulate the relationships between character, narrator, and reader in order to produce irony, ideology, and ultimately meaning in a universe depicted as absurd, unstable, and devoid of sense.

Style as Irony: Part 1 of *Madame Bovary*

Madame Bovary begins unexpectedly. Instead of encountering the married woman of the work's title, the reader shares the perspective of a schoolboy as he observes a "new boy" arriving in the middle of a lesson. This incongruity between expectation and presentation creates a sense of irony, primarily at the expense of the new arrival, a country bumpkin whose ill-fitting clothes and uncomfortable actions clearly show him to be an outsider.[3] But unlike, for example, Fielding or Stendhal, who might have referred to the misfit with obvious irony as "our hero" or another equally inapplicable expression, Flaubert uses oblique means to construct an ironic commentary that is as subtle as it is silent. Before taking such standard steps as revealing the new boy's name or his role in the plot, the narrator unexpectedly pauses to describe the character's hat, an unlikely conglomeration of styles, each more preposterous than the preceding. The lengthy description culminates with a simile likening the hat's "mute ugliness" to the "face of an imbecile," a comparison the alert reader does not fail to extend to the character himself.[4] As Flaubert tosses the new boy's hat into the ring, so to speak, the reader, like an apprentice, helps the master magician to extract the meaning, like a white rabbit, from the hat. In effect, the reader not only laughs at the joke but helps to play it, thus becoming a willing and necessary participant in the text.

The irony of the new boy's situation is reinforced by the observer's repeated use of "we," a pronoun that encompasses the entire group of classmates, along with the narrator and the reader, while excluding the newcomer alone. Flaubert also uses italics to highlight clichés, such as "new boy" and "our way," by which the group asserts its mastery of certain coded ways of speaking and thereby stakes out the school as its exclusive territory. These italicized "quotes" pass from the schoolboys via the narrator to the reader, thus bypassing the uninitiated new boy, whose command of language is shown to be so inadequate that he can barely stammer out his own name, which sounds to the teacher and classmates like "charbovari" and looks to the reader like "charivari," the name of a satirical magazine, but turns out to be Charles Bovary, the heroine's future husband.[5] The boy's exclusion functions like dramatic irony in the theater, where one character's ignorance creates a sense of distance, detachment, and thus collusion between the audience and the characters who are in the know, ultimately leading to a comic effect at the unenlightened character's expense.

The pervasive irony in *Madame Bovary* soon turns, however, against the schoolboys themselves, who are also shown to lack certain essential information. Immediately after setting up the schoolboys as ostensible observers of the classroom scene, the narrator states that the new boy was "remaining in the corner, behind the door, so that we could barely see him." When this limitation in viewpoint is followed by a detailed description of the new boy, down to the nails in his shoes, the puzzled reader wonders just who is meant to be observing the scene after all. Similarly, we are told later in no uncertain terms that "it would now be impossible for any one of us to remember anything at all about him," only to be given a lengthy description of the new boy's habits, down to the color of ink and number of seals he uses in writing privately to his mother. Clearly the joke is also on the schoolboys, who themselves do not possess all of the information necessary for seeing, remembering, reconstructing, and recounting the actions described in the story. Only the narrator completely commands the fictional terrain, which he is prepared to share with the reader willing to follow him in distancing himself from the characters and seeing the story from "above," from the dizzying heights of an omniscient, divine perspective.

Flaubert's choice of viewpoint and his subsequent decision to undercut it create a highly problematic beginning to the novel and suggest, from the outset, a master plan to subvert the characters and assert the narrator's superior position, the only position from which Flaubert can realize his goal of remaining a silent but omnipotent god in his fictional universe, through the elevating agency of style.

Style, put simply, is a matter of choice among the various possible ways of expressing something. In this case, the choices clearly work against the characters—against Charles, since the narrator chooses an event that casts him in the worst possible light, and especially against Emma, since we know from the outset the bleak fate that awaits her. Her role is fixed from the start by the title, which uses neither her first name (Emma) nor her maiden name (Mademoiselle Rouault) but the name that designates her role as a married woman in a world of rigid constraints, impassable barriers, and impossible divorce.

As the details of Charles's early life unfold, they paint a picture of mediocre achievement ("by dint of working hard, he always managed to stay in about the middle of the class") and of domination by women, first by his doting mother ("he had to have a wife. She found him one") and then by his first wife, an ugly crone considerably older than he and extremely demanding ("But his wife was the master").

Charles has little say in his life, a trait Flaubert reinforces through his masterful use of *style indirect libre* (free indirect discourse). With this technique, pioneered by Stendhal and perfected by Flaubert, the characters' expressions are not quoted directly but are mixed in with the narrator's voice. Consider this scene, in which an overwhelmed Charles takes a break from his medical studies in Rouen and stares out the window of his meager apartment:

> Opposite, beyond the roofs, the pure sky spread out, with the red sun setting. How pleasant it must be back home! How fresh under the beech tree! And he expanded his nostrils to breathe in the good smells of the country, which did not reach him.[6]

While the first and last sentences are standard examples of the third-person narrator's impartial voice, the second and third are clearly

Charles's expressions, as evidenced by the repeated exclamatory word "how," the exclamation points, and an incomplete third sentence that has no verb. Instead of quoting Charles directly ("Charles said to himself, 'How pleasant it must be back home!' ") or indirectly ("Charles said to himself that it must be very pleasant back home"), Flaubert merely inserts the character's expressions into the narration, without any markings to indicate the shift in voice.

Although this "seamless" narration makes great demands of the reader, who must negotiate the vocal shifts without the author's assistance, its advantages are numerous. First, the technique allows Flaubert to avoid both repetition (a constant concern of his) and sudden shifts in voice (thereby preserving the text's unity). Furthermore, the narrator can assist the character by verbalizing notions slightly beyond the character's reach, without specifying whether the expression is a spoken word, a thought, or a half-thought. Finally, by muffling the character's words, by making them pass through the filter of the narrator's voice, Flaubert reinforces the sense of distance between character and reader, while strengthening the bond between reader and narrator. In this case, the stifling of Charles's voice makes his loneliness all the more poignant; in most others, it simply enhances the predominant sense of irony.[7]

In addition to situational irony, the novel is rife with verbal irony (in which the narrator or characters state the opposite of the facts). When the previously studious Charles turns to a life of debauchery (mild, of course!), the narrator tells us, "Thanks to these preparatory labors, he failed his *officier de santé* exam completely. He was expected that very evening at home to celebrate his success!" Not only does the expression "preparatory labors" contradict the previous episode that describes Charles's carousing, but the positive introduction "thanks to" is at odds with the negative result described in the second clause. Furthermore, the success his family expected, which is expressed in free indirect discourse (note the exclamation point indicating their emotional involvement), is the opposite of what actually occurs. Although Flaubert uses such verbal irony frequently, it is the structural or situational irony that prevails in the novel, guaranteed by the cross-purposes of narrator and characters and by the reader's usual distance from the latter.

Flaubert is also adept, however, at modulating the voice and viewpoint in order to encourage the reader to identify with the characters at significant moments, thereby signaling the importance of certain events. When we next encounter Charles, installed in the village of Tostes with his new wife and medical practice (both arranged by his mother!), he is called to the countryside to mend the broken leg of Old Rouault, a farmer of some means who has an educated daughter called Emma. We meet the young woman through Charles's viewpoint; the repressed doctor's focus on various body parts ("Charles was surprised by the whiteness of her nails") and actions ("her full lips, which she was in the habit of biting") clearly reveals his fascination and, at the same time, Emma's sensuousness. When his good wife, who turns out to have lied about her means, has the good timing to die unexpectedly, Charles finds himself returning to the Rouault farm and, inevitably it seems, asking for Emma's hand. Even this simple act, however, reveals Charles's inadequacy with language; he approaches not Emma but her father and manages only to stammer, leaving the father to guess his intentions. The old man, only too happy to get rid of his daughter, agrees to ask her, and the young woman, mostly out of boredom with farm life, accepts.

The wedding plans reveal a conflict in value systems between daughter, who longs for a midnight wedding with torches, and father, who wants a huge outdoor feast. In this clash between characters, involving generation and gender, it is the father who prevails, while Emma is equally thwarted on another level: the narrator spends several pages detailing the revelry but skips the wedding ceremony entirely and describes the wedding night only in terms of the pranks played, not the emotions experienced. In essence, the description of the wedding turns away from the very aspects that would have most interested Emma and focuses on those that she would have liked least, which suggests another conflict in value systems, between narrator and character.

A highlight of the wedding description is the cake, whose three tiers can be read as an ironic forecasting of Emma's future: a temple on the base symbolizes the sanctity of marriage, a dungeon on the second level suggests the imprisonment of married life, and a cupid balancing on a chocolate swing on the upper platform foreshadows Emma's escape into adultery.[8] This technique of focusing on an aspect (the cake) of an event (the wedding), which reveals more than the event itself, is typical of Flaubert's art, as we already witnessed in the case of Charles's hat.

It is not until chapter 5 of the novel's first part (of three) that Emma assumes the viewpoint. It is the narrator, however, who describes what she sees, rather than have us "see" events and characters through her; she is depicted as too unobservant to be a reliable "viewer." It is also typical for the narrator to express Emma's thoughts rather than to present them directly through her expressions, either through dialogue (typical of Balzac) or interior monologue (typical of Stendhal); Emma is portrayed as too inarticulate to formulate her own thoughts.

Chapter 6 contains a flashback to Emma's convent days, thus establishing a parallel with Charles's schooling in chapter 1 and providing, together with the earlier episode, a picture of gender-separate education in Flaubert's time. The convent is depicted as a place isolated from real life, which causes Emma to develop a mystical, even sensuous approach to religion: she invents sins in order to linger in the confessional, and she is moved by such terms as "celestial lover" and "eternal marriage," details that the prosecuting attorney in Flaubert's trial for transgressions against public morals characterized as part of the writer's "lascivious painting."

Although the narrator makes several generalizations about Emma's personality and behavior, they tend to be evaluative and analytical rather than judgmental:

> She had to be able to extract from things a sort of personal benefit; and she rejected as useless whatever didn't contribute to the immediate satisfaction of her heart's desires,—being of temperament more sentimental than artistic, seeking emotions not landscapes."[9]

Flaubert's opinion of Emma's values emerges unequivocally, however, as always, through the vehicle of his style. The following excerpt describes the effects on Emma of the novels she and the other girls read secretly:

> There were only loves, lovers, lovely ladies, persecuted women fainting in lonely pavilions, postilions killed at every relay, horses ridden to death on every page, dark forests, heartaches, vows, sobs, tears and kisses, boat rides by moonlight, nightingales in groves, *gentlemen* brave as lions, gentle as lambs, virtuous as never before, always well-dressed, and weeping like urns. For six months, at fifteen, Emma dirtied her hands with the dust of old lending libraries. With Walter Scott, later on, she was taken with historical events, dreamed of old chests, guardrooms and minstrels. She would have liked to live in some old manor-house, like those long-waisted chatelaines who, under clover-shaped arches, spent their days, elbow on ledge and chin in hand, watching a white-plumed knight galloping from the distant countryside on his dark horse.[10]

The restrictive "only" reads ironically in the wake of the extensive, incoherent list of images, the rhythm of which suggests the frenzied imagination of the young schoolgirl, whose fascination for *messieurs* is captured by the use of italics. The four similes (comparisons involving "as" and "like") that end the first sentence are as banal as can be and thus constitute a silent condemnation not only of the mind that harbors them but of the source that generated them, which is revealed to be Emma's readings. Here the British novelist Walter Scott is singled out, but throughout the chapter allusions to the French writers Bernardin de Saint-Pierre, Chateaubriand, and Lamartine, show Flaubert's target to be the literature of the entire romantic period (a period whose writings he himself relished as an adolescent). Like Cervantes's Don Quixote, who reads novels of chivalry, Voltaire's Candide, nourished on Leibniz's philosophy of optimism, and Stendhal's Julien Sorel, brought up on the writings of Rousseau and Napoleon, Emma fits the paradigm of the fictional character whose reading of the preceding generation's literature has left him or her unable to cope with present-day reality. Unlike her male counterparts, however, who inherit images of idealism and action, Emma is assigned the passive role of a woman waiting for her knight (the chatelaine), headed for adultery (the ill-fated Héloïse is among her heroines), and destined for martyrdom (she reveres Joan of Arc). Without having recourse to the narrator's judgment, Flaubert has created, through style (that is, choice) alone, the portrait of a banal, vague, incoherent, incomplete dream doomed to passivity and tragedy, while allowing the reader to witness the socialization of a young woman through her readings and educational setting. Indeed, the term "bovarysm" has come to signify a dream that is as banal and self-serving as the reality it purports to replace and destined to wither in the face of that reality.[11]

It soon becomes clear to Emma that Charles fails to match up to the romantic images of her readings, many of which reveal stereotypical gender roles, both male and female. In the following example, Emma's ideas, expressed in free indirect discourse, reveal both her dependence on men and her impossible expectations of them, as well as, by implication, her perception of what women lack: "A man, on the contrary, should he not know everything, excel in all kinds of activities, initiate you into the energies of passion, the refinements of life, all of its mysteries?" Flaubert also makes heavy use of simile and its companion figure, metaphor, to chart Emma's progressive disillusionment: Charles's conversation is as flat as a street on which everyone else's ideas go walking; Emma's thoughts wander about aimlessly like her greyhound; her life is cold, like an attic facing north, where boredom, the silent spider, spins its web in the shadows of her heart. According to the early-twentieth-century French novelist Marcel Proust, himself a great stylist, "there is perhaps not a single beautiful metaphor in all of Flaubert."[12] Certainly, the three mentioned above are far from decorative, but they are highly functional, effective in capturing the emptiness of Emma's existence. Her dreams fading fast, she asks herself, all too soon after her wedding: "My God, why did I get married?"

Yet for one brief moment (as the cliché goes), her romantic dream is slated to be fulfilled, when Emma and Charles are unexpectedly invited to a grand ball, at the Chateau Vaubyessard. The ball episode, depicted in chapter 8, picks up many of the elements already encountered in the description of Emma's early readings, from the luxurious setting, upper-class guests, fabulous clothing, sumptuous food, and exotic drink to such specific romantic bric-a-brac as swans, love notes, travel talk, and especially, the dances! In describing the latter, Flaubert displays a technical wizardry designed to capture the movement of the dance and its impact on Emma, while setting up threads to be rewoven later. In the first instance, "feet fell in rhythm, skirts swelled and rustled, hands took hold, let go; the same eyes, turning away from you, returned to gaze upon you." Here disembodied parts—feet, skirts, hands, eyes—seem to detach themselves and move independently, merely hinting at the people to whom they belong. By focusing on parts, Flaubert not only underscores the movement of the dance as seen by one of the dancers, no doubt Emma, but also suggests a fragmenting of human beings and thus a dehumanizing of experience that permeates much of the novel. Later, the reluctant Emma is convinced by a distinguished viscount to try to waltz:

> They started out slowly, then picked up the pace. They were turning: things were turning around them, the lamps, the furniture, the wainscoting, the floor, like a disk on a pivot. While passing near the doors, Emma's dress, at the bottom, caught on his trousers; their legs intertwined with each other; he lowered his eyes toward her, she raised hers toward him; a torpor was seizing her, she stopped. They took off again; and, at a quicker pace, the Viscount, sweeping her away, disappeared with her to the end of the gallery, where, panting, she almost fell, and, for an instant, steadied her head on his chest. And then, still turning, but more slowly, he guided her back to her seat; she leaned back against the wall and put her hand in front of her eyes.[13]

Here the circular movement of the waltz and its dizzying effect on Emma is suggested by the use of simile ("like a disk on a pivot"), antithesis ("he lowered . . . she raised"), action verbs, and especially in the original French, the rhythm of the sentences, which Flaubert crafts through the length and number of clauses, the punctuation, and the repetition of sounds and words (especially "turning"). The actions themselves, in addition to causing Emma's vertigo, are highly suggestive, loaded with the type of sexual innuendos ("their legs intertwined . . . sweeping her away . . . panting") that did not escape the prosecuting lawyers during Flaubert's trial.

Although Emma is lost in her dream world for most of this fleeting night, there persist certain remnants and reminders of reality: Charles, whose advances she rebuffs by convincing him that it would be improper for a doctor to dance; a senile, drooling old man with whom Emma is enraptured because he is reputed to have been the queen's lover; and the faces of peasants peering through the window, which remind Emma of her past life on the farm, a memory she represses vigorously in order to better preserve the present experience of the ball. As she looks out her window after the ball, leaning on her elbow, striking the very pose of the waiting chatelaine of her readings, Emma is determined to prolong the illusion of this magic moment, only to have it inevitably slip away just as surely as she and Charles must drive away the next day. The reader may recognize in this episode similarities to Cinderella at the prince's ball, but here the story is tinged with several ironies: Emma's prince, the viscount, rides away, and her only remembrance, not a glass slipper but a cigar case, cannot resurrect this dream scene doomed to disappear into the shady alcoves of Emma's dimly lit memory.

In the following chapter, the final one of part 1, Flaubert silently but systematically pursues the degradation, disintegration, and destruction of Emma's dream world. Fueled by the experience of the ball, Emma frantically attempts to remake reality in the image of her dream: she caresses the cigar case, buys a map of Paris, subscribes to women's magazines, reads the romantic novels of Eugène Sue, Honoré de Balzac, and George Sand, trains a new maid in the ways of high society, and imagines future successes for Charles and thus herself. All to no avail, as the reader soon discovers by following the path of her futile efforts through Flaubert's meticulous descriptions of the monotonous people, events, places, and atmosphere that constitute life in Tostes. Finally, toward the end of the chapter, we come to measure the extent of her failure through Flaubert's deft use of suggestive scenes and symbolic objects. Perhaps the most celebrated of such scenes involves Emma and Charles seated at the dinner table:

> But it was especially at mealtimes that she couldn't take anymore, in this small first-floor room, with the stove smoking, the door creaking, the walls sweating, the humid flooring; all the bitterness of existence seemed to her to be served up on her supper plate, and, with the steam of the boiled beef, there arose from the depths of her soul other waves of weariness.[14]

Rather than simply have the narrator conclude that Emma was bitter, as might many an earlier writer, Flaubert lends her bitterness substance by making it a noun, giving it weight through alliteration (the repetition of *s* is very noticeable in the original French, "*semblait servie sur son assiette*"), and lending it form by having it appear as food on her supper plate. Nor is Flaubert's use of scenes and similes involving eating to represent the mundane reality that threatens Emma's dreams arbitrary. Beginning with the wedding scene, in which Emma's desires for a romantic ceremony are counterweighted by her father's plans for a huge feast, Flaubert consistently uses food to thwart Emma, who seeks more spiritual nourishment: Charles is said to "ruminate" his happiness, like those who chew and digest their food; his predictable kisses are compared to an ordinary dessert following a monotonous meal; his dinner habits become increasingly coarse and irritating; Emma, who barely eats, even takes vinegar to make herself thinner in hopes of convincing Charles that she is ill and needs to move from Tostes.

In his classic study of modern realism, *Mimesis,* Erich Auerbach examines in some detail the scene of the couple at the dinner table, touching on such technical matters as viewpoint and voice as well as on such human questions as realism and relevance:

> here . . . the two distinguishing characteristics of modern realism are to be found; real everyday occurrences in a low social stratum, the provincial petty bourgeoisie, are taken very seriously. . . . [and] everyday occurrences are accurately and profoundly set in a definite period of contemporary history. . . . Nothing particular happens in the scene, nothing particular has happened just before it. It is a random moment from the regularly recurring hours at which the husband and wife eat together. They are not quarreling, there is no sort of tangible conflict. Emma is in complete despair, but her despair is not occasioned by any definite catastrophe . . . such formless tragedy . . . probably Flaubert was the first to have represented it.[15]

We might add that several of the main constituent elements of modern tragedy that occur throughout *Madame Bovary* are well illustrated here: entrapment, boredom, alienation, and lack of communication.

Another scene Flaubert constructed to comment ironically on Emma's situation involves an organ grinder who occasionally passes by her window:

> In the afternoon, sometimes, a man's head would appear outside the living room window, a swarthy head with black sideburns, smiling slowly with a large gentle smile showing his white teeth. A waltz would soon begin, and, on the organ, in a little room, dancers the size of a finger, women in pink turbans, Tyrolians in jackets, monkeys in evening dress, gentlemen in knee-britches, were turning, turning amidst the armchairs, the sofas, the tables, reflected in small pieces of mirrors held together at the corners by strips of gold paper. The man would turn the handle, looking to the right, to the left, and toward the windows. From time to time, while spitting out a long stream of brown saliva against the milestone, he would use his knee to lift up his instrument, whose hard strap was tiring his shoulder.[16]

Here Flaubert's principle of internal associations comes into play, as he constructs a web of similarities that link this scene to the ball episode in the previous chapter. The reference to the waltz, reinforced by the repetition of the verb "turning," catches the reader's attention, which is then rewarded with a host of other repeated details: the women dressed in turbans, the evening dress, the knee britches, the mirrors, all appear in the earlier scene as well. Here, however, the situation is reversed, and reversal, as we have seen, produces irony because it thwarts expectations: Emma is now merely a spectator; the participants are miniaturized and caricatured (it is now monkeys, not gentlemen, who wear the evening dress) and serve no doubt to comment on the pettiness and grotesqueness of Emma's experience. These marionettes are manipulated much as Flaubert controls Emma and Charles, and the organ grinder's long brown stream of saliva expresses, perhaps, Flaubert's disdain for his own characters' dilemma. In short, Emma's dream is shown to be a grotesque lie, diminished and degraded by the ironic coupling of this scene with the earlier ball episode.

Similarly, Flaubert invests objects with symbolic resonances, which the reader must detect from echoes that resound within the text. One such object is a statue barely mentioned in passing: "In the little fir trees, near the hedge, the priest in his three-cornered hat reading his prayer book had lost his right foot, and the plaster itself, peeling off with the frost, had left white scabs on his face." Here the definite article alerts the reader that the statue has been mentioned before and sets him or her off on a trail that leads back first to the day after the ball, when

Emma stares at it in despair, and finally to her first day in her new home, where it acquires its meaning as a symbol of the sanctity of marriage and home life. In the form it takes in this chapter, it symbolizes the disintegration of Emma's marriage and home life, which the once-proud wife now neglects. The initiated reader will not be surprised to learn that the statue falls and breaks during the Bovarys' move from Tostes to Yonville-l'Abbaye at the beginning of part 2 nor to discover later episodes involving the loss of a leg and facial scabs, both of which we shall examine in due course.

Finally, the chapter ends with one of Flaubert's most frequently cited descriptions, that of Emma's wedding bouquet. The reader may already recall that, on arriving at her new home, Emma discovered the former Madame Bovary's wedding bouquet and wondered, with its removal, what would happen to her own when she died:

> One day while she was tidying up a drawer in preparation for her move, she pricked her finger on something. It was a metal wire in her wedding bouquet. The orange blossoms were yellow with dust, and the satin ribbons, with silver borders, were fraying at the edges. She threw it into the fire. It flared up more quickly than dry straw. Then it was like a red bush in the cinders, slowly consuming itself. She watched it burn. The little cardboard berries were bursting, the brass wire was twisting, the gold braid was melting; and the paper petals, shrivelled, floating along the fireback, like black butterflies, finally flew off up the chimney.
>
> When they left Tostes, in the month of March, Madame Bovary was pregnant.[17]

If the wedding bouquet is a traditional symbol of marital harmony and hope, then Flaubert clearly perverts its symbolism here. Not only is the fraying bouquet already in a state of disintegration, it actively irritates Emma: she pricks her finger. Her burning of it can be seen as symbolizing the destruction of her marriage through the flames of passion and thus as representing a gesture of liberation and escape, as suggested by the verb phrase "flew off." The comparison of the bouquet with the black butterflies, however, strikes an ironic note of foreboding (can the reader doubt that a butterfly simile will recur at an equally crucial moment later in the novel?), which is reinforced by the textual link of this bouquet with that of the deceased first wife.

The final sentence in this first part of the novel, set off in a separate paragraph, sounds a double note of irony; Emma's gesture of liberation tinged with a hint of death is undercut by the news that she is pregnant, a reminder of her ever-present marital ties and of the sign of life that is in her, presented almost as an afterthought.

Style as Ideology: Part 2 of *Madame Bovary*

Whereas part 1 focuses almost entirely on Charles, Emma, and their respective family members, in part 2 Flaubert expands the novel's scope to depict a panorama of provincial life. Although Flaubert prefers to dissect his specimens rather than to classify them, as does Balzac, there is in this central and longest part of *Madame Bovary* a remarkably coherent and comprehensive array of characters who represent different professions and segments of society: pharmacists, doctors, clergymen, clerks, notaries, innkeepers, merchants, tax collectors, and country gentlemen. They embody various value systems, which are embedded in their different types of discourse, the clichés of which Flaubert does not fail to explore and expose: the bourgeois, the scientific, the religious, the political, and the literary. Flaubert continues to wield irony as a powerful weapon, but directed as it is here at social types as much as at individuals, it takes the form of satire, an ideological arm with which to penetrate the various forms of cultural armor of his time.

Part 2 marks a new stage for the Bovarys as they move from Tostes to Yonville-l'Abbaye, and Flaubert calls attention to the event by utilizing a technique normally reserved for the opening chapter of a novel, the progressive presentation of a new place as it would be seen by a traveler. Unlike Emile Zola's *Germinal,* however, in which the novel's main character is designated as the traveler, or Stendhal's *The Red and the Black,* in which a cosmopolitan visitor is meant to approach a provincial village, part 2 of *Madame Bovary* has an anonymous viewer, referred to only by the pronoun "one," who travels to Yonville-l'Abbaye. As "one leaves the highway," one first perceives Yonville from afar, then approaches the outskirts before seeing such local highlights as the notary's house, complete with a statue of cupid in the garden (thus recalling Emma's cake and the symbol of adultery adorning it), and finally, in the middle of town, across from the inn, the spectacular pharmacy, resplendent with its mystifying paraphernalia, lights, and labels.[18]

The traveler's itinerary parallels, of course, the trip of Charles and Emma, who are about to arrive in Yonville. Why then, one might ask, does Flaubert choose not to describe the trip through the eyes of Emma and Charles, whose fantasies and banalities, respectively, would no doubt have produced interesting impressions that Flaubert could then undercut? Not only is Flaubert's choice consistent with his master plan of creating distance between the characters and the reader by shifting to the narrator's perspective at critical moments, but the characters' viewpoint would have limited the amount of information Flaubert could convey about Yonville, since presumably all they know about it is what the local pharmacist wrote in response to their letter of inquiry, mentioned in the previous chapter. After all, the reader already knows about Emma and Charles and is curious to learn about their fate in Yonville, and Flaubert rewards this curiosity not only with copious detail but with a language that at once reflects and undermines the values and mentality of the characters' new roosting place.

Again, similes play a major role in characterizing the new setting: the thatch roofs are like fur bonnets pulled down over the eyes, an image that recalls Charles's hat from the opening chapter and suggests here a close-minded attitude. Yonville itself is like a cowherd taking a siesta at water's edge, a description that reinforces the village's sleepy character and contains two potential puns, quite obvious to the French ear: the cow recalls the similarity between Bovary and bovine (cowlike), and the French *au bord de l'eau* (at water's edge) is identical in sound to *au bordello* (at the brothel).

Apart from its suggestive use of similes, a technique familiar to the reader by now, the text's language is marked in several ways that lend the narration, particularly in the first half of the chapter, a definite though barely detectable quality of strangeness, often signaled subtly by punctuation and typography. In the very first sentence of the chapter, for example, the reader encounters a parenthesis: "Yonville-l'Abbaye (named thus because of an ancient Capuchin abbey the ruins of which don't even exist anymore) is a village eight leagues from Rouen." The parenthesis contains the type of historical detail usually given by a guide, but it ends on the rather negative note that there is no trace of the abbey that gave the village its name.[19] Similarly, other parentheses contain information that seems to belittle the village—the main street, we are told, is "(the only one)"—or to poke fun at its residents: the cemetery caretaker is both church official and grave digger "(thus deriving a double benefit from the cadavers of the parish)". Indeed the narrator, breaking uncharacteristically with the novel's general aura of impartiality, makes a number of overtly negative judgments, particularly involving the agricultural products and practices of Yonville and the surrounding area: "the lazy village"; "it's there that the worst Neufchâtel cheeses in the entire region are made"; "instead of improving the soil, they persist in using it for pasture."

The reader is also struck by the fact that the first sentence, like much of the first half of the opening chapter, utilizes the present tense. Because the narrator's territory has previously been separated from the fictional universe by the conventional use of the past tense (which marks the story as belonging to another time and place), the use of the present here gives the reader the feeling either that the narrator is addressing the reader directly or, more likely, that the voice adopted for this part of the narration comes directly from the fictional universe, as if a character, albeit an unidentified one, were speaking (as is the case in a dialogue, a letter, or an interior monologue). The text is also replete with italics and quotation marks, which seem to suggest that the narrator is citing a particular person or type of discourse: some cases register a sense of community pride, as in "*gift of the Minister of the Interior*" and "*based on the design of a Parisian architect*," whereas others underscore words that are highly technical and slightly pompous, as in "*high access*" and "*new outlets*." The narration itself contains several examples of unmarked though quite distinctive scientific (or pseudoscientific) terms, such as "physiognomy" and "ferruginous."

From the above examples emerges a pattern of similes, parentheses, and direct judgments that tend to criticize the village for its traditional practices, coupled with a vocabulary, sometimes italicized, that mixes seemingly scientific terms with praise of progress. In short, the discourse appears to embody a value system disparaging the old and praising, in semiscientific terms, the new. Thus, in addition to the physical description of the village, Flaubert has given us the portrait of its dominant mentality—backward—and a voice, albeit anonymous, that is opposed to it in the name of progress.

Finally, although no specific character has as yet been introduced, there is an example of free indirect discourse, marked as such by an exclamation point: "But what catches the eye the most is, opposite the *Lion d'or* inn, the pharmacy of M. Homais!" Moreover, in the paragraph describing the pharmacy, there are several more examples of quotes and italics, all related to this establishment, which is presented as the local highlight. This focusing and clustering raises the intriguing possibility that the voice that has penetrated the narration belongs to none other than the pharmacist, Monsieur Homais.

Indeed, when we encounter Homais in the second part of the chapter, which depicts a scene involving local residents assembled in the inn to await the arrival of the Bovarys, the narrator singles out his pomposity in no uncertain terms: "his face expressed nothing but self-satisfaction." The highly opinionated Homais, like the anonymous voice earlier in the chapter, extols the virtues of progress ("one must keep up with one's century!") and criticizes such citizens as the clergy, who remain bound to tradition ("if I were the government I'd like to have priests bled once a month"), and the tax collector, whose silence is a breach of social etiquette ("no imagination, no wit, nothing that makes for a sociable man!"). Homais's speech is both laden with clichés propounding "new ideas" ("My own God is the God of Socrates, Franklin, Voltaire, and Béranger!") and what we would call today "family values" ("our duties as citizens and as heads of family"), and strewn with scientific jargon ("phlebotomy," "laws of physics").

In the next chapter, when Homais describes the area to Charles, his long-winded monologue is loaded with these same scientific terms and laced with a good dose of parentheses: in addition to standard Réaumur scale, the temperature has to be given in "Fahrenheit (English measure)"; the air is described as containing "considerable ammonia, that is to say nitrogen, hydrogen and oxygen (no, make that nitrogen and hydrogen alone)." In short, Homais's discourse, full of pompous "techno-talk" and parenthetical pronouncements, matches in many ways that of the anonymous voice encountered in the previous chapter. Flaubert does not, however, quote Homais directly, as he could have done by using Homais's letter describing Yonville to the Bovarys or simply by postponing a description of the village until Homais's conversation with Charles; Flaubert chooses, rather, to infuse the narration with Homais's ideas and manner of speech, which thus go beyond the individual character to reflect a certain philosophy and discourse prevalent in Flaubert's time: positivism. Formulated in France by August Comte in the 1830s, positivism is based on the belief that the only worthwhile truths are those obtained and expressed through scientific inquiry and method, which must therefore be applied to all domains of human endeavor, be they the human mind (psychology), social groups (sociology), language (linguistics), or even religion, which amounts to a faith in humanity and progress (Comte even established a Temple of Humanity in Paris). Needless to say, with his belief in the transcendence of art, Flaubert is far from being a partisan of positivism and thus sets about parodying the concept in *Madame Bovary*. By lending a positivistic turn to the language of the narration in this opening chapter of part 2 of the novel, Flaubert's irony cuts in several directions at once: it comments on Yonville's backwardness and Homais's pretentiousness, while the presence of both bode poorly for the dream-seeking Emma. But here, unlike its use in the first part of the novel, the irony also cuts a broader swath, becoming a commentary on provincial life and positivism as well, and thus taking irony to the heights of social satire. In the sense that it exposes the value systems underlying entire segments of society, Flaubert's style can be said to be an iconoclastic and even ideological tool.

Homais plays yet a second role in Flaubert's parody of contemporary discourse, a role he epitomizes but shares with nearly all of Yonville's residents, including the newly arrived Bovarys: that of "the bourgeois." The speech of all of the characters is both rife with clichés propounding the moral order of society and tinged with timid new ideas. In many cases Flaubert merely borrows these worn expressions from his future *Dictionary of Inherited Ideas* (*Dictionnaire des idées reçues*), a volume he began compiling in 1850 that contained banal definitions, in cliché form, of all manner of social roles and issues, from "artists" ("They are all wild!") to "religion" ("One of the very ramparts of society!"). He readily attributes these pronouncements to each of the characters, reserving the most pretentious for the ever-pompous Homais.[20]

In keeping with his expansion of irony toward the bounds of social satire in part 2, Flaubert soon broadens his covert attack on romanticism by introducing a soul mate for Emma, the clerk Léon Dupuis, with whom she has a lengthy conversation shortly after her arrival at the inn, at the very moment that Homais is haranguing Charles about the village. Léon's discourse, like Emma's and completely unlike Homais's, turns to spiritual matters, sunsets, the seaside, infinity, ideals, ecstasy, Paris, music, and novels! As Léon expounds on his manner of reading by identifying with the characters (precisely what Flaubert discourages the reader from doing) and Emma expresses her dislike for commonplace characters (precisely the type with which Flaubert has surrounded her), we sense not only Flaubert's irony directed against the two interlocutors but a type of metaliterary commentary on his part, through which he subtly reinforces his principles about literature by having his characters, of whose opinions the reader is more than wary, espouse the opposite.

Emma's spirits, elevated by the discovery of a kindred spirit, are soon dashed when she enters her new abode in Yonville and feels the cold plaster "fall on her shoulders, like humid laundry." Indeed, the dominant structure of part 2, as of the entire novel, amounts to a conflict between "her dreams too high, and her house too narrow."

As Emma's delivery date approaches, she dreams of having a son, the reasons for which, expressed in free indirect discourse, are revealing, not only in terms of her own desires but as an indication of the rigid conception of gender roles that characterizes her society:

> A man, at least, is free; he can sample passions and countries, overcome obstacles, taste the most remote forms of happiness. But a woman is continuously held back. Inert and flexible at the same time, she has against her the weaknesses of the flesh with the dependencies of the law. Her will, like the veil of her hat held back by a string, flutters in the wind; there is always some desire that pulls her along, some convention that holds her back.[21]

Here the male's mobility and freedom is set against the inertia and constraints that befall the woman, and the reader senses clearly that what is most insidious about societal roles is that, although they originate from without (family, schooling, laws, the media), they are maintained from within the victim herself or himself, whence they derive their overwhelming power. Of course (given Flaubert's penchant for mordant irony), Emma gives birth to a daughter, and, in caricaturally "feminine" fashion, she faints at the news.

Emma continues to be torn between her kindred feelings for Léon and an intermittent sense of family duty to Charles, an intermediate situation that Flaubert captures by often placing her at her window, which looks out afar but is confined within the walls of her home. In wrestling with her dilemma, she seeks help from the country priest, Abbé Bournisien, but as she tries to express her needs for spiritual nourishment, he continues to talk of food and family, the very elements that thwart her, while spouting implacable and inapplicable religious jargon: "we are born to suffer, as Saint Paul says"; "the way of our Lord, as indeed he recommended it himself through the mouth of his divine Son . . ." As Emma leaves the church in despair, the priest and catechism class recite memorized words about the comforts of religion, but religion fails to comfort Emma. Once again, without direct commentary, Flaubert uses the disparity between religious language and practice, philosophy and application, to comment ironically on religion (as the prosecution at his trial did not fail to point out). Once again, the scene is structured according to the principle of conflicting purposes and discourses and thus underscores a fundamental lack of communication.

Flaubert undoubtedly deemed the structural device of contrasting discourses, which occur simultaneously but do not intersect (as in the case of Homais and Charles conversing while Léon and Emma talk at the same time), as simply too good an idea to abandon. He uses it throughout the novel to contrast Homais and Bournisien and develops it as the basis for what has become perhaps the most famous episode in the novel, the country fair (*comices agricoles*), recounted in chapter 8.

In the final paragraphs of each of the two preceding chapters, mention is made of an upcoming agricultural fair (complete with exclamation points signaling its importance for the community). This long-awaited event finally occurs, as does the return of the roguish country squire Rodolphe Boulanger de la Huchette, whose intentions to seduce Emma were made all too obvious near the end of the previous chapter, in which we also learned of Léon's departure for Paris to further his studies. Intent on carrying out his plan of attack against Emma's virtue, Rodolphe invites her to accompany him to the second floor of the town hall, where they can observe the festivities without interruption. Here (about halfway through the chapter), Flaubert begins to interweave two "speeches," the councillor's, which celebrates agricultural progress, and Rodolphe's, in which he plies Emma with romantic drivel. Below, in the town square, the councillor's rhetoric is all too mundane, while above, in the "council room," Rodolphe musters up and manipulates all the romantic clichés already associated with Emma's dream world in order to win her favors. By interweaving the two speeches, by juxtaposing them rather than presenting them in separate contexts, Flaubert creates a double irony that cuts in two directions: the political parlance of the councillor is seen as a "seduction" of the populace, while Rodolphe's would-be romantic discourse takes on the banality of agricultural talk. Flaubert reinforces the reader's association of the two speeches by further relating them in several ways, notably through parallelism (a theme or word, such as "duty," occurs in both), word games ("bovine" recalls Bovary, just as "boulanger," the baker, matches Rodolphe's last name), and contiguity (just after Rodolphe says, "I followed you and stayed," an award is made "for manures!"). The final award winner, the aged peasant woman Catherine Leroux (whose name recalls Emma's maiden name Rouault), is at once the antithesis of Emma and her double: she appears as the tired target and ultimate victim of the political jargon, just as Emma is exploited by Rodolphe's ability to activate romantic rhetoric. To the speakers, to the masters and manipulators of discourse, belong the spoils in the spoiled society of provincial France. The agricultural fair is capped by fizzled fireworks and Homais's pompous reporting for the district newspaper, the journalistic discourse becoming yet another, along with the positivist, the political, the religious, the romantic, and the bourgeois, to be burlesqued in this part of the novel.

In the middle of the interwoven speeches, there appears a single paragraph, a portion of which follows here, that describes in detail and depth the complexity of Emma's inner reactions to Rodolphe's advances:

> it seemed to her that she was turning again in the waltz, beneath the glow of the lights, in the arms of the Viscount, and that Léon wasn't far off, was going to come . . . and yet she still felt Rodolphe's head beside her. The softness of this sensation thus penetrated her past desires, and like grains of sand before a gust of wind, they formed a whirlwind in the subtle wave of perfume that spilled over her soul.[22]

Unlike Stendhal, who characteristically presents the characters' conscious thoughts, or Chateaubriand, who describes their feelings, or Zola, who depicts their perceptions, here Flaubert shows the mixture of inner phenomena, their movement (a thought in the process of forming, a feeling defining itself, an image focusing), and their overall mode, represented by the metaphor of the whirlwind, which captures both the circularity and downward spiral so typical of the major movements that characterize the novel. Flaubert is among the first writers to depict the complex mechanisms by which the diverse aspects of the human psyche form, interrelate, and resonate with the outside world in the process that modern thinkers term human "consciousness."[23]

This short passage stands out in this novel because of the narrator's exceptionally privileged position inside Emma's mind and because of the unusual amount of psychological analysis. In representing Emma's inner life, Flaubert is more apt to use oblique means, especially similes, often ones that involve spatial configurations. Earlier, when Léon left, for example, the sadness reverberating in her soul was likened to the winter wind howling in an empty chateau; as her memory of him invariably fades, it is compared at great length to an abandoned campfire on a wintery Russian landscape. In this latter comparison, a lengthy one sustained over two full paragraphs, Flaubert is able both to track the gradual disintegration and destruction of Emma's memory (a process recalling the wedding bouquet) and, by the very length of the comparison, to parody the technique itself, a typical tool of romantic discourse.

The verbal and mental "seduction" of Emma by Rodolphe at the country fair is followed in short order by Rodolphe's physical seduction of her. Her downfall occurs during a horseback ride, a scene that perhaps recalls, in somewhat degraded form, the image of the knight from her dreams and that also suggests the traditional symbolism of unbridled passion associated with the horse, purchased to relieve her boredom by Charles, who unwittingly puts his wife at Rodolphe's "disposal" and insists that he be "accommodating." A mere amusement for Rodolphe, adultery marks for Emma an escape from reality into the dream world of her romantic readings: "Then she remembered the heroines of the books she had read, and the lyrical legion of adulterous women began to sing in her memory with the voice of sisters that charmed her."

The steamy and unseemly affair, consummated frequently at such trysting spots as Emma's garden and Rodolphe's chateau, soon passes from discovery to habit and eventually disillusionment, a process that, coupled with a nostalgic letter from her father, prompts Emma's repentant return to family life. Thus, spurred on by the glory-seeking Homais, she attempts to boost Charles's reputation and fortune (and thus her own lot in life) by encouraging him to undertake an experimental operation, recounted in chapter 11.

Hippolyte, the stable boy at the inn, has a clubfoot, a genetic defect that Homais (who, unlike Charles, keeps up with medical journals) believes can be cured by a new operation, which he and Emma convince Charles to perform. As the country practitioner, clearly beyond his capabilities, begins to study the procedure, he comes across a stream of medical jargon so obscure that the narrator is obliged to explain it to the reader twice in plainer terms: "he was studying equus, varus and valgus, that is to say strephocatopody, strephensopody and strephexopody (or, to put it better, the different deviations of the foot, either from below, the inside or the outside)."

The operation, described in graphic terms that only the son of a doctor like Flaubert could master, fails so miserably that a "real" doctor has to be called in to amputate Hippolyte's leg, which then becomes a grotesque symbol of the further crippling of Charles and Emma's marriage. Moreover, the reader may well recall the statue with the missing foot in the Bovarys' garden, which now takes on an additional layer of symbolic meaning as a precursor of this failure. Emma, whose return to family life and dreams of future status were riding on Charles's success, turns all the more ferociously to Rodolphe, acquiring expensive gifts from the unscrupulous merchant Lheureux (whose name means "the happy one" in French). Emma even manages to convince Rodolphe to run away with her and to take her daughter Berthe with them, but on the eve of their planned departure he writes her a letter, the composing of which shows clearly his capacity for manipulating romantic lingo (as he blames "fatality" for his failure to run off with Emma, he tells himself, "There's a word that always has an effect") and gestures (he lets a drop of water fall on the letter to simulate a tear). The interweaving of Rodolphe's thoughts with his words, not unlike the juxtaposition of discourses during the country fair, reveals not only Rodolphe's duplicity and the hollowness of romantic discourse but the disparity between thought and word that cripples the human capacity for expression, even if intentions are sincere. As the distraught Emma, having gone to the attic to read the letter, contemplates suicide, Flaubert again penetrates into the depths of her consciousness to reveal the hallucinatory attraction of death:

> She had leaned up against the frame of the mansard window and reread the letter with chuckles of anger. But the more she studied it the more her ideas became confused. She saw him, she heard him, she wrapped him in her two arms; and her heart beats, striking her in the chest like the huge blows of a battering ram, were accelerating, one after the other, at unequal intervals. She cast her eyes about her in hopes that the earth would crumble. Why not end it all? Who was holding her back? She was free. And she moved forward . . . [24]

Again, the familiar confusion of ideas, memories, hallucinatory images, and physical sensations leads to questions (expressed in free indirect discourse) and finally to a sense of vertigo, a pattern that has come to characterize Emma's mental workings. Ironically, it is Charles's voice calling her to supper that prevents her from leaping to her death, but she soon lapses into a state of semiconsciousness that lasts for several months before she begins to show signs of recuperation. During her convalescence, she once again turns to religion, but with a sensuous passion that betrays a displacement of her desires from Rodolphe to Christ: "When she kneeled down on her gothic prayer stool, she addressed to the Lord the same suave words that she used to murmur to her lover, in the throes of adultery." (Needless to say, the prosecuting attorneys seized on this passage and neighboring ones to support their contention that Flaubert's novel was antireligious.)

Eager to encourage her recuperation, Charles takes Emma to the opera in Rouen, where, in the final episode of part 2, Flaubert again tracks her mental meanderings. The luxurious setting and wealthy patrons, like those of the ball at the Vaubyessard chateau, look like a staging of Emma's childhood fantasies, and indeed, the opera playing—

Donizetti's *Lucia di Lammermoor*—is based on a novel by Walter Scott, which makes Emma "relive the readings of her youth." As she succumbs to the poetry of the music and identifies with the tragic heroine, whose story "had something of her own life," the reader watches her slip back into her fantasy world as reality fades away. Here, however, Emma displays a rare sense of detachment and seems to perceive, for the first time in the story, the boundaries between fiction and reality ("she knew now how petty were the passions that art exaggerated"). Emma's experiences seem to have modified her unrealistic approach to life; she appears to have a heightened understanding of human experience; she may be cured of her romantic delusions! Suddenly, her fantasies, thwarted on the level of fiction, are displaced from the character, Edgar Ravenswood, to the actor, Edgar Lagardy, as she is drawn into the lurid details of his life. As she cries out to herself, "Take me away . . . all my passions and my dreams are yours!," the curtain falls, seeming to bring yet another end to Emma's fantasies. This break in the flight of her fancy, however, merely leads to another detour, to another displacement of her emotions; Charles, sent off to seek refreshments, runs into none other than Léon Dupuis, onto whom Emma quickly transfers her reawakened passions and dreams, now linked to her own memories and to the unfulfilled promise of her once-budding love for Léon. At the end of part 2, the ever-complacent Charles convinces Emma to stay over in Rouen to accompany Léon to the final act of the opera, which their excitement at running into each other had caused them to miss.

Style as Fatality: Part 3 of *Madame Bovary*

If irony is directed primarily at the main characters in part 1 and is expanded in part 2 to target value systems embedded in various types of discourse, in part 3 Flaubert uses dramatic irony to create a sense of foreboding that shrouds the protagonists' fate. The clear presence of a definite sense of fatality raises the irony above the earlier individual and social targets to a metaphysical level, at which the novel exposes the ultimate irony: that life itself inevitably contains the germs of death.

If the reader is momentarily tempted to find hope for the heroine in the return of the once-kind and -kindred Léon, the narrator quickly dispels such notions with a portrait that is uncharacteristically direct in its negative assessments. The narrator sometimes appears to hesitate in making judgments, but this often occurs when the choice is between two equally negative possibilities—"To show off, or by a naive imitation of the melancholy that stimulated his own . . ."—or when a negative possibility overshadows a positive one: "As for excesses, he had always abstained, as much from cowardice as from discretion." In other cases, a feigned hesitation ("no doubt" or "perhaps") merely softens a negative assessment: "With a Parisian woman . . . the poor clerk, no doubt, would have trembled like a child"; "Perhaps he no longer remembered his suppers after the ball, with loose women." In still other cases, however, the narrator abandons his usual discretion and makes a judgment or a generalization about Léon's character bold enough to make even Balzac or Stendhal, noted for their blatant interventions, blush: "Self-confidence depends on the environment where it occurs: one doesn't speak downstairs as one does upstairs, and a rich woman seems to have around her, to protect her virtue, all her bank notes, like a piece of armor, in the folds of her corset." In short, Emma seems fated from the start to reconstruct the fantasy and fall of her earlier affair. She displays a moment of virtue during which she writes Léon a letter of good-bye, but since she doesn't know his address, she must deliver it herself to the previously arranged and presumably safe meeting spot in the Rouen cathedral.

While Léon sees the church as a gigantic boudoir surrounding Emma, she kneels to pray in the chapel of the Virgin. Such mild ironies are capped by the appearance of a guide, who hounds the couple, spouting his rote spiel, much to the chagrin of Léon, who has other plans. Once again, we encounter the pattern of interweaving value systems and types of discourse, as Léon's plans for seduction and growing anger are juxtaposed with the intruder's speech presenting the cathedral's wonders in typical guidelike jargon, which is often italicized: he insists that the cathedral must be visited "*in the correct order,*" and he tries to sell them works "*that concern the cathedral.*" Many of the segments of his presentation contain familiar tourist-attraction clichés: "It would be impossible, don't you agree, to imagine a more perfect representation of the emptiness of death." Yet it is precisely the mention of death that lends the guide, otherwise merely one more representative of bourgeois patter, another, more somber dimension. His talk, sprinkled with such pregnant terms as "final judgment" and "flames of hell," contains the words "death" and "tomb" four times each, thus striking a lugubrious note of premonition that will resound throughout the final part of the novel.

In effect, the opening chapter of each part of the novel, designating a pivotal point in the plot, is inaugurated by a "voice," clearly marked by clichés and italics, which then serves to set the tone for the rest of that part. The guide's pitch, which captures a commercial discourse that dominates part 3 of the novel, is as banal, bourgeois, and territorial as the language of the schoolboy in part 1 or Homais in part 2, and as such serves as a counterpoint to Emma's dreams and desires. But the guide's speech sounds a somber note of death as well.

As Léon tries to flee "the eternal guide" and pursue his plan to seduce Emma, he has a cab hailed and convinces the reluctant Emma to take a ride with him on the grounds that "it's done in Paris." This famous seduction scene, set in a horse-drawn cab, a further degradation of Emma's ideal horseman, drew an incensed cry from the prosecution at Flaubert's trial that "the fall takes place in a cab!" Yet the genius of Flaubert, both in thwarting would-be censorship and in creating a delightfully comic episode, lies in his manner of presentation: he shows nothing directly but suggests everything obliquely, through his stylistic choices.[25] First, he chooses a viewpoint that is neither Emma's nor Léon's from within but that captures the scene from outside the coach; it alternates between the bourgeois residents of Rouen, startled at the spectacle of a coach with drawn curtains, the coachman, who can't understand what "locomotive fury" is pushing his passengers, and a general vantage point, much like a camera tracking a moving object from afar. In one sense, the technique creates an effect that is the opposite of dramatic irony, in that information known to the characters is withheld from the reader, but this applies only to the prudish reader, like the prosecuting attorney, or to the voyeur, who reads luridly on the level of plot, not to the initiated reader of Flaubert, who derives his or her pleasure from deciphering the clues that lend the scene its suggestivity. Despite the distance and resulting detachment, Flaubert lets the reader know what is occurring through such details as Léon's voice, as he shouts with increasing fury to the coachman, and Emma's "bare hand" (the adjective extending itself, no doubt, to other parts of her anatomy), strewing over the countryside pieces of torn paper that the reader understands to be her letter renouncing further contact with Léon, now shredded like her virtue. The ambiguity of the French pronoun "*elle*" (she), which is used for the cab but can be applied to Emma as well, enables Flaubert to create a sustained effect of double entendre, in which the cab's movements may well suggest Emma's, as in the following (tactfully chosen!) examples: "suddenly she leapt forward with a bound"; "She came again; and then, without decision or direction, haphazardly, she wandered" (a verb used twice before to describe Emma). The places the coach visits are equally suggestive: some are comic, as with the earlier pun "*au bord de l'eau*" (which means "at water's edge" but sounds like "at the bordello"), Sotteville (Stupid City), and Gaillardbois (Bawdywoods), whereas others recall the name Bovary (la rue d'Elbeuf, le boulevard Bouvreuil, le quartier Beauvoisine). Some places parallel Emma's desire for escape (the railway station, the river, the islands), whereas others suggest the theme of death that is beginning to dominate this part of the novel (the statue of the tragic playwright Pierre Corneille, the hospital gardens with old people dressed in black, and the final stop mentioned, the Monumental Cemetery). Indeed, the similes describing the coach as "more closed than a tomb and buffeted like a ship" contain the same mixture of death and escape, as does the comparison of the pieces of torn paper to "white butterflies," the insects suggesting flight but recalling the black butterflies used to characterize Emma's charred wedding bouquet, itself an earlier premonition of death.

The entire movement of this third and final part of *Madame Bovary* can be defined by the twin trajectories of love and death (eros and thanatos), by Emma's increasingly desperate affair with Léon, fed by growing expenditures, and by increasingly frequent and blatant signs of impending doom. Even in a chapter like the second, which does not directly involve Emma's affair with Léon, episodes tend to be grouped around the themes of sex (Homais discovers and denounces a book on conjugal love that fell from the pocket of his apprentice, Justin, who also has had a long-standing crush on Emma), death (Homais callously announces to Emma the death of Charles's father, while chastising Justin for using a pot stored near the pharmacist's supply of the deadly poison arsenic), and finances (Emma is visited by the merchant Lheureux, who suggests ways in which she can expand her credit). Lheureux's speech is replete with commercial jargon and financial terms, frequently italicized to further parody yet another form of discourse. Emma, who "had profited by Lheureux's lessons," imitates his language in order to convince Charles of the need to monitor their finances by consulting with Léon in Rouen, but she hardly masters the substance of Lheureux's financial philosophy, instead falling further and further in debt to him.

Following her initial three-day "financial consultation" with Léon, Emma is able to convince the ever-gullible Charles that she needs to take piano lessons in Rouen every Thursday. Although the weekly trips to Rouen may appear to mark an expansion of Emma's horizons, in fact, the spaces in which Flaubert depicts her are more and more enclosed, as prefigured by the tomblike coach and continued by the claustrophobic hotel room in which they spend their time, "shutters closed, doors locked." Consequently, Emma's actions become increasingly "extreme" and "extravagant," leading to the "lascivious" scene cited with indignation by the prosecution:

> She undressed brutally, tearing off the thin lace of her corset, which whistled round her hips like a slithering snake. She went on the tips of her bare feet to see once more whether the door was locked, then with a single movement she would let all her clothes fall off;—and, pale, speechless, serious, she would fall against his chest, with a long shudder.[26]

At the same time that her passion grows more frantic, her desires become more unreal. As she writes to Léon she imagines another man, a phantom composed of her wildest dreams, strongest desires, and most vivid readings, a god who lives in bluish surroundings whose presence she feels strongly but whose appearance escapes her. Inevitably, she grows tired of Léon, whom she had dominated from the outset ("he was becoming her mistress rather than she being his") and for whom she eventually loses all respect: "she was as disgusted with him as he was tired of her. Emma found in adultery all the platitudes of marriage." Rather than abandon her dying affair, however, she frantically tries to fan the fading flames by increasingly extravagant actions (she goes to an all-night masked ball dressed in an outlandish costume) and lavish expenditures, thus falling deeper into the trap of the unscrupulous Lheureux, who finally has his covert colleagues foreclose on Emma. Desperately trying to avoid the seizure of the family's belongings, Emma vainly seeks money from Léon, the notary Guillaumin, the tax collector Binet, and as a last straw, Rodolphe, whose refusal sends her into a state bordering on madness, which Flaubert explores in depth with yet another plunge into her consciousness:

> She remained lost in a stupor, and no longer conscious of herself except through the beating of her arteries, which she thought she heard escaping like a heavy tune that filled up the countryside. The earth, under her feet, was softer than the sea, and the furrows seemed like immense brown waves, that were unfurling. Everything inside her head like memories, ideas, was escaping at once, in a single bound, like a thousand pieces of fireworks. She saw her father, Lheureux's office, their room back there, another landscape. Madness was seizing her. . . .

> It seemed to her suddenly that fiery spheres were bursting in the air, like exploding balls, falling down, and were turning, turning, before going to melt in the snow, among the branches of the trees. In the middle of each one appeared the face of Rodolphe. They were multiplying, and they were drawing nearer, penetrating her.[27]

The reader will recognize the same patterns defining Emma's consciousness, the same mixture of inner and outer phenomena, the same circularity marked by the repetition of "turning, turning."[28] But here these patterns are pushed to an extreme, with an eccentric movement that spells the loss of one's center, one's sanity, one's self. Emma regains her composure long enough to head straight for Homais's pharmacy, where she consumes a quantity of arsenic, the location of which had unwittingly and ironically been revealed to her during Homais's lecture to Justin on its dangers. Emma returns home to find her household in disarray because of the impending seizure, and she calmly awaits what she assumes will be a peaceful death, an escape into nothingness that has long been forecast during this part of the novel by all sorts of signs.

In effect, twice during her trips to Rouen, Flaubert describes at some length a strange character who comes to symbolize Emma's fate:

> There was in the area a poor devil wandering with his stick, amidst the coaches. A pile of rags covered his shoulders, and an old battered hat, rounded like a bowl, covered his face; but, when he took it off, it revealed, instead of eyelids, two gaping bloody sockets. The flesh was fraying in red strands; and running from it were liquids that congealed in green scabs down to the nose, whose black nostrils sniffed convulsively. To speak to you, he reared back his head with an idiotic laugh;—then his bluish eyeballs, rolling in continuous movement, hit each other, toward the temples, on the edge of the open wound. He would sing a little song while following the coach:
>
> Often the heat of a nice day above
> Makes many a young maiden dream of love
>
> And all the rest was filled with birds, sunshine, and greenery.[29]

The reader immediately grasps the irony of this grotesque figure singing a song about young maidens dreaming, clearly an allusion to Emma. What's more, the blind man seems to be an ironic commentary on Emma's own blindness, on her refusal to see reality. By combining this interpretation with the conventional symbolism of the blind beggar as a truth bearer, the reader can construct a message about the grotesque and doomed nature of Emma's fantasies, much as we did with the earlier episode of the organ grinder. Moreover, as in the earlier example, the full meaning of the blind man can be established only by his relationship with other elements in the novel. One example of this type of inner relationship occurs in this same textual segment: in describing the powerful effect of the blind man's voice on Emma, the narrator tells us that "it descended to the depths of her soul, like a whirlwind in an abyss." In the very next paragraph we learn that Emma is overcome by sadness, shivering with cold, "with death in her soul"; the recurrence of the word "soul" brings the blind man's voice and the notion of death together. In effect, Flaubert constructs a sort of stylistic syllogism: since the blind man's voice reaches Emma's soul, and since death is in Emma's soul, then the blind man's voice is linked to death. The reader will soon see, during Emma's death scene, just how deadly this logic proves to be.

The blind man's description also echoes other elements in the novel from more remote textual segments: the unusual French verb *vagabonder* ("to wander"), for example, has been used several times to describe Emma's actions and thoughts; the green scabs recall the scabs on the disintegrating statue of the priest; and the vague sound of the blind man's voice hovering in the night evokes a similar sound Emma hears when she succumbs to Rodolphe for the first time. Especially striking, the tapping of the blind man's stick directly recalls the sound of Hippolyte's wooden leg, which serves as a constant reminder of failure to Emma and Charles. Indeed, the term "poor devil" used here for the blind man was applied earlier to Hippolyte, and the "howl" when the blind man falls is identical to the sound of Hippolyte's scream as his leg is amputated.

In short, apart from the conventional symbolism of the blind beggar and his obvious use both as a grotesque counterpoint to Emma's dreams and as a grim image of her own blindness, Flaubert constructs additional layers of meaning from within the text. In the immediate context, the blind man is linked to death, and in the larger context he is associated with images of disintegration, adultery, and failure. A great work invests words with new meanings; in essence, it contains its own dictionary, which the reader must consult in order to grasp all of the layers of signification that the word can embody. For Flaubert, *le mot juste* is, among other things, one that is highly charged with possible meanings, that is polyvalent.

The blind man reappears when Emma returns from her vain attempt to borrow money from Léon and is described in similar terms while performing a "comedy act," which involves rolling his eyes, sticking out his tongue, rubbing his stomach, and howling like a hungry dog, gestures that Emma herself will not fail to repeat precisely during her death scene, thereby confirming the symbolic value of the blind man both as Emma's double and as a death figure.[30] Indeed, it seems inevitable that, at the very moment of death, Emma will hear the tapping of the stick and the song of the blind man, who has come to Yonville because Homais has promised to cure him. Thus the final image that Emma carries with her into the awaiting heavens is that of her grotesque double, the symbol of her own blindness, disintegration, and death, the embodiment of her fate.

Just as the novel began without Emma, the final chapters trace the consequences of her actions. The distraught Charles adopts her romantic terms and gestures, raising the intriguing possibility that it was he, after all, who was her soul mate, and when he dies soon thereafter of grief, he leaves barely enough money to send their daughter Berthe to an aunt, who herself is so poor that the young girl must go to work in a cotton mill. As the novel ends, the reader learns that Homais continues to prosper and has just been named to the Legion of Honor. These final words are written in the present tense, suggesting the ongoing triumph of those who, unlike Emma, manage to espouse the prevalent norms and discourses of society.

Before his death, Charles, having discovered letters that clearly reveal Emma's affairs with both Léon and Rodolphe, encounters the latter and pronounces what the narrator terms to be the only great word that he ever uttered: "It was the fault of fatality!" The word *fatality* is among the most banal clichés of romanticism and one that figures prominently in Flaubert's *Dictionary of Inherited Ideas;* it is the word that Rodolphe used in his letter of good-bye "for the effect" and the one that he now finds to be "quite debonair . . . even comic, and a little vile"; in this passage, then, the use of the word "fatality" appears to be yet another example of Flaubert's famous irony.[31] And yet even more ironic is the fact that the word holds true, that Emma's tragic downfall does appear to have been fated from the start. Like any "great word," *fatality* is immensely polyvalent (not to say ambiguous); it is as if Flaubert were inviting the reader to explore the word's many meanings before judging its relevance. While we might readily reject the conventional sense of the hero victimized by the gods, we have, during the course of our discussion of the novel, identified several forces that weigh fatefully on Emma: her overactive imagination, the readings that produced it, and the convent school that fostered it while contributing to her socialization as a woman, a role sealed by the institution of marriage, particularly to a dolt like Charles; a society at odds with imagination, beset by banality, rules, and roles, governed by unscrupulous manipulators of discourse and finances, who prey on unwitting victims or on those who, like Emma perhaps, victimize themselves. In a broader sense, we may interpret fatality as what twentieth-century existentialists term "the human condition" (indeed, the title of the Nobel Prize winning author André Malraux's novel *La Condition humaine* has been translated as *Man's Fate*). Emma is condemned to solitude, unable to articulate and communicate her feelings in a life doomed from the outset to exploitation, uncertainty, disintegration, and death. On another level, the literary, Emma can be said simply to be the victim of Flaubert's art, of a narrative system that isolates her and of a structural system that puts organ grinders and blind beggars in her path. But if the novel's style marks Emma's downfall, it also points to the path of salvation for Flaubert.

Style as Salvation

Throughout *Madame Bovary* language itself plays a major role in Emma's destiny. In the early days of her marriage, when she first begins to feel disappointment, she is unable to formulate or express her thoughts linguistically: "Perhaps she would have liked to confide in someone about all these things. But how to describe an elusive uneasiness, that changes form like the clouds, that spirals like the wind? The words were lacking, the opportunity, the courage." She is both seduced, during the fair, and rejected, through the contrived letter, by meaningless words manipulated by Rodolphe. During her affair with Léon, the narrator warns us that "language is a rolling pin that always stretches out feelings," and when Emma later writes letters to Léon, her words are merely substitutes, not signs, for the feelings they describe. In a particularly moving and famous passage, after summarizing Rodolphe's opinion that Emma's words are trite, the narrator moves from her situation to a generalization about the limits of human expression:

> as though the fullness of one's soul didn't sometimes overflow with the emptiest of metaphors, since no one, ever, can give the exact measure of one's needs, one's conceptions, one's sorrows, and since human language is like a cracked kettle on which we beat melodies to set a bear to dancing, when we would like to touch the stars.[32]

Here, the rare use of "we" shows that Flaubert is talking as much about the difficulties of writing as about Emma's failure to communicate her desires and dreams. The example goes far in justifying Flaubert's reputed (and oft-disputed) dictum "*Madame Bovary, c'est moi*" ("I myself am Madame Bovary"). In the sense that we also grapple with the desire to communicate and the inadequacies of language, we ourselves are Madame Bovary as well.

But if language is an element of fatality, it is also, in its highest form, literature, the means of escaping it: as Malraux put it, "art is an anti-destiny." Malraux's statement stresses the notion that the art work is eternal, that it defies the ravages of time by outlasting its author; similarly, Stendhal believed that he was writing for a future, more enlightened reader. Flaubert's belief in the redemptive power of art is, however, more immediate. We might say for Flaubert that art defies destiny, that, through style, art resists the very forces that define the human condition. Where life is rife with misunderstanding, art offers communication, especially for the initiated reader who can follow the narrator in distancing himself from the characters and plot in order to piece together the puzzles posed by the artist. Where reality is fraught with disintegration, style produces permanence, or, as Flaubert put it, "continuity constitutes style just as constancy defines virtue."[33] From the chaos of reality, style wrests order and reconstitutes the meaningless matter of human experience into a coherent, significant whole. Style is the means by which the threatened writer can achieve detachment and elevation to become a god in his fictional universe. Style can be, for the writer reciting in his "yelling room" ("*gueuloir*"), not only an ecstatic torture but a sort of transcendental chant that raises him above the fray. In a world devoid of meaning, style generates meaning, accompanies meaning, underscores meaning; indeed, style is meaning, or, as Flaubert put it, "an absolute manner of seeing things." Above all, it is through work itself, the dedication to stylistic perfection, that, armed with inadequate language in an imperfect world, Flaubert defies destiny. Like Camus's Sisyphus, Flaubert pushes his rock up to the brink of the mountain only to have it roll back down and thus make him begin the task again; and we must imagine that, like Sisyphus, Flaubert is happy.[34]

Chapter Four

Salammbô: Veiled Meaning

Salammbô (1862) is a troubling and enigmatic work. Based on a historical event, the war between Carthage and her Mercenary armies after the North African republic's defeat at the hands of Rome in the First Punic War, it ranges in tone from epic to mystic and from heroic to sadistic. Its characters are never fully developed, and although the motives of some are patently obvious (reducing them to mere role-playing ciphers), the psyches of the protagonists remain impenetrable—to the reader, to each other, and to themselves. The novel's natural setting is at times breathtaking in its stark beauty, but Carthage's urban landscape is unsettling in its oppressive geometric precision and obsessive opulence. The book's action ranges over vast territories but is difficult to visualize given the modern reader's unfamiliarity with the region's topography and ancient geography. Scenes of frenetic movement alternate and even coexist with a pervasive sense of immobility and stasis. Stylistically, the novel's spare and symmetrical structure contrasts with its descriptive excess.[1] In short, the reader of *Salammbô* is confronted with a series of contradictions and enigmas capped by an overriding sense of the unfamiliar, the "other," that leads us to question the author's intentions and the book's meaning and relevance.[2] Is *Salammbô* merely a historical novel, undertaken by the author either as a respite from the banality and ennui of contemporary reality as portrayed in *Madame Bovary* or as an opportunity to show off his erudition? Does the choice of Carthage reflect the author's attraction to the beauty and aura of North Africa, or does it simply give him a pretext to explore the cruelty and violence he found so fascinating in the work of the Marquis de Sade? Is Carthage, a vanished antique culture with bizarre and at times unspeakably horrible rites and customs, simply too exotic, too alien, to spark any interest or understanding in the modern reader? How, if at all, does this work relate to the recurrent themes of the ideal, art, and the difficulties of communication that characterize Flaubert's other works?

An Emblematic Beginning: The Themes Unveiled

Salammbô opens as hoards of Mercenary soldiers celebrate the anniversary of one of their victories on the grounds of the palace of Hamilcar Barca, the Carthaginian general and suffete (a supreme executive magistrate) who had valiantly commanded their forces in Sicily during the First Punic War. This is not, however, a typical civic or military celebration, for the event is marked from the beginning by a threatening undercurrent of resentment and frustration. Carthage has shown considerable reluctance to pay the Mercenary armies that fought on its behalf: having lost the war, the avaricious mercantile republic cannot easily pay the bill and resents those to whom it owes money. The debt owed the soldiers-for-hire has even become confused in some citizens' minds with the tribute demanded by Rome; hence the former allies have come to be viewed as enemies. The Mercenaries, stung by this attitude and impatient at the delay, are restless and suspicious. Hamilcar himself is absent from the festivities, his palace having been offered, in response to the Mercenaries' demand for a reunion, by the "peace party" as an act of vengeance for the general's support of the war and his reluctance to accept defeat. Beyond burdening him with the expense, these political enemies hope, by association, to attach to him the disdain and hatred the populace feels for the foreign soldiers.[3]

The banquet scene is one of profusion and confusion. A seemingly endless array of exotic foodstuffs is presented in Flaubert's typical catalog style, which emphasizes excess and betrays an erudite fascination with rare and evocative words not unlike that of the poet Stéphane Mallarmé:

> First they were served birds in a green sauce on red earthenware plates decorated with black designs, then every kind of shellfish found on the Punic coast, porridge of wheat, beans and barley, and snails with cumin on yellow amber plates.
>
> Then the tables were covered with meats: antelopes with their horns, peacocks with their feathers, whole sheep cooked in sweet wine, legs of she-camel and buffalo, hedgehogs in garum, fried grasshoppers and pickled dormice. In wooden bowls from Tamrapanni floated large chunks of fat surrounded by saffron. Everything overflowed with brine, truffles and assa foetida. Pyramids of fruit collapsed over honey cakes, and they hadn't forgotten a few of those little pot-bellied, pink-bristled dogs fattened on olive pulp, a Carthaginian delicacy that others found repugnant.[4]

The Mercenaries, who hail from "every nation . . . Ligurians, Lusitanians, Balearics, Blacks, and fugitives from Rome," attack the food with gusto, even if they aren't always quite sure what to do with it: long-haired Gauls devour whole watermelons, peels, seeds, and all, while Blacks who have never before seen crayfish scratch their faces on the claws. Meanwhile, a cacophony of languages fills the air: "One heard, next to the heavy Doric dialect Celtic syllables ringing out like battle chariots, and Ionian endings clashing with desert consonants, harsh as jackal cries."

As the evening progresses, the Mercenaries become increasingly drunk—and increasingly bitter about their recent treatment by Carthage. As their behavior turns rowdy, some soldiers run off to free Hamilcar's slaves, one of whom—the Greek, Spendius—delivers a thank-you speech in several languages that ends up inciting the Mercenary mob to aspire to one of the treasures of the republic, the cups of the Sacred Legion. They demand the presence of Giscon, the suffete in whose charge the absent Hamilcar has left the foreign armies. When Giscon refuses to yield to their demand for the cups, a Gaul, Autharite, rushes at him brandishing two swords; Giscon knocks him down by hitting him over the head with a heavy ivory baton, thereby provoking the wrath of the other Gauls. Disdaining a fight with such drunken animals, Giscon and his bodyguard of legionnaires withdraw. This incident does nothing to improve the Mercenaries' attitude about their treatment at the hands of Carthage, and when they remember Hamilcar's absence they begin to suspect that it is yet another sign of treachery. The absent general becomes the focus of all of their "unsatisfied hatred."

Shortly thereafter, when one of the Mercenaries falls to the ground, foaming at the mouth, rumors of poisoning abound. Suspecting the worst, the drunken soldiers let loose a whirlwind of destruction: they attack the slaves they have just freed and set fire to the trees by hurling torches at their branches; they massacre Hamilcar's lions by shooting them with arrows and mutilate his elephants, cutting off their trunks and tusks; they walk through the serving dishes, smashing them to bits and demanding wine, gold, and women, raving in a hundred different languages.

One group wanders off looking for other things to pillage and happens upon the lake where are kept the Barca family's sacred bejeweled fish, reputed to be descendants of "the original conger eels that had hatched the mystic egg in which the Goddess lay hidden." Delighted at the idea of committing a sacrilege, the soldiers snatch the fish from the water and take them back to the banquet area, tossing them into pots of boiling water and amusing themselves by watching the creatures' agonized struggle. Suddenly, Hamilcar's palace door opens, and his daughter Salammbô appears, accompanied by the eunuch priests of the moon goddess Tanit.

As Salammbô walks among them, the Mercenaries are cowed by her pale presence ("Some emanation of the gods enveloped her like a fine vapor") and enthralled by her words: murmurs of mourning for the fish, cries of recrimination directed at her ungrateful guests, sighs of regret for the old days of Carthage's strength and prestige, and a song recalling the adventures of the god Melkarth, the original ancestor of her family. Nonetheless, they do not understand a bit of the old Canaanite dialect in which she speaks:

> They wondered what she might be telling them with the frightening gestures that accompanied her words . . . they tried to grasp these vague stories that swayed before their imagination, through the obscurity of theogonies, like phantoms in the clouds.[5]

Two men appear particularly taken with the strange but compelling virgin in their midst: Narr'Havas, a young Numidian chief, who is in Carthage less as a Mercenary than because it is his family's tradition to send its sons to live among other great families in the hope of preparing suitable marriages, and Mâtho, a Libyan soldier of colossal stature with a bloodstained face. Later, when as a gesture of reconciliation with the foreign troops Salammbô offers the Libyan a cup of wine, the same trouble-making Gaul who had earlier attacked Giscon suggests that she is symbolically offering Mâtho her bed. Narr'Havas reacts to this suggestion by hurling his javelin at the Libyan, pinning his arm to the table. By the time the unarmed Mâtho can free himself and make his way through the crowd, Narr'Havas has disappeared, as has Salammbô.

Mâtho rushes up the steps of the palace, only to find the doors locked, the building impenetrable. He is joined by the wily and manipulative Spendius, who binds the Libyan's wounds and declares Mâtho to be his new "master." The former slave understands politics and the complexities of Carthage's plight, and as the sun rises in splendor, he urges Mâtho to take charge of the Mercenary armies and conquer the republic. Mâtho, however, has no interest in political intrigue or military conquest; his only thoughts are of Salammbô, as he regrets having sensed in her eyes the curse of Moloch (the sun god and rival of Tanit, the moon goddess of whom Salammbô is a devotee) weighing heavily on him. As the chapter ends, Spendius stifles a cry when he recognizes in the distance two women fleeing the city and trailing a large veil, an allusion that Flaubert leaves unexplained for the bewildered reader.

Thus in the first chapter all of the major themes of the novel are already in place: violence, treachery, and excess; the tension between the sacred and the profane (or even the sacrilegious); the difficulties of communication and comprehension, which can cause one to act for the wrong reason on incomplete or incorrect information; the rivalry between Mâtho and Narr'Havas; the attraction of Salammbô, the otherworldly virgin (who nonetheless closes her eyes and presses her breast as she savors the excitement of the crowd of soldiers), to and for Mâtho; and through Salammbô and Mâtho, the antagonism between the moon and the sun, between the cult of Tanit and the cult of Moloch, between the feminine principle and the masculine principle.

Indeed, superimposed onto the tremendously complex plot of the war, intertwined with episodes involving the love/hate relationship between Salammbô and Mâtho, is a deceptively simple symbolic schema that links characters, characteristics, nations, nature, and the supernatural. On the one hand, Salammbô and the goddess Tanit, linked to Carthage and the moon, constitute the feminine principle; on the other hand, Mâtho and the god Moloch, the masculine principle, are associated with the Mercenaries and the sun. At times the schema works so well that a statement about one element can also be applied to elements in the same network (by similarity) and in the other network (by contrast): a sentence like "Moloch possessed Carthage" suggests the sun beating down on the city, the defeat of Tanit, and the sexual conquest of Salammbô by Mâtho. The reader soon discovers, however, that the symbolic associations do not always hold: Carthage also has a cult of Moloch, and the Mercenaries temporarily capture Tanit's veil. Moreover, the transparent symbolism is often underlain with, even undermined by, a more opaque suggestiveness, whose meaning remains inaccessible. A key example is Tanit's veil, with which Salammbô is obsessed throughout the novel. Linked clearly to the ideal nature of the goddess and to the fate of Carthage, the veil is also more vaguely but surely tied up with Salammbô's sexuality. Yet the precise nature of this sexual symbolism remains unstated, unclear, indecipherable, marking the veil, ultimately, as a symbol of its own unreadability, its own veiled meaning.[6]

The Early Stages: Unveiling the Veil

Salammbô's plot develops inexorably from the events and relationships established in the first chapter. The Carthaginian leaders convince the

Mercenaries that their number is overtaxing the city's physical and fiscal resources and that they should leave the city so as to avoid a famine and the complete ruin of the Carthaginian treasury. Each soldier is given a gold coin and the promise that taxes will be raised immediately to fulfill the city's debt. The Barbarian armies set up camp at some distance, just outside the sacred city of Sicca, and wait to be paid. Narr'Havas reappears, and although Mâtho initially wants to kill him, Spendius is able to convince his master to accept the Numidian's apologies and overtures of friendship. Narr'Havas's true motives remain somewhat ambiguous, however: one day he hides a dagger beneath his cloak when going hunting with Mâtho and Spendius, and another time he leads them a long way from camp and then claims to be lost. Such unexplained clues lead the reader to conjectures that are not answered, to effects that do not produce causes, thus thwarting his or her normal deductive reading habits and making the text frustrating. Spendius, more flexible than the reader, senses that the Numidian is undoubtedly up to something and wonders only whom he will betray: the Carthaginians or the Barbarians. Nonetheless, "expecting to profit from whatever disorder might ensue, he was grateful to Narr'Havas for the future perfidious deeds he anticipated from him." Meanwhile, the melancholy Mâtho, totally obsessed by his passion for the seemingly unattainable Salammbô, wanders about "constantly irresolute and overcome by an unshakable torpor, like someone who has taken a drink of some substance destined to kill him." Thus, while individual motives remain unclear, the general sense of foreboding is unmistakable.

Finally, a delegation of Carthaginians arrives, led by Hamilcar's rival, another suffete—the pompous, obese, and leprous Hannon. He pontificates at great length to the assembled troops about all of the republic's fiscal trials and tribulations, but neither the soldiers nor their captains can understand the Punic dialect in which he speaks. Suddenly Spendius intervenes and purports to translate the suffete's speech into five different languages, claiming that the Carthaginian has insulted them by calling them cowards and thieves, blamed the republic's losses on them, and threatened them with hard labor. This is, of course, a complete misrepresentation, but the suffete doesn't object since he can't understand any of the languages into which Spendius translates his message. The reader is reminded of the numerous pitfalls of language that figure in Flaubert's works, from Rodolphe's mendacious manipulation of Emma in *Madame Bovary* to the Spanish patriot's incomprehensible diatribe that drowns out Frédéric's political speech in *Sentimental Education*. At this point a tattered Balaeric named Zarxas arrives quite by coincidence to tell the tale of how a contingent of his compatriots was horribly massacred by the Carthaginians after the rest of the Mercenary troops left the city. Provoked to fury by Spendius's lies and Zarxas's account of the republic's atrocities, the Barbarians ransack the baggage of the Carthaginian delegation, claiming their just due, and when they find—instead of the money owed them—a partial accounting in leather chits, they turn on the suffete and his entourage. Hannon flees in terror, and the Barbarians break camp to go attack Carthage.

Meanwhile, Salammbô has continued her life of pious devotion under the direction of the high priest Schahabarim. Living in seclusion in the palace, cut off from human contact except for the priest and a personal slave, Salammbô's dedication to Tanit has become a form of identification: "An influence had come down from the moon upon the virgin; when the star waned, Salammbô grew weaker. Languishing all day long, she revived in the evening. During an eclipse, she had nearly died." Overwhelmed by a vague sense of longing, she has become obsessed with penetrating the most secret mysteries of the goddess's cult—with seeing the idol and her sacred veil, the "zaïmph," on which the destiny of Carthage depends. Schahabarim, however, rejects these desires as sacrilege, reminding her that touching the veil brings certain death.

The Barbarians set up camp outside the walls of Carthage, and Mâtho, respected for his strength and courage, takes charge of the army. More negotiations take place between the Carthaginian council, which seems to have come to understand the seriousness and the immediacy of the threat posed by the Barbarian armies, and the captains of the various Mercenary groups regarding the question of their pay. As the council makes more and more concessions, the Barbarians' demands extend beyond money and goods: they ask for Hannon's head and for the marriage of their chiefs to the virgin daughters of the republic's great families. As outlandish as these requests might seem to the Carthaginians, they are not entirely evidence of bad faith, for Hamilcar made many extravagant, albeit vague, promises to the Barbarians. Finally, a payout is begun under Giscon's direction, but discontent continues to grow in the Barbarian camp as the duplicitous Spendius makes his way from one group to another, convincing each that it is being shortchanged or that the Carthaginians plan to exact vengeance on it when the other groups have dispersed. Before long, the Mercenaries turn on Giscon; he is shot in the ear with an arrow, and the Carthaginians accompanying him are chained around the waist and thrown into a garbage pit.

As the Barbarians await reprisals from Carthage, national antipathies and personal grudges continue to flourish among them during the continual harangues of the war councils: "everyone talked, no one listened." One evening Spendius secretly offers to sneak Mâtho into the city (in other words, into proximity to Salammbô) if the Libyan promises to obey him without question during the excursion. They climb the aqueduct and are carried into the city's cisterns by the flowing water. Once inside, they make their way to Tanit's temple, from which Spendius proposes to steal the sacred zaïmph. His project has a double purpose: to diminish Carthage's power (which is believed to depend on possession of the veil) and to allow Mâtho to avenge himself on Tanit for his unrequited passion for Salammbô.

During their search for the veil, Mâtho, a somewhat unwilling participant in this sacrilegious enterprise, is nearly overcome by the temple's warm and stifling atmosphere, by its perfumes and symbols of fecundation. As he experiences the holy site's dazzling mysteries, he thinks only of Salammbô, confusing her in his mind with Tanit, the goddess herself. Once the theft is accomplished, he decides to sneak into the palace and present the veil to Salammbô, acting contrary to Spendius's advice (and in violation of his promise to follow the Greek's every order on this adventure). It is unclear, however, whether Mâtho's motivation is to seduce the devout virgin with such a precious gift or to dominate her into submission with the powers conveyed by the sacred object. When Salammbô is first awakened by his presence in her room, she is fascinated by the prospect of achieving her ambition of seeing something of the goddess's tangible form. She orders Mâtho to bring the veil closer, to give it to her. Yet when Mâtho declares his love and reaches out with the zaïmph to embrace her, she is seized with horror, either at the sacrilege she is about to commit or at her dawning realization that Mâtho's intentions are far from pure. Summoning the palace slaves, with fanatical rhetoric she heaps curses on the Libyan's head, especially the curse of Moloch ("the Other"), always seen in opposition to Tanit:

> Curses upon you who have stolen from Tanit! Hatred, vengeance, slaughter and pain! May Gurzi, god of battles, tear you apart! May Matisman, god of the dead, suffocate you! And may the Other—who must not be named—burn you![7]

Because no one is willing to touch the veil, Mâtho is able to escape with it from both the palace and the city, and with great dismay the Carthaginians line the walls to watch their city's "fortune" blazing in the sun as it is carried away. This image recalls the disappearing veil that ended the opening chapter, though the parallel is neither underscored nor explained by the narrator.

Possession of the zaïmph makes Mâtho the undisputed leader of the Barbarians, while its absence from Carthage encourages her neighbors, tired of paying tribute and obeying the republic's dictates, to ally themselves against her. Even Narr'Havas appears, declaring his intention to join the Mercenaries since Carthage is a potential threat to his kingdom. He and Mâtho make a blood pact whose symbolism is overwhelmed by its goriness:

> A white bull and a black ewe were brought in, one the symbol of day, one the symbol of night. Their throats were cut at the edge of a pit. When it was full of blood, they plunged their arms into it. Then Narr'Havas spread out his hand on Mâtho's chest, and Mâtho his on Narr'Havas's. They repeated this mark on the canvas of their tents.[8]

A plan is set to lay siege to Carthage and subdue her once and for all. As a first step, the cities of Utica and Hippo-Zarytus, which have refused to ally themselves with the Barbarians, must be conquered because their geographic locations would allow a besieged Carthage to continue to supply herself. Thus three groups set out: one led by Spendius to attack Utica; a second led by Mâtho to attack Hippo-Zarytus; and a third, led by the Gaul Autharite, to occupy the plain of Carthage. Narr'Havas returns to his kingdom to collect elephants for battle.

The war effort in Carthage is put in the hands of Hannon, who spends months on fastidious and showy preparations. Finally he sets out to rescue Utica, leading the elite guards of the Legion, squadrons of citizen warriors, and assorted Elders. A first skirmish seems to give certain victory to Spendius's troops:

> The Barbarians broke through their lines; they cut their throats with two-edged swords; they tripped over the dying and the dead, blinded by the blood spurting into their faces. This heap of pikes, helmets, breastplates, swords, and confused limbs spun around and around, expanding and retracting with elastic contractions . . . finally the Suffete's litter (his grand litter with the crystal pendants) that one had been able to see from the beginning, swaying among the soldiers like a small boat on the waves, all of a sudden foundered. No doubt he was dead?[9]

As with many of the descriptive passages in the novel, the controlled style, with its detached tone, uniform rhythm, meticulous lists, and mechanical patterns ("elastic contractions") seems at curious odds with the gore and chaos, not to mention the personal (though unattributed) note struck by the use of free indirect discourse in the final sentence.[10] As a result it is difficult for the reader to situate the viewpoint.

When the dust clears, Hannon reappears, astride the lead beast in an onslaught of charging elephants. The Barbarians are quickly dispatched to the hills, and Hannon enters Utica a victorious savior. He quickly repairs to the baths, where his leprous body presents a most disconcerting spectacle, the details of which Flaubert, in his fascination with rotting flesh, does not spare the reader. This same fascination also characterizes the descriptions of the blind beggar in *Madame Bovary* and, especially, the leper/father figure in "Saint Julian," who, like Hannon here, is depicted as having burning eyes:

> From his purplish lips escaped a breath more noxious than the stench of a corpse. Two embers seemed to burn in place of his eyes, which no longer had brows; a clump of wrinkled skin hung from his forehead; his two ears, sticking out from his head, had begun to swell, and the deep wrinkles that formed semi-circles around his nostrils, gave him a strange and frightening look, like a wild beast.[11]

Hannon has three Barbarians who were captured during the battle brought to him, and he harangues them at great length. They, of course, can't understand a word he says, and their seeming impassivity serves only to work him up into a greater fury.

Meanwhile, the tide of battle has turned again: the Barbarians, after regrouping, have used flaming pigs to frighten the Carthaginian elephants into crushing the Punic army against Utica's gates. When Hannon learns of this reversal of fortune, he has the three captive Barbarians decapitated and smears his knees with the "warm slime" of their blood to profit from its remedial powers before sneaking out of Utica to join the remnants of his army. On the way back to Carthage they encounter Narr'Havas, who, although he bows in greeting, does so making a sign that Hannon doesn't understand and that Flaubert doesn't explain, leaving the reader in the lurch as usual.

Carthage's losses have been heavy—"400,972 silver shekels, 15,623 gold shekels, eighteen elephants, four members of the Grand Council, three hundred of the Rich, 8,000 citizens, grain for three months, a large amount of baggage, and all the war machines"—but although tradition would have Hannon crucified for this defeat, the city is too weakened and vulnerable to act on its anger. It is nonetheless determined that only one man can save the republic, and the peace party itself "votes holocausts" for the return of Hamilcar Barca.

When Hamilcar does return he meets with the Elders and the priests of the four major cults in the Temple of Moloch. The discussion turns acrimonious as various factions attempt to cast blame on one another for the series of losses and defeats that have humbled the republic. Hamilcar berates the Elders for the dishonorable and shortsighted way they treated the Mercenaries and declares his unwillingness to take command of the Punic forces because he finds the Carthaginian leaders to be "cowardly, greedy, ungrateful, pusillanimous and crazy." Out of spite, certain among the Elders cry out that his reluctance is undoubtedly due to the fact that his daughter takes her lovers from among the Mercenaries, either a lie or a misreading of the episode involving Mâtho's theft of the veil. Hamilcar is staggered by the thought that Salammbô would have any lover at all, but recovering his aplomb, he jumps up on the altar and swears before Moloch that the accusation is so groundless and meaningless he will not even deign to mention it to Salammbô.

Barca then returns to his palace, where he encounters his daughter. They have a strained, vague, and entirely ambiguous conversation in which Salammbô might be confessing an indiscretion or in which she might be lamenting the loss of the zaïmph or the threat posed by the Barbarians. Out of pride Hamilcar refuses to break his oath and ask for the truth, but he ends up erroneously interpreting her remarks and gestures as proof that the Elders' accusations were true. Leaving her in a state of emotional turmoil, he stalks off to inventory his riches. He wanders past pits of grain, through chambers filled with gold, silver, and bronze coins, and into a vault "where mysterious things were kept, things without a name and of inestimable value." His mood improves briefly as he basks in his accumulated wealth but quickly shifts to dismay and then to anger as he becomes aware of the losses and damage inflicted by the Barbarians, which seem to confirm in his mind "the thing he had forbidden himself to know." Unable to strike out at the real source of his anguish, he finds a target for his wrath in those around him: the garden slaves are all condemned to the mines, the slave master is sent to be suffocated in a dungheap, the governors of the estate are flogged and branded as cowards, and the chief steward is threatened with crucifixion for having failed to protect the elephants. That evening he notifies the assembly of the Rich that he has changed his mind and that he will accept command of the Punic forces in their conflict with the Barbarians, a decision seemingly based more on a sense of personal affront than on national allegiance.

Hamilcar undertakes new preparations for battle, while the Barbarians, aware of his return, wait and try to guess his tactics so they can position themselves to outmaneuver him. Mâtho displaces his passionate fascination with Salammbô and his resentment of her indifferent rejection of his advances onto her father. Narr'Havas's loyalties continue to puzzle Spendius: the Numidian has not fully lived up to his promises to supply horses and elephants, and when an unknown man suddenly appears and breathlessly recounts some tale in "an unintelligible dialect," Narr'Havas simply takes off without a word, galloping away on horseback, leaving Spendius, and the reader, clueless once again.

One evening Hamilcar and his troops take advantage of the winds and currents to cross the Macar River, taking by surprise the Barbarian armies camped before Utica. The battle is fierce. The surprise factor initially helps the Carthaginians to take the upper hand, as the Barbarians find themselves crushed against the phalanx of Punic lancers. Yet after extended and ferocious hand-to-hand combat, the Barbarians begin to take control. Soon, however, they are definitively crushed by Hamilcar's charging elephants, a gory episode depicted by Flaubert with typical matter-of-factness:

> To better resist, the Barbarians rushed into a compact mass; the elephants charged impetuously into the middle of them. . . . With their trunks they choked men, or tearing them from the ground, flung them up to the soldiers in the towers; using their tusks, they disemboweled them, threw them in the air, and long entrails hung from their ivory fangs like bundles of rigging on masts.[12]

When Mâtho finally arrives the next evening from Hippo-Zarytus there is nothing to be seen on the plain before Utica but heaps of corpses. When he catches up with Spendius and the remnants of his army, he is dismayed by the defeat, distraught at having missed the battle, and discouraged by Spendius's shortcomings as a military tactician and battlefield leader. The Greek makes excuses (Hamilcar attacked at the absolutely worst moment) and tries to reinstate himself in Mâtho's good graces by reminding him of past triumphs (the mistranslation of the suffete's speech at Sicca to provoke the Barbarians against Carthage, the theft of the zaïmph) and by encouraging him to view the current disaster as a temporary setback.

The Carthaginians and the Mercenaries continue to scheme and maneuver. Mâtho, possessed with the spirit of Moloch and imagining that he is obeying the god's voice, commits such appalling deeds as having lancers attack the women following the army so as to eliminate them as a distraction and a strain on resources. Narr'Havas returns to join his Barbarian allies, furious that Hamilcar has attempted to foment revolt in the Numidian kingdom. For his part, Hamilcar finds himself increasingly isolated. After a period of initial adulation when the two thousand captives from the battle of the Macar were delivered to Carthage, he now encounters resentment and resistance. Requests for men and supplies, deemed to be excessive and unduly burdensome, are ignored or denied. His army scours the countryside, looking to take by force what the republic won't provide. Meanwhile, the Barbarians, not to mention the reader, find the Carthaginians' marches and countermarches incomprehensible. It is unclear whether they are pursuing Hamilcar or whether he is leading them on.

Eventually the Barbarian armies succeed in surrounding Hamilcar's forces. The suffete sends word blaming the war on the Elders, offering the Barbarians their choice of Utica or Hippo-Zarytus to pillage, and declaring that he has no cause to fear them because, having won over certain traitors, he is certain to prevail over the rest of the Mercenaries. The Mercenary soldiers are tempted by the thought of easy spoils but unnerved by the idea of traitors. Rather than suspecting Hamilcar of bravado, they begin to suspect one another, abandoning former comrades, realigning themselves according to whim, shunning in particular those of different custom or dialect. The four Barbarian chiefs cannot agree on a course of action, and Mâtho, who sees the war against Carthage as his own personal affair, becomes increasingly frustrated that the others involved refuse to obey him.

One morning the Barbarians line up the three hundred Carthaginian rich men taken captive during the debacle at Sicca—by this time a dazed, motley, vermin-infested crew—and use them as a living rampart from behind which to throw spears at the Punic troops. Infuriated by this provocation, the Carthaginians rush out of the protective stockade they have constructed but are quickly driven back by an onrush of Mercenary soldiers. In the confusion, the Balaeric Zarxas manages to grab one of the legionnaires, plunges a dagger into his throat, and placing his mouth over the wound, drains the body of blood.

The surrounded Punic army ventures no more sorties but sits watching its supplies dwindle as it waits in vain for reinforcements. Public opinion in Carthage turns more and more against Hamilcar, to the point where "the Suffete would have been less execrated if he had allowed himself to be beaten from the start." Full of hate, they abandon the cult of the goddess Tanit and turn to Moloch, "the killer." There is even talk that Salammbô should be punished—immolated as an offering to the gods—given her involvement in the loss of the zaïmph. Every evening unknown men invade Hamilcar's gardens to look up at Salammbô's terrace and cry against her, "like dogs baying at the moon."

Salammbô Unveiled

Meanwhile, Salammbô is filled with a combination of despair and joyful pride at having seen the zaïmph and a certain regret at not having touched it. She is filled also with worry about her python (a national and personal fetish), which seems to be wasting away, and with a vague and general sense of boredom, sadness, desire, jealousy, and fear. She seeks solace from Schahabarim, who is undergoing his own crisis of faith. Having observed the sun's position above the moon in the sky in conjunction with the events transpiring on earth, he has become convinced that the "male exterminating principle" is, in fact, supreme and thus feels all the more strongly the loss of his virility. Doubting Tanit, he nonetheless wants to believe in her and longs for some kind of proof of her power. In time, he imagines a scheme that could save both his faith and his country: Salammbô must go to the Barbarians' camp and retrieve the zaïmph.

Salammbô is initially overcome with terror at the suggestion:

> An indeterminate horror held her back; she was afraid of Moloch, afraid of Mâtho. This man of gigantic stature, who was master of the zaïmph, dominated the Rabettna as much as did the Baal and he seemed to her surrounded by the same lightning flashes; after all, the soul of the Gods sometimes visited men's bodies. When Schahabarim spoke of the man, didn't he say she must conquer Moloch? They were mixed together; she confused them; both were pursuing her.[13]

As the days pass, however, the idea of serving Tanit in this way begins to grow on her, and as it does, her python, which has shed its old skin, begins to revive and flourish. She finally assents and seeks orders from Schahabarim on how to proceed. The usually verbose priest is not very forthcoming in his explanation; he first tries to communicate through facial expression and posture, then looks for words to let him talk around the point. When it becomes clear that Salammbô isn't getting the message, he finally elaborates: "You will be alone with him. . . . Fear nothing! And whatever he tries, do not call out. Don't be afraid. You will be humble, do you understand, and submit to his desire which is the order of the heavens."

On the evening of her departure for Mâtho's camp, Salammbô undertakes an extensive and mysterious series of preparations and ablutions ordered by Schahabarim. She first rubs her ears and heels with the coagulated blood of a black dog "slaughtered by barren women on a winter's night in the ruins of a tomb." Next she unfastens her gown, loosens her hair, and begins to sway to the repetitive, frenzied music being played outside her door as her python wraps itself around her, its head and tail under her arms and between her knees, its sexual symbolism somewhat obvious:

> it tightened round her its black coils striped with golden patches. Salammbô gasped beneath this heavy weight, her back bent, she felt she was dying; and with the tip of its tail it gently flicked her thigh; then the music stopped and it dropped off.[14]

Finally, dressed in a tunic embroidered with bird feathers, her hair covered in gold dust and her hands and feet dripping jewels, she sneaks out to join her guide.

When she arrives at the Barbarian camp, so hidden beneath veils and draperies that she appears to be a ghost rising from the shadows of the night, she declares herself to be a deserter from Carthage and demands to see Mâtho. He does not recognize her until they reach his tent and she tears off her veils and demands the zaïmph. Although she presents her demand with considerable eloquence, he is too enthralled by her presence to hear her words and wants only to touch her, embrace her, absorb her. Repelled by his desire and masculinity, she continues her verbal assault, reproaching him first for the destruction the Barbarians have wrought—"The provinces quake at your fury, the furrows are full of corpses. I followed the trail of your fires as if I were walking behind Moloch"—and then for implicating her in the theft of the zaïmph—"I didn't understand your words; but I saw that you wanted to drag me towards something dreadful, to the bottom of an abyss." In response to the latter reproach Mâtho explains that the garment seemed to belong to her since he finds her to be as "omnipotent, immaculate, radiant, and beautiful" as the goddess and asks if she is not, in fact, Tanit. He goes on to speak of his passion for her, which both frightens and wearies Salammbô. Eventually she makes a move to simply take the zaïmph and leave, which provokes the amorous Mâtho to such fury that he threatens to kill her, before breaking down in sobs and begging for pity. As he kneels before her with tears in his eyes and his hands roving over her, she finally succumbs:

> A limpness came over Salammbô and she lost all consciousness of herself. Something both intimate and superior, an order from the Gods, forced her to give herself up to it. . . . Mâtho seized her heels, the golden chain broke apart, and the two ends, flying off, struck the canvas like two vipers recoiling. The zaïmph fell down, covering her. . . .
>
> "Moloch, you are burning me!" and the soldier's kisses, more devouring than flames, ran over her; she was as though carried away in a hurricane, caught in the power of the sun.[15]

As they lie together, Mâtho spots the moon and confesses to having spent countless nights gazing at it, trying to see through its veil to Salammbô's face: "Your memory mingled with its rays; I could no longer distinguish between the two of you!" When he falls asleep, Salammbô spots a dagger lying beside the bed and is excited with an urge for blood. She seizes the weapon, but before she can act, Mâtho is awakened. Loud cries from outside the tent call him to action: Hamilcar has set fire to Autharite's camp.

Left alone, Salammbô contemplates the zaïmph at length and is surprised to feel only melancholy as her long-held dream is realized. Suddenly a strange figure appears crawling under the canvas of the tent; it is Giscon, still a prisoner of the Mercenaries, who has overheard her encounter with Mâtho and has come to curse her for her treachery and her sacrilege. Frightened, Salammbô gathers up the veil and rushes out of the tent. Schahabarim's guide has waited for her and they flee.

Touching Tanit's Veil

Meanwhile, Narr'Havas has decided to defect from the Barbarian cause and has gone to prostrate himself before Hamilcar. Hamilcar accepts this new alliance, seeing in it not only a solution to his current desperate strategic situation but a potential asset toward the realization of his long-term plans. Suddenly, Salammbô appears in her father's tent, brandishing the zaïmph. Hamilcar is at first overwhelmed with gratitude at the recovery of Carthage's "fortune" but then horrified when he spots the broken chain dangling from her ankles and realizes the implication of her lost virginity. Maintaining his impassibility, he offers his daughter in marriage to his newfound ally the Numidian king, who of course accepts.

With Narr'Havas's help Hamilcar's forces succeed in besting the Barbarians, leaving behind a scene of unbelievable carnage: "Hideous weapons had inflicted complicated wounds. Greenish strips hung from their foreheads; they were hacked to pieces, crushed to the marrow, turned blue by choking, or split open by the elephants' tusks." Yet this gruesome victory, far from complete, proves to be transient. As a result of misjudgments, jealousies, missed opportunities, and shifting alliances the Punic troops retreat to Carthage without pursuing their psychological or strategic advantage. The depleted Barbarian forces are given new hope and follow the Carthaginians to the gates of the city. Reinforced by opportunists and revenge seekers from among the republic's former allies and enemies, the Mercenaries undertake to lay siege to the great city, and when Spendius succeeds in destroying Carthage's lifeline—its aqueduct—it appears that the Barbarians may be destined to become the ultimate victors.

The siege drags on as the Barbarians construct ever more elaborate but always unsuccessful machines for penetrating the city's defenses, while the Carthaginians, nearly overwhelmed by hunger and thirst, continue to resist. Every contact between the two sides results in yet more carnage. Within Carthage the usual blame-fixing and second-guessing intensifies. Schahabarim, who is increasingly obsessed with his impotence and who has every reason to suspect all that transpired in Mâtho's tent, arrives at the palace to berate Salammbô, ostensibly for having provoked Mâtho by stealing back the zaïmph—"but that was not what the priest really meant." Hamilcar visits his daughter to discuss Mâtho, on the pretext of garnering military information, but she tells him little more than that during her visit to the Barbarian's tent he shouted a lot and then fell asleep. She fails to mention his other advances—because she is ashamed, because her value system attaches little importance to such things, or because the whole memory is so hazy and dreamlike that "she could not have found the means or the words to express it." During this period her serpent dies, and she handles the loss with surprising detachment.

One evening Iddibal, one of Hamilcar's most trusted slaves, appears at the palace with a young boy whom he has sneaked into the besieged city via the gulf. This child is Hamilcar's son Hannibal, who had been hiding in the provinces until the widespread war made his position there too precarious and who now will be hidden in Salammbô's room.[16] The palace turns out not to be a safe haven, however, for unbeknownst to Hamilcar, someone spotted the boy's arrival.

Meanwhile, the people of Carthage are becoming desperate. Since the return of the zaïmph has not proved sufficient to restore the republic's good fortune, it is determined that the fate of the city rests with Moloch, the bloodthirsty god for whom no pain is too excessive. The Elders decree (by paraphrase, "since some things are more awkward to say than do") that every great family must sacrifice its young children, and Hamilcar is not exempt. Determined not to lose his cherished son, Hamilcar has the child of a slave disguised as his own and delivered to the priests to be burned alive at the altar of the Baal. During the mystic and horrific frenzy of the immolation ceremony, Schahabarim briefly appears and, renouncing Tanit, declares his allegiance to the virile and ferocious Moloch. His gesture, which seems to indicate a severing of the "last bond that linked men's souls to a merciful deity," is futile since his impotence precludes his participation in the virile cult of Moloch. Nonetheless, the sacrifice of the children does not appear to be without effect; the skies open up, and the city is born anew as a deluge replenishes its water supplies: "the thunder rumbled; it was the voice of Moloch; he had conquered Tanit, and now made fertile she was opening her vast womb from the heavenly heights." The parallel with Mâtho's "conquest" of Salammbô is unmistakable, although its significance remains unclear.

Hamilcar and a contingent of Carthaginians break out of the besieged city via the gulf, while the Barbarians struggle with the storm and its muddy aftermath. Fickle allegiances once again shift; fear that a Barbarian victory could lead to a general state of anarchy provokes the republic's African neighbors to lend their support, in the form of men and supplies, to Hamilcar and his troops. Narr'Havas reappears and manages to get 6,000 men and 40 elephants, all laden with foodstuffs, into the still-besieged city. The Carthaginians are particularly pleased to see the elephants, whose presence they take as a sign that Baal is now looking on them with affection. Narr'Havas attempts to visit his betrothed but is turned away because Hamilcar has left orders that he is not to see her until the end of the war. For her part, Salammbô finds it difficult to understand how the Numidian will ever become "her master," especially since she is still fascinated by Mâtho: "Although she asked Tanit every day for Mâtho's death, her aversion for the Libyan was lessening. She felt in a confused way that the hatred with which he had persecuted her was something almost religious."

Hamilcar succeeds in maneuvering the Barbarians into a narrow gorge, which his soldiers then seal off with boulders. Trapped, the Mercenaries now face the same dangers of famine and thirst that earlier confronted the besieged Carthaginians, but in a compressed time frame since they had few supplies with them when they entered the gorge. Within days they are reduced to cannibalism, fighting off the vultures to pick strips of flesh from the rotting corpses of their comrades. By the end of the third week, when fully half of the Barbarian army has died, the Carthaginians appear at the edge of the precipice bordering the gorge and offer to present terms to a delegation of Barbarians. Egress from the gorge is made possible as the Carthaginians push down large boulders to form an improvised staircase.

Hamilcar's terms are surprisingly clement: 10 unarmed Mercenaries, of his choosing, are to be turned over to him to be dealt with at his discretion. The delegation, which includes Spendius, Autharite, and Zarxas, readily assents, only to discover that they themselves are the 10 he demands. When their spokesmen fail to return, the rest of the Mercenaries fear they have been betrayed. After waiting a few days, one group gingerly picks its way up the boulders to the top of the gorge, where it encounters an ambush. Caught in a mass of attacking elephants, the Barbarians in this group are quickly vanquished; even those who surrender and beg for mercy are killed, tied down and trampled out of sheer vengeance. When another group appears, Hamilcar uses a different strategy, offering to take some of them as replacements for his own decimated troops. However, since he needs only a few, he declares that the best will have to prove their worth by surviving a fight to the death with their comrades. When there are only 60 left, they are stabbed to death by 60 Carthaginians during a water break, an act of treachery by which Hamilcar hopes both to satisfy his army's instinct for violence and to bind it to him out of fear.

The Carthaginians now head for Tunis, where Mâtho has taken refuge. The Elders, fearing the power of Hamilcar should he and Narr'Havas achieve victory on their own, send Hannon to join them. The Numidian troops and the two Carthaginian armies take up positions outside the walls of Tunis, and Hamilcar has the 10 Barbarians from the delegation at the gorge crucified side by side as a message to the remaining Mercenaries about how they can expect to be treated. Nonetheless, Mâtho and a group of Barbarians manage to sneak out of the city and surround Hannon's army. The suffete and a group of 30 Elders who have accompanied him are taken prisoner, and in spite of Hannon's efforts to buy mercy either with money or by betraying Hamilcar, the entire group is crucified.

Mâtho's group cannot withstand an assault by the combined forces of Narr'Havas and Hamilcar; chased away from Tunis, they take to wandering the countryside in search of a refuge. Red sores appear on some of their faces; although the sores may come from having touched the leprous Hannon, some maintain they are punishment for having eaten Salammbô's sacred fish—and "far from regretting the deed, they dreamed of even more appalling sacrilegious acts." After three frustrating months of meandering through the countryside, punctuated by inconclusive skirmishes with the Carthaginians, Mâtho is prepared to propose a final great battle to end the war once and for all—and Hamilcar accepts the challenge.

As they prepare to fight, Narr'Havas and Mâtho are both preoccupied with thoughts of Salammbô: the Numidian has received a gift from her that he interprets as a sign of love (although in truth she sent it merely to stimulate his courage in battle, so that Mâtho and his hold over her can be destroyed once and for all); the Libyan attempts to displace his impossible affection for her onto his comrades-at-arms; as a result both Narr'Havas and Mâtho enter the fray with a sense of increased strength and power.

At first, Mâtho's clever battle plan and the Barbarians' invincible courage portend a victory for the Mercenaries, but just as Hamilcar is beginning to despair, there appears a ragtag collection of old men, young children, and women—accompanied by an elephant mutilated during the Barbarians' rampage in Hamilcar's garden. At this gesture of patriotism from the Punic people, the Carthaginians are seized with renewed fury that enables them to quickly vanquish the Barbarians. Soon, only Mâtho remains; surrounded but determined to fight on, he is ensnared in a net thrown by Narr'Havas.

As the novel closes, the Carthaginians are celebrating their victory over the Mercenaries and Salammbô's marriage to the Numidian king. The political and the personal are merged in the event: Salammbô's wedding is a day of national rejoicing because of her role in saving the homeland by recovering the zaïmph, and the highlight of the day's festivities is to be the execution of Mâtho. Various means of torture and death—filling him with molten lead, flaying him alive, setting him afire—have been proposed and then rejected on the grounds that too few citizens would be actively involved. The Elders finally settle on a plan that allows everyone to participate: he is to walk through the city, arms tied behind his back, as the assembled Carthaginians attack him in any manner they choose. The only restrictions are that no one may strike him in the heart (so he lives to suffer as long as possible) or in the eyes (so he sees his torture to the very end).

As Mâtho is released from his prison cell, the sun begins to sink in the sky and is replaced symbolically by the crescent moon. He is pushed along, torn apart by the Carthaginians' delirious rage, in the direction of the square where the wedding party is centered. There, a resplendent Salammbô, "no longer distinguishable from Tanit, seems to be the very genius of Carthage, her soul incarnate." When he finally reaches her, barely alive, she looks into his eyes and suddenly understands all he has suffered for her. She remembers being in his tent and wishes that she could once again feel his arms around her and hear his gentle words. At the moment that her longtime wish for his death is about to be fulfilled, she realizes that she does not want him to die. Schahabarim, dressed in the mantle of a priest of Moloch, rushes towards Mâtho's inert body and tears out his heart, offering it to the sun: "The sun was dropping behind the waves; its rays, like long arrows, struck the crimson heart. The star progressively sank into the sea as the beating of the heart lessened; at the last quiver, it disappeared." At this evidence of Mâtho's destruction, all of Carthage is convulsed with a spasm of titanic joy. Narr'Havas puts his arm around his bride and raises his cup to drink to the genius of the city. As Salammbô raises her cup in response, she suddenly falls to the ground, struck dead "for having touched Tanit's veil."

The abrupt and ambiguous ending produces several layers of meaning, none entirely satisfactory.[17] In one sense, Salammbô is simply stricken by the goddess's curse (though at some remove from the actual deed), yet when the reader lifts this veil Salammbô seems to die for having glimpsed the ideal and having found it hollow. Behind this layer of meaning lies the suggestion that the veil merely represents her own sexuality, which, inextricably linked with Mâtho, must expire with him. Indeed, the masculine and feminine principles can neither coexist nor exist the one without the other. Ultimately, the text's meaning remains hidden behind the swirl of elusive symbols that veil it.

Art and Chaos

Despite these symbolic impasses and the apparent chaos that characterizes much of the novel's plot (with its alliances that shift like the desert sands and its battlefield reversals of fortune), its structure is tightly symmetrical. The book is divided into 15 chapters, and parallels of theme, setting, or action are established between chapters 1 and 15, 2 and 14, 3 and 13, and so on. For example, feasts combining festive celebrations with acts of violence are the subjects of the first and last chapters; in chapter 2 the Barbarians pass a line of crucified lions on their way to Sicca, and in chapter 14 Hamilcar has crucified the delegation of Mercenaries, and lions attack and devour the last Barbarians who straggle out of the gorge; in chapter 3 Salammbô's devotion to the cult of Tanit is explored, whereas in chapter 13 the bloodthirsty practices of the cult of Moloch are revealed; in chapter 4 Spendius sneaks Mâtho into Carthage via the aqueduct, and in chapter 12 he destroys the aqueduct; in chapter 5 Tanit's veil is stolen by Mâtho, and in chapter 11 it is stolen back by Salammbô; in chapter 6 the power of the zaïmph seems to be confirmed as the Carthaginians under Hannon's command are routed by their enemies, while in chapter 10 Schahabarim berates Salammbô for the veil's loss and plots its recovery; in chapter 7 Hamilcar is welcomed back to Carthage and hailed as the city's only possible savior, whereas in chapter 9 the city second-guesses his tactics and turns against him. Chapter 8, the only chapter not to be paired, depicts the Barbarians' first significant loss in the war, and by its central and unparalleled position it presages the action's eventual outcome, providing a sense of direction through the chaos that follows. A similar symmetry governs the encounters between Salammbô and Mâtho, which occur in chapters 1, 5, 11, and 15.[18]

On another level certain elements of Flaubert's style serve to counterbalance the frenzied activity that characterizes his novel's plot. For example, the imperfect tense, which suggests an action whose duration continues in the past rather than one that is accomplished at a specific moment, permeates the text, fixing even the most active scenes in a kind of netherworld of perpetual becoming. Also, the tight and extended series of oppositions (between Salammbô and Mâtho, between Tanit and Moloch, between Carthage and the Barbarians) and parallels (between Salammbô, the moon, and Tanit, between Mâtho, the sun, and Moloch) that Flaubert establishes create a network of interrelationships, a tangible framework that ensnares the vagaries of human action and the vicissitudes of war described in the plot. Even on the sentence level the rhythm, sonority, and grammatical symmetry of Flaubert's prose create an aura of stability that attenuates the plot's overriding sense of movement and change. For example, the opening sentence of the novel—"It was at Megara, a suburb of Carthage, in the gardens of Hamilcar"—is marked by a tripartite rhythm, symmetrical punctuation, the repetition of the sound "ar" in each of the three parts, and a verb in the imperfect tense. All of these elements interact to create a sense of solidity, balance, and stasis that clearly anchors the text in the immutable realm of art rather than in the chaotic realm of reality.[19]

Is then the ability of art to dominate the flux, the unpredictability, the slipperiness of life *Salammbô*'s real message? Certainly there is no redeeming message in the plot: like an antique Emma Bovary, Salammbô pursues an ideal (Tanit), haunted by forbidden or seemingly unattainable desires (to touch the goddess's veil) that not only prove to be hollow when realized but that ultimately bring about her destruction. At the novel's end Salammbô and Mâtho both die, each in some measure responsible—without really wanting to be—for the other's death; Schahabarim renounces his god but is excluded from the cult to which he aspires; Carthage wins the war but, as the modern reader knows, will eventually lose everything, from its identity to its very physical existence. Yet if art is the answer, the antidote to life, it doesn't emerge unscathed, for throughout the novel Flaubert systematically undermines the usefulness of language—the medium of his art—in the pursuit of communication and understanding. Like Schahabarim, Flaubert, the high priest of the cult of art, is besieged by doubts while longing to believe. No wonder then that *Salammbô,* which constitutes both a testimony to the power of language and an incarnation of its shortcomings, remains such an enigmatic and intriguing work. Ultimately, as in a dance of veils, it is the dance itself, not what lies behind the veils, that constitutes the true beauty of the performance.

Chapter Five

Sentimental Education: A Sentimental Journey

When we first encounter Frédéric Moreau, the protagonist of Flaubert's 1869 novel *Sentimental Education* (*L'Education sentimentale*), the future law student is about to embark on a boat trip from Paris to his home in Nogent-sur-Seine. It is fitting that the novel begins with a journey, since its title echoes that of Lawrence Sterne's *Sentimental Journey* (1768) and since the journey is the main organizing principle (some might say the only one) that holds Flaubert's seemingly formless work together.[1]

The journey is a literary commonplace that structures narrative works as diverse as the ancient epic poems of Homer and the medieval romances of Chrétien de Troyes, the picaresque tales of Denis Diderot and the philosophical stories of Voltaire, the scientific fantasies of Cyrano de Bergerac and Jules Verne, and such modern existentialist novels as André Malraux's *The Royal Way* (*La Voie royale*) and Louis-Ferdinand Céline's *Journey to the End of Night* (*Voyage au bout de la nuit*). There is hardly a famous French writer who hasn't authored an aphorism about travel; notable examples include Michel de Montaigne's "I travel for pleasure," Alphonse de Lamartine's "the complete person is one who has traveled a lot," Charles Baudelaire's "travel for the sake of traveling," and André Gide's "perception begins with a change in sensation, whence the necessity of travel." Flaubert's *Sentimental Education* adds to this anthology an exploration of the motivations for traveling, the impulses behind the journey, which, for the sake of analysis, can be categorized as discovery, displacement, and recovery. Although these modalities overlap considerably, each can be said to dominate in turn one of *Sentimental Education*'s three parts, extending from the novel's plot to the character's perceptual and psychological patterns and finally to Flaubert's vision of human experience.

The Journey as Discovery: Part 1 of *Sentimental Education*

The novel opens with a precise notation of time and place, a hallmark of realist fiction: "The 15th of September 1840, toward six o'clock in the morning, the *Ville-de-Montereau,* nearing departure, was wafting huge billows of smoke along the Saint-Bernard dock."[2] Along with the precision of detail and the suggestion of industrialism conveyed by the steamboat, there is also a heightened sense of anticipation ("nearing departure") affixed to the boat (*Ville-de-Montereau*), whose name already contains that of the main character (*Mo . . . reau*). In introducing Frédéric several paragraphs later, Flaubert draws his portrait, not by analysis, opinion, generalization, and conclusion, as did most novelists before him, but with seemingly insignificant details that the reader must evaluate in order to construct the character's personality traits:

> A young man of eighteen years, with long hair and holding an album under his arm, was standing near the helm, immobile. Through the fog, he contemplated steeples, edifices whose names he did not know; then he embraced, in a final gaze, l'île Saint-Louis, la Cité, Notre-Dame; and soon, with Paris disappearing, he let out a long sigh.[3]

The long hair suggests a student, whose album indicates perhaps an interest in the fine arts. Although his position near the helm may reflect a desire for control, he appears to be meditative ("he contemplated") rather than active ("immobile"), and the fog through which he peers may hint at a certain vagueness of perception on his part. Although new to Paris, since he knows only the most familiar landmarks, his gaze betrays an ardent desire for the capital, and his sigh reflects his disappointment in having to leave; his departure is rendered poignant by the effect of Paris "disappearing," an image that captures Frédéric's perception from the moving boat. We learn later that Paris is merely a stopping point in Frédéric's trip, an intermediate stage in a journey he has purposely prolonged by taking "the longest route," partly to avoid returning to the boredom of his provincial village but also, we come to realize, in anticipation of the potential adventures afforded by travel.

First among the discoveries that begin to materialize during the journey is a middle-aged man dressed flamboyantly whom Frédéric observes flirting with a peasant girl and eventually engages in conversation. The stranger introduces himself as Jacques Arnoux, owner of an art gallery called Industrial Art, a name that is an oxymoron and that would have been anathema to Flaubert, who believed that art must remain independent of economics. Arnoux's self-satisfaction and taste for modernism, reflected in his trendy opinions and trite expressions, clearly mark him as a descendant of Homais and of all the other characters epitomizing bourgeois behavior in Flaubert's works.[4] Nonetheless, the boredom-prone Frédéric finds him fascinating, all the more so since "he had traveled" and thus "knew" about everything from restaurants to artists. The link between travel and knowledge is far from insignificant in a novel whose title relates to education, and the words "travel" and "traveler" ("*voyage*" and "*voyageur*") occur four other times in the opening chapter alone, marking the journey as a major theme, not just an element of the plot. Furthermore, the narrator refers several times to the boat's "bridge" ("*pont*") and "passway" ("*passerelle*"), which, like the journey, designate positions of passage between two points, a state of suspension that mirrors Frédéric's state of mind throughout the novel.

After Arnoux disappears below deck, Frédéric makes the ultimate discovery, an "apparition," as the narrator phrases it, that will forever seal his fate. Seated alone on a bench, silhouetted against the blue sky, is an unknown woman, slightly older than he, with dark hair and a straw hat. Frédéric becomes immediately and totally obsessed with her, although the narrator is quick to point out that the young man's attraction is not just physical but reflects "a deeper desire, a painful curiosity that had no boundaries." She is, for Frédéric, no less than "a discovery, an acquisition"; she is, as the reader may have guessed, Madame Arnoux, and thus the two characters who preoccupy Frédéric during his journey home are linked; she will remain Frédéric's ideal woman throughout the novel. After attempting numerous maneuvers to be near her, engage her in conversation, and learn more about her, Frédéric must leave the boat, along with the other passengers, who continue their separate journeys: Madame Arnoux and her husband are en route to Switzerland, and Frédéric goes by carriage to his home in Nogent, where he is eagerly awaited by his doting mother. At this point we learn that Frédéric's father died before his birth; it is possible, then, that the young man saw in Arnoux, who spoke to him in a "paternal tone," a sort of father figure. This in turn suggests that Madame Arnoux may play a motherly role in the novel, a working hypothesis to be confirmed or rejected by the reader according to future textual evidence.[5]

Unlike the earlier novels *Madame Bovary* and *Salammbô,* in which Flaubert presents the characters mainly from the narrator's elite perspective, in *Sentimental Education,* beginning with the initial chapter, Flaubert entrusts the viewpoint primarily to his main character and, unique to the novel at that time, explores the dynamic interplay between character and setting, observer and object, in the act of observation. As Frédéric observes the passing countryside from the moving boat, the reader discerns an evolving pattern of perception. First Frédéric sees the surroundings as a neutral landscape composed of phenomena that reflect at once nature (hills), industry (floating logs), and human activities (a man fishing). Next, his perception of residential properties begins to provoke fantasies of a future filled with artistic endeavors and amorous affairs. It is at this moment that he encounters Arnoux, whose abrupt departure is followed by a perception of the countryside as empty and boring; this is the background against which Madame Arnoux becomes an "apparition," as if Frédéric's curiosity has been heightened by the emptiness of his surroundings before fixing itself on his new "discovery." When Frédéric next turns to the landscape, he views it as a setting in which he walks with Madame Arnoux, his arm around her waist, a fantasy shattered by the boat's imminent docking and the travelers' departures in separate directions. Later, as Frédéric continues his journey home by carriage, he again inspects the passing countryside, only to have it fade before the powerful memory of Madame Arnoux, whom he now associates with the romantic heroines of his readings and has thus positioned at the center of his own fictional universe: "the luminous point where everything converged."

In the sense that Frédéric Moreau is a dreamer whose fantasies coincide with his readings, he is not unlike Emma Bovary, despite the differences in gender (hence opportunity) and class (Frédéric's mother is from "an old aristocratic family, now extinct"). Frédéric, however, is more intelligent than Emma, more articulate, and his dreams, as we have witnessed, are interwoven with reality, which is at once a catalyst for his desires and a screen on which he can then project his crystallized fantasies. Thus, whereas *Madame Bovary* is characterized by the outright conflict between dream and reality, *Sentimental Education* is structured by subtle modulations, by pulsations between dream and reality, past and present, movement and immobility.

Unlike Emile Zola, who follows the impact of the outside world on the character's perception and ultimately on his or her personality, or Marcel Proust, who uncovers the various layers of memories, fantasies, and images that the individual projects onto the outside world, Flaubert traces the movement back and forth between inside and outside individual and reality, observer and object, such that "consciousness" is perched in between, in an intermediate zone, much as the traveler is situated between points of a journey. Indeed, Frédéric Moreau is depicted throughout the novel as a man positioned between the many alternatives afforded by the journey that constitutes human experience.

The very evening of his return to Nogent, much to his mother's dismay, Frédéric receives a message to join his former schoolmate and inseparable friend, Deslauriers. Three years older than Frédéric, less wealthy and refined, more active and practical, interested in philosophy and politics rather than the arts, Deslauriers is, in many ways, Frédéric's alter ego. Their conversation, recounted in chapter 2, ranges from reminiscences of school life to plans for the future and takes place, significantly, as they walk back and forth on Nogent's two bridges, which again suggests a position of suspension between two points, in this case the two banks of the river: one is occupied by Nogent and its small closed properties; the other looks toward Paris and a highway that stretches toward the horizon in the night vapors, as if beckoning the young men to future discoveries. The short chapter ends with the characters gazing at a light in a house on the Nogent side, which sparks an allusion to a shared escapade that sets them laughing but is not explained to the reader, who is thus propelled forward, much as on a journey.

Chapters 3, 4, and 5 describe the first three years of Frédéric's life as a student in Paris, including his initial failures but eventual success in obtaining his law degree. The chapters are not, however, divided neatly by year, and the chronology is often hard to follow, mirroring no doubt the rhythms of life but increasing the confusion of the reader, who invariably seeks the type of focal point and discernible plot line found in more traditional novels. Although nothing eventful (in the usual novelistic sense) occurs in these three chapters, Flaubert introduces the main characters who reappear throughout the novel, while depicting typical aspects of the student lifestyle.

When Frédéric arrives in Paris in November 1840, he runs an errand for his mother's neighbor, "Papa" Roque, which leads to his meeting the wealthy aristocrat-turned-industrialist Monsieur Dambreuse, whom Frédéric hopes to cultivate for his connections and who will become yet another father figure for him. During this first year in Paris, beset by inertia and boredom, Frédéric sees several acquaintances: the handsome social climber Martinon, the superficial aristocrat Cisy, and the rigid republican Sénécal. He stumbles across Arnoux's establishment and spots him at the theater with two unidentified women, but doesn't manage, despite his efforts, to engage him in conversation or to encounter the elusive Madame Arnoux. One day, early in his second year, Frédéric happens on a student demonstration in the heart of the Latin Quarter, where he meets a sarcastic fellow student, Hussonnet. Frédéric and Hussonnet observe and attempt to rescue a herculean young worker, Dussardier, an innocent victim of police reprisals. Since it turns out that Hussonnet does part-time work for Industrial Art, Frédéric finally manages to get himself introduced into Arnoux's circle, in which he encounters several other characters destined to reappear throughout the novel. The punctual and morose Regimbart is as factual in approaching politics as Sénécal is theoretical. The artist Pellerin is also given to theories, assimilated pell-mell, which punctuate and flavor his conversation but distort his paintings ("it was quite impossible to understand anything in them"); he recalls the painter Frenhofer in Balzac's *The Unknown Masterpiece* (*Le Chef-d'oeuvre inconnu,* 1834) and foreshadows Claude Lantier in Emile Zola's *The Masterpiece* (*L'Oeuvre,* 1886). Frédéric also recognizes the tall, slender Mademoiselle Vatnaz as one of the two women he spotted with Arnoux at the theater, and he is able to seize allusions to a "deal" she is working on for Arnoux, the details of which escape both Frédéric and the reader. (Such elliptical and cryptic constructions are typical of Flaubert's narrative style in *Sentimental Education* and often prove frustrating even to Flaubert's most ardent admirers.) Finally, Frédéric is able to see Madame Arnoux once again, when he is invited with several other guests to dinner at the family's apartment. Flaubert continues to assign her the role of a discovery for Frédéric: "Each word that came out of her mouth seemed to Frédéric like a new thing"; "The contemplation of this woman made him nervous, like using too strong a perfume. It descended into the depths of his being, and became almost a general way of feeling, a new mode of existing."

The student life, which Flaubert paints so vividly in the novel, has little to do, we learn, with classes, and although Flaubert does sketch out the exam procedure, he dwells very little on the courses Frédéric takes or the subjects he studies. In addition to the student demonstration described in chapter 4, Flaubert depicts several other aspects of student life, including the get-togethers at Frédéric's apartment, which he now shares with Deslauriers and where talk turns inevitably to politics and women, and evenings at the public dance-hall at the Alhambra, where Frédéric runs into Arnoux in the company of Mlle Vatnaz and again overhears allusions to the mysterious deal. Among the most recurrent events of Frédéric's life are his "interminable walks," each a journey in itself, through the streets of Paris, motivated in general by "the hope of a distraction" and in particular by Frédéric's belief that he might run into Madame Arnoux. These scenes afford Flaubert the opportunity to create several canvasses of Paris, much as Manet and the impressionist painters Monet, Morisot, and Renoir painted cityscapes, often involving a stroller (*flâneur*), in the late sixties. Like these painters, Flaubert often shows how effects of light and color transform the city's appearance:

> Behind the Tuileries, the sky was taking on the tint of slate. The trees in the garden formed two enormous masses, tinged with violet toward the summit. The street lamps were lighting up; and the Seine, greenish over its entire width, was streaked with silvery ripples near the bridges.[6]

In addition to painting this vivid picture of visual effects, which abound in the late-nineteenth-century French novel, Flaubert is able to integrate the motifs of the walk and the cityscape into the novel by linking them to the twin themes of journey and discovery.

The journey motif itself continues to operate throughout these chapters on several textual levels. Travel dominates conversation at the Arnoux's dinner: "[Frédéric's] taste for travels was caressed by Dittmer, who spoke about the Orient." In a song interpreted by the "expressive singer" Delmas, travel becomes a theme that parallels Frédéric's own story: "It was a villager recounting his own trip to the capital." Flaubert also uses travel as a simile to link Frédéric and Madame Arnoux: "like a traveler lost in the middle of a wood where all paths returned to the same spot, he continually rediscovered behind each idea the memory of Madame Arnoux." Frédéric's perception of reality often leads to projected images of him and Madame Arnoux traveling: "When he went to the Jardin des Plantes, the sight of a palm tree would carry him off to faraway lands. They were traveling together, on the backs of camels, under the parasols of Elephants, in the cabin of a yacht among blue archipelagos . . . " Finally, on the level of plot, walks, trips, and travel continue to link Frédéric to Madame Arnoux. After the dinner at the Arnoux's, as Frédéric wanders the streets at random (*au hasard*), he discovers his vocation to be a painter, an attractive possibility due to Madame Arnoux's proximity to the art world.

Significantly, Frédéric comes to his decision during this night journey, while suspended again on a bridge, "in the middle of the Pont Neuf." Of course, his subsequent painting lessons do little for his law studies, and he fails his exams on his first try. The combination of journey and bridge figures prominently in yet another significant scene, as Frédéric, his hopes temporarily dashed by his lack of success with Madame Arnoux, wanders through the streets (*il vagabonda dans les rues*) and stops on the Pont de la Concorde, where he contemplates suicide. A later trip to see Madame Arnoux in the countryside, during which he experiences for the first time a genuine sense of communication with her, inspires him to study ardently, and he passes his doctor of laws exam on the final try. In short, the link between the journey, discovery, and Madame Arnoux, heralded in the opening chapter, continues to dominate part 1 of the novel and brings Frédéric the promise of success.

Just as Frédéric begins to realize his dreams and relish the future, however, he returns home for summer break, only to learn from his mother that the family's financial situation has deteriorated to the point that he must abandon his plans to live in Paris and find employment in Nogent. The short final chapter of part 1 recounts his failure to adjust to provincial life during his several years of exile ("considering himself a dead man, he ceased doing absolutely anything") and his wanderings through the countryside, often in the company of Louise Roque, a wild young neighbor who has a crush on him. Finally, on 12 December 1845 he receives a letter informing him that since his uncle has died without leaving a will, Frédéric has inherited a small fortune that will allow him to live comfortably in Paris, where alone could be found "art, knowledge, and love (those three faces of God, as Pellerin would say)." That his fortune has come by chance, due to no plan on either his uncle's part or his own, betrays a legacy of indecision that will plague Frédéric, just as the death of Louise's mother, on the eve of his departure, casts a foreboding pall over his good fortune.

The Journey as Displacement: Part 2 of *Sentimental Education*

Part 2 begins like part 1, with Frédéric traveling, this time in the opposite direction, from Nogent to Paris. This reversal of direction is significant in that Frédéric's motivation for travel this time is not the joy of the journey itself but the desire for displacement, for being elsewhere—a desire that stems less from a sense of discovery than from disappointment. This pattern of Frédéric's disillusionment with his situation (whether in love, art, or career, the "three faces of God" that continue to bedevil him) followed by displacement, or a shift of attention to another object of desire, marks the major behavioral characteristic and thus structuring principle for part 2 of the novel.

Rather than prolong his journey as he did earlier, Frédéric is impatient this time to see it end, to be elsewhere ("He asked the driver several times how long, exactly, before one would arrive"). Similarly, in this scene Flaubert does not dissect Frédéric's consciousness into a series of steps but paints him as consistently overwhelmed ("he sensed a drunkenness submerge him") by profusion ("a prodigality of things") and overtaken, as he falls asleep, by confusion ("But, bit by bit, his hopes and his memories, Nogent, la rue de Choiseul, Madame Arnoux, his mother, all became mixed together"). This pattern of profusion and confusion, in addition to describing Frédéric's perception of reality throughout part 2, also defines the reader's task: to sift through mounds of detail in an often futile effort to wrest meaning from the novel's seemingly endless and pointless episodes. Indeed, much to the reader's frequent dismay, Flaubert manages to capture the rhythms, rituals, and riddles of modern bourgeois society by displaying a dizzying array of goods, events, people, and ideas before the overwhelmed, seduced consumer.

The most striking characteristic of Frédéric's mode of consciousness in the opening journey in part 2, however, lies not in the give and take between object and observer that we witnessed at the novel's outset but in the obliteration of reality before the individual's imagination: "and this contemplation was so profound that the exterior objects had disappeared." In effect, at this stage of the novel, Frédéric's perception does not interact with reality or embellish it but replaces or displaces it in favor of a powerful inner vision composed of ideals crystallized by memories into images. For example, at the end of a long paragraph in which Flaubert takes great pains to detail the artifacts of a nascent but already crumbling industrial society ("posters covered the corners of the walls, and, three-quarters ripped, trembled in the wind like rags") and to describe the uncomfortable weather ("a fine rain was falling, it was cold, the sky was pale"), Frédéric's perception is dominated by an inner vision unrelated to the surroundings: "but two eyes worth more to him than the sun were glowing behind the fog." Any perceptive reader can surmise that the eyes are those of Madame Arnoux, but the trained reader of Flaubert will embark on a journey backward into the text, into the memory of his or her reading, and be rewarded by the discovery (or recollection) of a passage during Frédéric's visit with Madame Arnoux in the countryside: "all that Frédéric could see of Madame Arnoux were her two eyes, in the shadows." Thus the reader, thwarted on the level of plot, is recompensed on the higher level of structure, as he or she discovers the web of associations, repetitions, and variations that constitute the text's true music, which can be heard beyond its often confusing and discordant melodies.

In typical Flaubert fashion, however, Frédéric's exaltation is followed abruptly by an ironic letdown: he arrives at the Arnoux's gallery, then their apartment, only to find they have moved without trace ("No more display windows, no more paintings, nothing!").[7] Frédéric then embarks on another lengthy journey across Paris, which can only be called a quest, futile at that, for Madame Arnoux, during which certain phrasings recall other memorable journeys in Flaubert's oeuvre. As Frédéric tries to find Regimbart, for example, in the hopes that he knows the Arnoux's whereabouts, the names of the various cafés the "citizen" frequents explode in his memory "like the thousand pieces of a fireworks display," the precise terms with which the narrator describes Emma's attack of madness prior to her suicide; when Frédéric finally has the Arnoux's address, he heads for their new apartment "with the extraordinary ease that one experiences in dreams," the very words used to describe Mâtho's movements before he steals Tanit's veil and Julian's before his massacre of the animals and encounter with the stag that will seal his fate. These examples of intertextuality not only gain the reader entrance into the pantextual web of associations that binds together all of Flaubert's works but by their frequency allow him or her to hypothesize about the patterns that define Flaubert's own manner of experiencing reality.

Frédéric's reunion with the Arnoux family is marked by a further letdown, prompted not only by the commercialization of art, since Arnoux has now become a fine-china merchant and manufacturer involved in the mass production and sales of art objects, but by the "degradation" of Madame Arnoux herself, who no longer seems the same outside of her former "milieu," which the reader interprets to mean both her old apartment and, especially, the ideal world in which Frédéric has housed her and enhanced her during his absence.

Shortly after this disappointment, however, Frédéric displaces his attention from Madame Arnoux to a bevy of beauties whom he encounters at a masked ball, recalling the earlier dance scene at the Alhambra.[8] It is Arnoux who serves as agent or intermediary of this displacement, since he is associated with both Madame Arnoux and the hostess of the ball, Rosanette Bron. Rosanette turns out to be Arnoux's mistress and, the reader assumes, the subject of the "deal" arranged years ago by Mlle Vatnaz, who also appears in this final scene of the opening chapter, along with Hussonnet, Pellerin, and the singer Delmas (who now calls himself Delmar). Frédéric's displacement or shift of desire is further facilitated by an old chandelier that formerly adorned Arnoux's gallery but now occupies Rosanette's living room, sumptuously furnished not only with bric-a-brac but with costumed women representing different body types and roles. The frozen Frédéric watches the swirling dancers, overwhelmed by a profusion of fragmented images that evoke all types of desire. A particularly striking image involves a woman costumed as a dock worker who "seemed to cover in her supple gestures and serious expression all the refinements of modern love, which has the exactness of a science and the mobility of a bird." Later Frédéric spies another woman, dressed like a sphinx, secretly spitting blood, a grim reminder of the harsh reality that lies beneath the luxurious surface of Parisian life. Unlike Emma Bovary, however, who refuses to see reality, Frédéric understands the sphinx's riddle, which involves the vulnerability of humankind, and persists in the pursuit of pleasure despite this "education."

It is especially Rosanette, dubbed la Maréchale (field marshal) because of her spurs and domineering personality, who fascinates Frédéric and appears as the central figure in the short but suggestive dream sequence that ends the chapter:

> Another thirst had come to him, that for women, luxury, and all that comprises Parisian life. He felt a little dizzy, like a man debarking from a boat; and, in the hallucination of falling asleep, he saw passing and repassing continuously the shoulders of the Fishwife, the hips of the Dockworker, the calves of the Polish woman, the hair of the Jungle woman. Then two large black eyes, which weren't at the ball, appeared; and light like butterflies, burning like torches, they came and went, vibrating, rising up to the ceiling, falling back to his mouth. Frédéric tried hard to recognize these eyes, without succeeding. But already the dream had taken him; it seemed to him that he was harnessed with Arnoux, to the yoke of a carriage, and that la Maréchale, standing astride him, was poking him with her golden spurs.[9]

Here the pattern of desire displaced to another object ("another thirst") and linked to the motif of the journey ("like a man debarking from a boat") is illustrated by the shift of attention from the dancing women to the eyes (which the reader, unlike Frédéric, recognizes as those of

Madame Arnoux) to the dominant figure of la Maréchale. It is typical of Frédéric's behavior that he is not a participant but a mere spectator, transfixed by the profusion of images comprised of fragmented body parts and female types; the women are thus rendered impersonal and artificial by the roles they play. Frédéric's inability to recognize the very eyes that earlier obsessed him and his failure thus to crystallize Madame Arnoux's image can be read, in the dream, as a form of repression that stems, no doubt, from a feeling of guilt in betraying his ideal woman; to complicate matters further, this ideal woman is herself confused, as we saw earlier, with the image of his mother, the ultimate taboo. In this context, it is interesting that Frédéric sees himself as bound to Arnoux, identified with Arnoux, the very figure (perhaps father figure) he must replace in order to gain the affections of either Madame Arnoux or Rosanette Bron.

This final paragraph not only brilliantly and unconventionally summarizes the events of a long chapter (the journey, the eyes, Madame Arnoux, the dance) but dramatizes the very patterns that will characterize Frédéric throughout part 2: the confusion of real and ideal, the inertia when faced with an abundance of images that lie before him like a spectacle, the compulsion to be elsewhere than where he is, other than who he is, and the tendency to displace his desire from one object to another.

The pattern of profusion continues throughout part 2, contributing substantially to the tedium of this part of the novel, which contains nearly twice the material of the first part stuffed into the same number of chapters (six). The soirees at the Dambreuse mansion, recounted in chapters 2 and 4, with their sumptuous settings and various women, provide an upper-class analog to the ball at Rosanette's and cause Frédéric to feel equally attracted to and confused by the abundance of alternatives. The gatherings of friends at Frédéric's apartment (chapter 2) and at Dussardier's flat (chapter 6) expose a plethora of political doctrines and artistic theories, none more (or less) compelling than the others.

Another public gathering is featured in the famous race track episode, recounted in chapter 4. As in the dance scenes, Frédéric is again depicted as the immobile spectator of events involving frantic, circular motion that leads nowhere. (Small wonder that these emblems of modern life, the dance and the horse race, also figure heavily in the paintings of Parisian life of two of Flaubert's contemporaries, Manet and Degas, as well as those of Toulouse-Lautrec a generation later.) Rosanette, Frédéric's companion at the races, leaves him for Cisy, whom Frédéric later challenges to a duel because of an insult regarding Madame Arnoux. The duel, like nearly all the events in this part of the novel, fails to come off: Cisy faints at first feint, and Arnoux, believing himself to be the cause of the trouble, arrives in the nick of time and begs the would-be duelists to desist.

Inertia besets Frédéric in all matters, from the investment and career opportunities offered in vain by M. Dambreuse and the bewildering choice of art forms and political doctrines espoused by his friends to his lack of commitment to one of the various women in his life. As the narrator explains it, "action, for certain men, becomes all the more impracticable as desire increases," and the reader further discerns a pattern of paralysis caused by too many options, each equally plausible and thus none particularly compelling. If Emma Bovary's fate is limited by a lack of possibilities imposed by her gender, her education, her financial circumstances, and her provincial milieu, then Frédéric Moreau's life is blocked by an excess of opportunities that emanate from his advantages in precisely the same domains. He remains suspended among the various options that confront him, looking either back to the past or ahead to the future, never fully residing in the present: "his afternoons were spent recalling last evening's visit, anticipating that of the coming evening."

This same state of suspension before multiple choices that leads to inertia also underlies the pattern of disillusionment and displacement that dominates this part of the novel. Numerous examples abound in chapter 2 alone: Frédéric no sooner leaves the charming Madame Dambreuse than, "needing a less artificial milieu," he goes to visit la Maréchale. Later, "not doubting that la Maréchale would soon become his mistress . . . this desire raised another; and . . . he wanted to see Mme Arnoux." As he acquires the habit of alternating between the households of Rosanette and Mme Arnoux, the narrator notes his penchant to associate the two women:

> Frequenting these two women made for two types of music in his life: one joyful, exuberant, entertaining, the other serious and almost religious; and, vibrating at the same time, they continued to grow, and bit by bit mixed together; because, if Mme Arnoux happened to touch him with so much as a finger, the other's image soon came to his desire, since his chances were less remote on that side; and, in the company of Rosanette, when his feelings became stirred, he immediately recalled his great love.[10]

The advantages offered by each of the two women lead to an equalizing that facilitates Frédéric's tendency to shift from one to the other, thereby, as with his inertia, avoiding a commitment. The narrator adds that their association is reinforced by similarities in the two households, both furnished by Arnoux. Displacement is often facilitated by a common trait, agent, or intermediary: thus, when Frédéric strolls with la Maréchale, he recalls the same walk with Madame Arnoux, a recollection that obliterates the present: "and this memory was so compelling, that he no longer saw Rosanette, no longer thought about her."

Similarly, at a soiree given by Madame Dambreuse, as Frédéric contemplates the various women, he focuses on Madame Dambreuse but thinks about la Maréchale. Moments later, the mention of Papa Roque makes him think of Louise, which in turn evokes the memory of how much he missed Madame Arnoux while he was in Nogent. Clearly, Flaubert has set up four types of women—the ideal Madame Arnoux, the mundane Rosanette, the naive Louise, and the sophisticated Madame Dambreuse—that are mutually exclusive yet each attractive in its own right; when Frédéric is with one woman, his attention tends to shift to another who is elsewhere. Flaubert uses the same patterning principle of an array of alternatives in presenting Frédéric's career possibilities, the various aesthetic theories spouted primarily by Pellerin, and the political doctrines propounded by Deslauriers, Dussardier, Hussonnet, and Sénécal.

Near the end of chapter 4, after a series of financial setbacks and women troubles, including an outright rejection by Madame Arnoux, Frédéric escapes his situation by returning to Nogent, a displacement that is both geographical and libidinal, as he soon shifts his affections to Louise Roque. Interestingly, the motif of the journey is accompanied by a simile linking the intermediary and the bridge: "There are some men whose missions in life include serving as intermediaries; one crosses them like bridges, and one moves along." By bringing together the three recurrent themes of the intermediary, the bridge, and the journey, Flaubert enables the reader to grasp the notion of suspension between points that joins them and that characterizes Frédéric's predominant state of being.

No sooner does Frédéric commit himself to Louise (by not declining her marriage proposal!), however, than he journeys back to Paris and, with yet another displacement, declares his love to Madame Arnoux. This time, having acknowledged her feelings for him when confronted with the news of his impending marriage (delivered by Deslauriers in a vain attempt "to substitute himself for Frédéric and imagining himself almost to be him"), Madame Arnoux does not reject Frédéric but allows him to visit her often in the countryside and even agrees to a clandestine rendezvous in Paris. After days of preparation, Frédéric spends hours waiting for her, managing to dodge a demonstration against the government and to avoid his friends who want him to participate, but he only experiences yet another letdown when she fails to show. As the final chapter of part 2 finishes, Frédéric ends up sharing the bed in the apartment he has prepared for Madame Arnoux with Rosanette, who takes his tears of remorse for an expression of joy at finally seducing her.

It is, no doubt, with a measure of relief on the reader's part that this long and often tedious part of the novel comes to a close; very little has occurred, due to Frédéric's inertia on the one hand and his displacement from one to another alternative—be it career, idea, or woman—on the other. Whereas the reader expects a novel to be eventful, to move forward, *Sentimental Education* lacks not only action but results, resolution, and even progress (all hallmarks of traditional fiction). Unless one counts Frédéric's seduction of Rosanette, a substitute for the real object of his desires and among the loosest women in Paris, this part of the novel has been highly uneventful in both the private and public domains.

For many readers, Flaubert's subtle stylistic modulations of voice (from narrator to character), presentation (from narrative to dramatic), time (from the precise to the elastic), and rhythm (from immobility to fluidity) are not sufficient to compensate for the deficiencies of an inert character, an indeterminate plot, and indiscriminate descriptions.[11]

The Journey as Recovery: Part 3 of *Sentimental Education*

Whereas part 2 of the novel moves rather slowly, part 3 begins with an event of cataclysmic proportions, the revolution of February 1848, which marked the end of the 18-year regime of Louis-Philippe. Given the revolutionary rhetoric of Frédéric's friends, one might expect him to participate, but he remains merely a spectator, again projecting his private fantasies onto the panoramic screen of historical events Flaubert depicts in luxurious detail.

As Flaubert paints evocative canvasses of the marches, the barricades, the exchange of gunfire, the sacking of the royal palace by the people, and the general chaos, "Frédéric, caught between two deep masses, wasn't moving, fascinated incidentally and enjoying himself tremendously. The wounded falling, the dead stretched out didn't seem to be really wounded, really dead. He had the feeling of attending a spectacle." The word "spectacle," underscoring Frédéric's passive role in relation to events, occurs four times in this opening chapter.

For the purpose of simplification, we can divide this chapter, more than 50 pages in length, into four segments: the insurrection, the aftermath, the journey to Fontainebleau, and the return to Paris. As in parts 1 and 2 of the novel, Flaubert uses this opening chapter to assemble his rather large cast of characters and to lay out the traits that will typify Frédéric's behavior throughout the final part of the novel. Once again the opening chapter involves patterns of profusion and inertia, and again the journey plays a significant yet slightly different role, which Flaubert continues to define through the interaction of Frédéric and the setting in which he is inserted.

The parts the various characters play in the revolution and their reactions to it recall their main characteristics, while affording Flaubert the opportunity to display (if not classify à la Balzac) different types of social behavior. Hussonnet remains as cynical in his attitude toward the common people as he was regarding the rich and powerful; Regimbart continues to be critical and pessimistic regarding everyone and everything; Dussardier, the most altruistic of the politically involved, is eternally optimistic; Deslauriers, as usual, sees the events in terms of personal gain; Arnoux, always the pragmatic survivor, embraces the new republic, even joining the National Guard; the profoundly vain Delmar sees politics as another forum for self-display; Pellerin continues to promote the arts; Mlle Vatnaz seeks to advance the cause of women; Dambreuse, ever the chameleon, changes politics to suit the times; and Martinon continues to follow him around, seconding him in convincing Frédéric to run for a National Assembly seat, which Dambreuse later obtains for himself.

As Frédéric seeks an official organization to sponsor his candidacy, faced as usual with a dizzying array of choices, he comes across the Club of Intelligence, whose name seems appropriate but whose president turns out to be the ever-rigid Sénécal, who thwarts Frédéric by questioning (with some justification, as the narrator points out) his convictions and commitment to the revolution. As Frédéric nonetheless rises to speak, a patriot from Barcelona simultaneously delivers a tirade in Spanish that thus becomes interwoven with Frédéric's words; the sustained juxtaposition of the two discourses underscores the lack of understanding and communication, all the more ironic in a club of such lofty pretensions.[12]

A frustrated Frédéric leaves the club in a rage and turns to la Maréchale for consolation, only to be struck by her inanity and infidelity; he has now suffered a double defeat, in first the public and now the private domains: "Under this avalanche of stupidity, Frédéric passed from his other disappointment to a deeper deception." Unable to understand Rosanette, he asks a question about his love life that might well apply to his public life and thus to life in general as well: "What is the sense of all of this?" Faced with profound disillusionment, Frédéric turns, typically, to displacement, to escape, here in the form of a journey with Rosanette: "Frédéric had a thirst for abandoning Paris. She didn't reject this fantasy, and they left for Fontainebleau the very next day."

The journey to Fontainebleau is marked, however, by more than mere escape; it involves a return to the past, to other historical periods, which Flaubert juxtaposes with the contemporary history being made, if not understood, in Paris. Unlike part 1, in which Flaubert details Frédéric's progressive interaction with the countryside, or part 2, in which he portrays Frédéric's projection of inner fantasies onto the screen of outer reality, here Flaubert shows Frédéric as receptive to and affected by the images projected by the setting.

The couple is immediately struck, even surprised, by the "tranquillity, replacing for them, the tumult of Paris." Unlike the Tuileries, which Frédéric saw destroyed, emptied of its contents and symbols, the Fontainebleau chateau, a former royal residence, strikes him by its "abundance," not only of luxurious objects but of memories of such patriarchal figures as popes, kings, the emperor, and great writers, so many paternal symbols of the order stripped from current society by the revolution. Certain art objects, like the tapestries, reach even farther back into the recesses of history to resurrect figures from ancient history and mythology: "the Gods of Olympus, Psyche, or the battles of Alexander." Finally, in the Fontainebleau forest, the trees and rocks take Frédéric still farther back, into a prehistoric period beyond the reaches of history, beyond the ravages of time: "Frédéric was saying that they had been there from the beginning of the world and would remain there until the end."

The return to the past marks a regression, a rejection of the chaos of modern times and a recovery of the stability of the past, the security of personal and cultural memory, which Flaubert marks throughout this section of the chapter by repeating words like "silence," "immobile," and "eternal," all of which figure in the following example:

> Royal residences have in them a particular melancholy, which stems no doubt from their size, too large for the small number of their occupants, from the silence that one is surprised to find there after so much fanfare, from their immobile luxury, proving by its age the fleeting nature of dynasties, the eternal misery of everything; and this exhalation of the ages, numbing and foreboding like the odor of a mummy, makes itself felt by even the most naive of minds. Rosanette was yawning inordinately. They went back to the hotel.[13]

Here the narrator momentarily assumes the viewpoint and voice to analyze overtly the nearly universal impact of the past (the inane Rosanette apparently being the exception), conveyed in the above passage by such words as "exhalation," "numbing," "foreboding," and "felt." It is primarily, however, through Frédéric's viewpoint, brought to life by the more subtle vehicle of the author's style, that Flaubert imparts meaning to the Fontainebleau setting, while tracing Frédéric's reactions to his surroundings.

Flaubert creates a sense of order by using a vocabulary based on geometric forms, not only for the chateau, where one might expect to find it, but also for the forest, where it is all the more striking: among the numerous examples are "rectangle," "squares," "pyramid," "line," "cone," "symmetrical," "cubic," and "dome." At the same time, Flaubert uses active verbs, attributed to natural phenomena, to suggest their power and impact on the observer. Among the many examples is a passage detailing the effects of light on the landscape:

> The light, in certain places illuminating the edge of the wood, left the depths in shadow; or else, attenuated in the foreground by a sort of twilight, it displayed a white burst in the violet vapors lying far away. At midday, the sun, falling straight down on the vast greenery, spattered them, suspended silver drops on the branch tips, striped the grass with trains of emerald, cast golden spots on the layers of dead leaves; in leaning backward, one could see the sky between the treetops. Some, of immeasurable height, took on the appearance of patriarchs and emperors, or, touching at the tips, with their long trunks, formed what seemed like arcs of triumph; others, pushed sideways at the bottom, seemed like columns ready to fall.[14]

The clear designation of spatial relationships ("depths," "foreground") and the subtle variations of light and color depicted with painterly precision are reminders that the Fontainebleau forest was among the cradles of impressionism, having attracted such precursors to the movement as Corot, Courbet, and Daubigny, and later, such outright impressionists as Monet, Renoir, and Bazille. In the final sentence, Flaubert uses personification and simile to lend the landscape a human quality, again suggesting the nostalgia for stability symbolized by such purveyors of paternal order as patriarchs and emperors.

Flaubert also describes the forest, not as a mixture of different types of trees, as it might appear visually, but in categories of trees, as the mind might order them: "There were huge rough oaks, which were distorted, stretched out from the earth, embracing each other, sending out with their bare arms cries of despair, furious threats, like a band of Titans, immobilized in their anger." Here again the personification and similes serve to humanize the forest, while suggesting the eternal presence of mythological figures; it is later in the same paragraph that Frédéric comes to reflect on the timelessness of nature.

As usual Frédéric displaces his feelings for the setting onto the woman occupying it. As he muses, for example, over the various symbols of Diane de Poitiers, Henry II's mistress, he quickly transfers his desire to Rosanette: "Frédéric was taken by an inexpressible retrospective urge. To distract his desire, he began to consider Rosanette tenderly." Later, he attributes the timelessness of the setting to his companion herself: "He had no doubts that he would be happy for the rest of his life, so much did his happiness seem natural, inherent to his life and to the person of this woman." Indeed, he sees their love as inseparable from nature and in contrast with the Parisian scene they abandoned: "all that agitation seemed to him pitiful beside their love and eternal nature."

In the midst of this happiness, however, remnants of Frédéric's personal past return to break the nostalgic spell cast by the retreat to Fontainebleau. Accusing Frédéric of having slept with Mme Arnoux, Rosanette inadvertently reawakens his dormant ideal, which leads to an irrevocable communication gap between the two lovers that provokes a generalized reflection by the narrator: "it is difficult to express anything at all; thus complete unions are rare." When Frédéric reads of an injury to his friend Dussardier, wounded during the workers' uprising against the fledgling republic, he is determined to rejoin him in Paris, thus bringing an end to the idle idyll with Rosanette.

The return to Paris is itself a journey fraught with peril; Frédéric has great difficulty finding transportation into the capital, which has been closed off by troops attempting to quell the workers' insurrection. On his arrival, Frédéric is, ironically given his lack of commitment, taken for an insurgent, held captive, and shuffled from group to group during the night, his experiences thus underscoring the confusion surrounding the political events. When he finally finds Dussardier, in the care of Mlle Vatnaz, he learns that the republican was wounded while attacking a barricade held by workers and now questions whether he acted on the side of justice after all. Sénécal is imprisoned, and Papa Roque, now a national guardsman in Paris, displays excessive cruelty in repressing the insurgents, all the while proclaiming his "sensitivity." His complaint, "Ah! these revolutions!" reminds the reader of the constant political turmoil in postrevolutionary France, the repetition of events that must have made history itself seem like a continual stream of insurrections and provisional governments, a perpetual state of suspension between political points and parties, an endless and fruitless journey leading nowhere.[15]

Chapter 2 is unusual in that it involves a single event, a soiree hosted by Mme Dambreuse. This focus enables Flaubert to muster his cast of characters and maneuver them toward the impending conclusion. The reader reencounters Martinon and Cisy (both suitors of M. Dambreuse's illegitimate daughter, Cécile, who passes for his niece and constitutes an inheritance threat to Mme Dambreuse), along with Pellerin and Hussonnet (who have done one deed or another for Dambreuse) and especially the various women in Frédéric's life. Louise, still thinking herself betrothed to Frédéric, is there in the company of Papa Roque, as is Madame Arnoux (accompanied by Arnoux), thinking herself jilted by Frédéric in favor of Rosanette. In a sense, even Rosanette is present, since discussion turns to her portrait, painted by Pellerin for Frédéric, whom everyone thus assumes to be her keeper. Faced with so much confusion, Frédéric acts (if so strong a word can be used) in typical fashion by diverting his attention to Mme Dambreuse, whose interest in him is in turn stimulated by that of the other women. As the guests leave, Frédéric heads for Rosanette's, while Louise sneaks out with her servant to find Frédéric, only to learn that he hasn't slept at his apartment for three months. Enlightened but crushed, she is consoled by her servant with a philosophy worthy of the fickle Frédéric himself: "If that one was gone, she would find others."

In chapter 3 several events actually occur in Frédéric's love life, but each appears to annul the others and thus negate advancement. Frédéric works up the courage to visit Mme Arnoux, and finally they share their first long kiss, only to be interrupted by Rosanette, who later that evening informs him that she is pregnant with his child. Frédéric feels a commitment to Rosanette but dreams of another child, whom he would have with Mme Arnoux, and later, of another life, "more amusing and more aristocratic," which he would share with Mme Dambreuse. Mme Dambreuse soon takes her place alongside the other objects of his wandering desire: "He didn't feel with her the same rapture of his entire being that attracted him to Mme Arnoux, nor the gay disorder that Rosanette had first given him. But he desired her like a rare and difficult thing, because she was noble, because she was rich." To court her, he feeds her lines borrowed from his previous affairs, and to awaken his own feelings, "he had to evoke the image of Rosanette or of Mme Arnoux." When he finally manages to seduce her, he is "surprised by the ease of his victory" and experiences a "universal suspension of things" into which other moments, other memories enter confusedly, constituting what one might call an emblematic representation of his general state of being. By chapter's end, a reunion with Deslauriers rekindles his political ambitions, and his confidence bolstered by his latest amorous conquest, he decides to run for a National Assembly seat, this time from the Nogent region and as a conservative!

Indeed, throughout the final chapters of the novel, we learn that Frédéric and many of his once-progressive friends have embraced various regressive political positions, marking yet another return to the past. When Deslauriers reveals that he now hates the common people, Frédéric declares the proletariat to be immature, weighs the merits of an aristocracy or an autocracy, and proclaims the conservatives to be the best bet for the moment. Pellerin, disgusted with modern times and nostalgic for the Middle Ages and for Louis XIV, supports a return to the monarchy. Even the once-radical Sénécal now favors authority and tyranny in the form of a benevolent dictatorship, making his position, as the narrator notes, indistinguishable from the conservatives of the Dambreuse clique. In fact, just such a political regression occurred in December 1851, when Louis-Napoleon Bonaparte engineered a coup d'etat that led to the downfall of the Second Republic and, eventually, to his coronation as emperor under the Second Empire; these events mirrored similar ones earlier in the century, namely the coronation of his uncle, Napoleon Bonaparte, as emperor in the aftermath of the French Revolution and the demise of the First Republic. Flaubert barely alludes to the December coup d'etat, thereby underscoring Frédéric's lack of interest ("He was so preoccupied with his own affairs that public affairs left him indifferent") and perhaps the ironic message that history's tendency to repeat itself is so inescapable that it hardly bears mentioning.

With the institution of the Second Empire, the historical journey has returned to the past, a trajectory that Frédéric's personal history is also fated to follow.

The final chapters, especially 4 and 5, are further marked by a distinctive pattern of death, "the great journey," according to Dambreuse, who is the first of the characters to embark on it. Soon to follow is Frédéric's infant son, whose dead body is captured in a grotesque painting by Pellerin, in which the artist's style rejects the new realism, embracing instead a mixture of models from the past. The child's death seems to Frédéric like a premonition of others to follow, and indeed, at the end of chapter 5 he happens to observe, during the reprisals against those who oppose Bonaparte's takeover, Sénécal kill, with a saber thrust, his former friend Dussardier. Dussardier's death symbolizes that of the republic itself, as the honest republican had previously forecast ("they're killing our Republic").[16]

The final chapters also depict the symbolic and quite precipitous deaths of each of Frédéric's love affairs. Madame Dambreuse's proposal of marriage to Frédéric on the day of her husband's death in the dead man's room not only reinforces Frédéric's passivity but provides a morbid premonition of their future together. He continues to lead a double existence with her and with Rosanette, however, taking considerable pleasure in the lies he feeds both, who, between them, help him forget the one he can't have but who continues to obsess him, Mme Arnoux. As for Arnoux, he has become proprietor of the Gothic Arts, a shop for religious objects (marking a further degradation of the arts and regression toward the past), and is beset by impending lawsuits involving his always shaky finances and financial dealings; Frédéric has rescued him on several past occasions from several such threats, primarily to prevent him from fleeing Paris with Madame Arnoux. Frédéric finally leaves Rosanette for good when he suspects her of having pressed the suit (filed, it turns out, by Mme Dambreuse in collusion with Deslauriers) that led to the Arnoux's departure. Significantly, Frédéric imagines Mme Arnoux on an endless journey to unnamed lands where he will never find her again. When Mme Dambreuse insists on stopping at an auction of the Arnoux belongings and persists, despite Frédéric's pleas, in purchasing a box that belonged first to Mme Arnoux, then to Rosanette, then again to Mme Arnoux,[17] Frédéric leaves her, abruptly and permanently, thus putting an end to all three of his affairs and provoking, typically, the desire to escape, to return home to Nogent:

> he hated Mme Dambreuse because she had almost caused him to commit a low deed. He forgot la Maréchale, wasn't even worried about Mme Arnoux, thinking only of himself, of him alone, lost in the debris of his dreams, sick, full of sadness and discouragement; and, in hatred of the artificial milieu where he had suffered so much, he longed for the freshness of the countryside, the calm of the provinces, a tranquil life spent in the shade of his birthplace with simple hearts.[18]

During the journey home the memory of Louise Roque begins to reappear, and as he stops in the middle of the Nogent bridge, again mirroring his state of suspension, he decides to look for her, only to discover her leaving the Nogent church in the company of her new husband, Deslauriers. As usual, Frédéric's disillusionment leads immediately to displacement, to the desire for escape: "Ashamed, vanquished, crushed, he returned to the train, and went back to Paris." It is on his return that he witnesses Dussardier's death, which represents the death of the republic and coincides with the death of all four of his loves, indeed, of his dreams.

Given how slowly the plot moves for so much of the novel, it is remarkable how quickly everything unfolds in chapter 5, as if an intricately constructed house of cards crumbled completely when one was removed. The reader is left with a kind of stupefaction and a sense of emptiness that allows him or her to simulate the experience of Frédéric's profound disillusionment.

Chapter 6 begins with one of the most celebrated passages in the history of the French novel:

> He traveled.
>
> He knew the melancholy of ships, the cold awakenings in a tent, the dizziness of landscapes and ruins, the bitterness of interrupted relationships.
>
> He came back.
>
> He socialized, and he had still other loves. But the continual memory of the first one made them seem insipid; and then the vehemence of desire, the very flower of sensation was lost. His intellectual ambitions had diminished also. Years passed; and he endured the idleness of his intelligence and the inertia of his feelings.[19]

Having depicted 11 years of Frédéric's life in 400 pages, Flaubert condenses the next 16 years into a few short paragraphs that occupy less than half a page. The compression is staggering: it not only serves as a commentary on the emptiness of Frédéric's middle years but, by its very spareness, puts the reader at an immense distance, as if he or she were suddenly viewing a faraway, isolated object through a telescope after sharing Frédéric's microscopic vantage point for most of the novel. The starkness of the style, captured by the finality of the past-perfect tense, the remarkably short paragraphs, the repetitive syntax (the pronoun "he" followed by the verb at the beginning of each paragraph), and hence the humdrum rhythm, underscore the bleak picture of Frédéric's life, the early part of which is, in a sense, simply recapitulated here in short form. As throughout, the journey (recalled by the phrase "He traveled") assumes the initial place, and as earlier, is linked to knowledge ("He knew"), an association the reader assumes to be significant in a novel that purports to deal with education.

But what has Frédéric learned? What has been his "sentimental education"? The passage quoted previously appears to make the answers bluntly clear: melancholy, coldness, dizziness, and bitterness, leading to (or stemming from) loss of desire and sensation, diminishing ambition, idle intelligence, and inert feelings. If this is so, his education has amounted to an "unlearning" of ideals, an abandonment of illusions, and the novel itself is a sort of "anti-Bildungsroman."[20]

But the germs of a solution to such ills lie within the very list of problems summarized so succinctly in the passage, in its only positive element: "the continual memory of the first one." Indeed, at the precise textual moment that Frédéric's precarious ideal appears about to topple, it is righted by its very incarnation: "Toward the end of March 1867, with night falling, as he was alone in his study, a woman entered.—Madame Arnoux!"

She now lives with the aging Arnoux in Brittany, and she has changed; her hair is now white, which comes as a great shock to Frédéric. As they stroll through the dimly lit streets of Paris, the narrator compares them to "those who walk together in the countryside, on a bed of dead leaves," thereby resurrecting an autumnal image that recurs throughout the novel and that suggests at once the approach of winter and the memory of summer. Indeed, as they reminisce about the past and recount their feelings, it is clear that they have retained, even increased, their closeness. They use similar metaphors to describe their recurrent memories of each other: for Madame Arnoux, Frédéric's words return like a distant echo, like the sound of a bell wafting on the wind; for Frédéric, the music of her voice and the splendor of her eyes have always been deep within him. When she tells him how she appreciated his restraint, "he regretted nothing. His past sufferings were redeemed." Yet when she offers herself to him physically, despite his overwhelming desire, the strongest he has ever felt, he declines. The narrator notes that Frédéric experiences a sort of repulsion, "like the fear of incest," reinforcing our early suspicions that she is a mother figure; moreover, his primary memory of her is with her children, and when she goes to leave, she kisses him on the forehead "like a mother." But the narrator further describes "another fear," another reason for not sleeping with Mme Arnoux, more telling in the final analysis: "in order not to degrade his ideal."

Frédéric has learned a sentimental truth after all, one evidenced throughout the novel and constituting perhaps its main message: that the ideal will invariably wilt in contact with reality and can be preserved only within the realm of memory, where it can remain intact, a lesson perhaps not so surprising in a novel written by a hermit who lived physically at Croisset but spiritually in the domain of art. Mme Arnoux leaves, untouched, her role as ideal safely sheltered in the vaults of memory, where, in fact, Frédéric first found her. Indeed, we are reminded that when he initially saw Madame Arnoux, on the boat journey, she was really a "memory" of an ideal woman from his boyhood dreams, "so that in seeing her for the first time, he had recognized her." The chapter ends with a paragraph as abrupt as the opening one—"And that was all"—a fitting ending, but the novel continues.[21]

Since there are six chapters in parts 1 and 2, the seventh and final chapter of part 3 assumes, structurally, the role of an epilogue. As Frédéric and Deslauriers, together again by the fireside, reminisce, they summarize the lives of most of the novel's characters. Mme Dambreuse has married an Englishman, and Louise has run off with a singer. Martinon has become a senator and Hussonnet an important journalist; Cisy, father of eight children, lives in his ancestral chateau; and Pellerin has given up painting to become a well-known photographer. Arnoux died recently, and Madame Arnoux has joined her son in Rome. La Maréchale, now overweight, married Papa Oudry, Arnoux's neighbor and successor as her keeper, and after his death adopted a son. Regimbart still spends his life going from one café to another, but no one knows what has become of Sénécal or Mlle Vatnaz. Deslauriers finally explains to Frédéric a political allusion, involving a calf's head, that comes up several times during part 3 and that neither Frédéric nor the reader has been able to understand until now.

Frédéric and Deslauriers then turn to their own lives, analyzing their failures with some degree of self-knowledge: Frédéric, too sentimental, has lacked direction; Deslauriers, too logical, has been overly rigid. Finally, as they "exhume" their youth, exclaiming, "Do you remember?" with each retrieved memory, they resurrect an event that occurred in 1837, three years prior to the start of the novel's action: there was at Nogent, much to the dismay of the upstanding citizenry, a brothel, located at riverside near the bridges and run by a woman known to all as "the Turk":

> Well, one Sunday, while everyone was at Vespers, Frédéric and Deslauriers, having had their hair curled, gathered some flowers in Mme Moreau's garden, then left by the back gate, and, after a long detour in the vineyards, came back by the Fish Market and snuck into the Turk's place, still holding their big bouquets.
>
> Frédéric presented his, like a lover to his fiancee. But the hot weather, the fear of the unknown, a kind of remorse, and even the pleasure of seeing, in a single glance, so many women at his disposal, moved him so much that he became very pale and remained without advancing, without saying anything. They all laughed, delighted at his embarrassment; thinking he was being made fun of, he took off; and, since Frédéric had the money, Deslauriers had to follow him.
>
> They were seen leaving. It made for a story that hadn't been forgotten three years later.
>
> They recounted it to each other at great length, each completing the other's memories; and, when they had finished:
>
> —That was the best we ever had! said Frédéric.
>
> —Yes, perhaps so? That was the best we ever had! said Deslauriers.[22]

It is with these words that the novel ends.

The passage is a fitting summary of Frédéric's behavior throughout his life: his idealism in the face of reality (flowers at a brothel), his paralysis when confronted by conflicting emotions (remorse and pleasure) as well as by profusion (so many women), his misinterpretation of others' reactions (the women's laughter), his paranoia, and his tendency to avoid confrontation by resorting to flight. That such a seemingly trivial event takes on such importance to the characters makes their lives seem all the more insignificant, a meaningless journey leading back beyond its point of departure. Furthermore, since the "best" of times seems to have occurred before those recounted in the novel, the ending appears to negate the very act of having read it, leaving many readers to wonder why they have bothered.

Yet there are two traits that elevate this event above the trivial, that rescue it from oblivion and bestow meaning on it: it is remembered, and it is recounted. By preserving, embellishing, and sharing the episode through memory and communication, much as with artistic creation, Frédéric and Deslauriers manage to find some solace, to salvage whatever happiness is to be found in a life doomed to disintegration, degradation, and failure. The final episode is, like the work of art, a reconstruction of the human mind and thus a testimony of the human spirit's capacity to persist. Although the event itself may be banal, its resurrection and sharing are uplifting, and the final episode of the novel is played in a minor but positive key.

For the reader who has committed time and sentiment to *Sentimental Education,* who has resisted the temptation to abandon the frustrating Frédéric, the final chapters of the novel can prove to be an immensely moving experience, matched only, perhaps, by the aging narrator's recovery of the past at the end of Proust's *Remembrance of Things Past* (*A la recherche du temps perdu*). In both cases, the sheer number and nature of pages that one has had to endure adds to the relief one feels at the end, the elation of a seemingly lost cause that is suddenly won at the last moment. Even more, the reading experience itself replicates Frédéric's journey backward, as the reader must return to an allusion at the end of the novel's second chapter, to a "common adventure" involving a house near the river, to retrieve the first signs that point to this final scene. Whereas plot, like life, carries us forward, structure, the hallmark of great art, moves us backward through memory toward the objects, events, and themes that constitute the web of associations within which, alone, meaning can be found. If the initial pleasure of reading is one of discovery, the ultimate satisfaction is, perhaps, that of recollection, of recovery.

This short chapter, highlighting a seemingly trivial episode resurrected from the past, confirms, then, that it is memory and representation, not reality and experience, that are the repositories of the ideal, the safeguards of sentiment and feeling. These are essentially the lessons of *Sentimental Education,* lessons that also apply, as is so often, so strikingly true of Flaubert's fiction, to art itself.

Chapter Six

The Temptation of Saint Anthony: The Matter of Form

Published in 1874, *The Temptation of Saint Anthony* (*La Tentation de Saint Antoine*), despite a gestation period of nearly 30 years and two earlier versions, remains a seemingly formless work.[1] Certainly its literary form is of dubious origin. Like a novel, the text is divided into seven sections and begins with a precise description of the setting: the isolated Egyptian mountain top overlooking the desert landscape where, in the third century A.D., the future saint, Anthony, has taken refuge from humanity. Unlike a novel, however, the lyrical style and fantastic images make the text read like a prose poem, while its typography is set up like a play: "staging" notations are given in small print, the dialogue appears in larger print, and the characters' names are centered on the page in capital letters. Yet this formal clue is undermined from the outset when the main character's name, typographically independent, runs grammatically into the description—

"SAINT ANTHONY
who has a long beard . . ."

—as in a narrated form. But any notion of narrative quickly dissolves in the eddy of images that sweeps up and entangles the thin thread of plot involving Saint Anthony's visions during one night of "temptation." Indeed, the vivid, surreal imagery suggests yet other formal analogies, with medieval paintings, such as the Breughel canvas *The Temptation of Saint Anthony,* which captured Flaubert's imagination when he first saw it in 1845 during a visit to Genoa.

This confusion of forms and genres is more than matched by an apparent lack of logical or chronological ordering principles: cascades of hallucinatory episodes succeed each other at a dizzying pace, in serial fashion, submerging the bewildered Anthony and depriving him of any discernible identity as a character. By the time Anthony, beset by a host of unintelligible figures, asks himself, "What are they getting at?" the reader has no doubt already posed the same question.

Subject Matter

Nonetheless, as the text unfolds, traces of order begin to emerge gradually from the threatening chaos. Each of the seven sections, for example, has a certain consistency in the grouping of its subject matter:

I. In an expository monologue, interspersed with stage directions indicating his movements and depicting the ever-changing setting, Saint Anthony describes his present condition (hunger, thirst, poverty, and abstinence) and recalls his past life (he left his mother and the beautiful Ammonaria to follow wise men and eventually acquired his own disciples before becoming a hermit). Questioning his path, he reads from the Bible "at random" and falls on scenes of destruction, sin, and temptation, which stimulate thoughts of his own lack of food, riches, adulation, and women. He begins to hear voices of temptation and to perceive tantalizing images.

II. The seven capital sins—gluttony, greed, envy, wrath, lust, sloth, and pride—appear in the form of hallucinations, first of a table laden with delicacies, then of precious objects, then of Alexandria, where Anthony witnesses, then participates in savage massacres before meeting Emperor Constantine and King Nebuchadnezzar, with whom he identifies. To dispel the visions, he whips himself in penitence, which serves only to awaken sexual desires that culminate in a final hallucination involving the Queen of Sheba, who tries to seduce him, not only with sexual favors but also with promises of riches and power.

III. Anthony believes he sees a child, who turns out to be his former disciple, Hilarion, who seems to know everything, first flattering Anthony, then analyzing his privations as perverse forms of desire. Hilarion fertilizes the already sown seeds of Anthony's doubt about his path, which grow like the image of Hilarion himself, who tempts Anthony with knowledge held by heretic wise men, whom he then evokes.

IV. The middle section, considerably longer than the three previous ones combined, features a parade of heretics, thinkers, philosophers, wise men, martyrs, sinners, and saints who represent a dizzying array of theological truths, most of which contradict Anthony's beliefs, as they do each other. Different conceptions of Jesus are followed by the appearance of a gymnosophist, then Simon and Helen, who fall into the abyss of nothingness, then Damis and his master Apollonius, whose claims to know everything attract Anthony, leading him to want to know the gods themselves.

V. The gods then appear in another substantial section. Guided by the ever-growing Hilarion, Anthony sees a parade of idols "of all nations and of all ages," beginning with the animal gods of primitive religions, and has extensive dialogues with the Buddha, the Egyptian goddess Isis, and a host of Greco-Roman deities, all of whom Hilarion relates to Christian beliefs, despite Anthony's protests. As the gods self-destruct before Anthony's eyes, Hilarion, transformed into a handsome archangel, reveals himself to be the possessor of all knowledge, the devil, and offers to show Anthony the wonders of the universe.

VI. Hilarion takes Anthony on a flight through the skies, revealing the secrets of physics and astronomy. He also meditates on such metaphysical matters as being and nothingness and, especially, form and matter, noting that "Form is perhaps an error of your senses, Substance a figment of your imagination."

VII. In the final section, Anthony, once again back on earth, is visited by two sets of temptations, staged as dialogues. In the first, two women, Death and Debauchery, argue, one preaching suicide, the other pleasure, both forgetfulness. In the second, the Sphinx confronts the Chimera, one representing reason and immobility, the other imagination and change, each expressing the desire to be the other. After seeing a series of figures that represent mutilations and mutations of all forms—animal, vegetable, and mineral—Anthony nearly yields to the ultimate temptation: to abandon his inner self, whatever the form, to become "matter." He is deterred, however, at daybreak, by the face of Jesus Christ radiating in the middle of the disk of the rising sun, causing him to make the sign of the cross and continue his prayers.

Traces of Form

This history of ideas may well be an intellectual tour de force, but it remains an artistic morass and a reader's nightmare due to its seeming incoherence. Lacking such literary amenities as a knowledgeable narrator, a discernible plot, or a coherent character, the book threatens to dissolve into the very nothingness that is among the saint's greatest temptations. For many critics who have tackled the tangled text, however, uncovering the text's forms, wresting order from chaos, has proven to be *Saint Anthony*'s ultimate challenge, the key to its meaning, and its greatest source of pleasure.

The French philosopher Michel Foucault, for example, in a brilliant essay about *Saint Anthony,* discerns, despite the seemingly endless linear succession of images strung together like the episodic scenes of the puppet shows that fascinated Flaubert in his youth, two complex and subtle organizational principles.

In addition to Flaubert's division of the text into seven sections, Foucault describes several patterns that contribute to the text's structure, of which Hilarion's growth is the most obvious. Others include a progressive monstrosity in the hallucinations; an expansion of space from the precise initial setting to the infinite universe; a gradual movement backward in time from Saint Anthony's youth through progressively more ancient civilizations to the very beginnings of life; conversely, a progressive gain in knowledge, which goes beyond the limits of Saint Anthony's time toward the scientific discoveries of the modern universe that were known in Flaubert's era; and a hidden theological order, derived by comparison with the earlier versions of the book, that marks the progressive defeat of the Christian virtues of faith, hope, and charity.

In another sense, for Foucault the visions are structured in "depth" by a series of intermediaries or spectators, each looking over the other's shoulder. Thus the reader scans the text, in which an implied spectator observes the playlike setting, which contains Saint Anthony, who, like the reader, reads from a book, the Bible, which produces its own images, which in turn generate the appearance of Hilarion, who becomes a sort of master of ceremonies, presenting visions of characters, who themselves describe their own visions. The linearly linked episodes thereby acquire a sort of "texture" or "relief," constituted by layers of spectators, each of whom in turn presents an image farther removed from the initial scene but every bit as textually vivid. Viewed from this perspective, the work has distinct levels—the book, the theatrical setting, the Bible, images of characters, and images described by the characters. The text can thus be seen as structured in depth, with different spaces each inserted within the other, different images inscribed within images, as with the different planes of a painting within a painting or with the scenes of a play within a play. Consequently, despite the seeming chaos, Foucault concludes that Flaubert's order is in fact "meticulous":

> The visible line along which file sins, heresies, divinities and monsters is only the superficial tip of an entire vertical organization. . . . Each element or each figure thus takes its place not only in the visible parade, but in the order of Christian allegories, in the development of culture and

> knowledge, in the inverse chronology of the world, in the spatial configurations of the universe. If one adds that *The Temptation* develops according to a process that envelops the visions within one another and lays them out in depth, one sees that, behind the thread of the discourse (text) and under the line of succession, there is a "volume" that is constituting itself.[2]

Further evidence of ordering principles stems from the fact that many of the novel's earlier episodes appear to generate later ones. Foucault, for example, traces the reappearance of Anthony's biblical readings from earlier scenes and concludes that Flaubert's work is ultimately a book comprised of books; similarly, other readers have pointed out Anthony's recollections of his past as the source of later episodes.[3] For example, Anthony believes he sees his mother in the image of the old woman who represents death in the final scene. Again, Anthony thinks he recognizes the sensuous image of the young girl Ammonaria ("the rings on her feet sparkled in the dust, and her tunic, open at the hips, floated in the wind") in a naked woman being whipped by soldiers, then later evokes Ammonaria's image while whipping himself, just before he encounters the Queen of Sheba, and finally he mistakes her for the young woman who becomes Debauchery in the culminating scene of the book.

Clearly such a reading based on Anthony's recollections posits the possibility that the figures he encounters, far from being independent entities, more than simple temptations, are projections of his own memories, his own desires. From this perspective, Anthony's psyche becomes the central organizing principle, not according to his visions, which remain incoherent, but according to the desires they reflect, which show remarkable consistency.

Forms of Desire

Perhaps what is most modern in Flaubert's treatment of the story of Saint Anthony, as is the case with the legend of Saint Julian, is the psychological dimension with which he underlays the original tale. By depicting the visions as possible projections on the part of the central character, Flaubert both renews ancient images and figures and uses them to crystallize modern thoughts and desires. Flaubert's process of visualization, reflecting, perhaps, elements of the Breughel painting he saw and the play he wanted to write, amounts to a "staging" of desire before the superimposed spectators Foucault identifies.

Flaubert does little to discourage a psychological reading of the text. The word "desire" occurs no fewer than 10 times in the text and its partner "envy" 5 times. The words often appear in notable passages, as when the Queen of Sheba describes her magnificent bird—"He flies like desire"—and promises Anthony that she will fulfill "all the imaginations of your desire," or when Hilarion tells him that "my desire has no limits" and the gymnosophist concludes that "existence stems from corruption, corruption from desire."

Moreover, the sequencing of events clearly links Anthony's visions to his obsessions. In the opening section, for example, his verbalized suppositions ("Maybe some {women} will come?") produce echoes, which become voices that formulate questions in terms of desires ("Is it women you want"?), which then engender vague images before fostering concrete ones. At the beginning of the second section, this process is condensed even further, as his question "Where's the bread?" leads him to find a piece of crust, which "in sheer fury, he flings to the ground. No sooner has he done so than a table stands there, spread with everything good to eat." As if the sequencing weren't clear enough, Flaubert goes so far as to have Anthony analyze his own temptations as forms of desire: "Why all this? It comes from urges of the flesh."

Not content with tracing the manifestations and crystallizations of desire, Flaubert explores the transmutations and interactions that characterize the curious workings of the psyche. In the hallucinations involving food or wealth, for example, lie the seeds of lust—"fleshy fruits come forth like amorous lips"; "With a jewel like this, even the Emperor's wife might be won," and in Anthony's vision of the seductive Queen of Sheba, who wears the very jewel just alluded to, she appeals to his desire for wealth and power as much as for sexual favors. Later, when Anthony refuses to discuss his faith, Hilarion identifies sloth as merely a form of pride: "you're falling into your habitual sin, sloth. Ignorance is the froth of pride."

Even penance is shown to be a form of pride ("the thirst for martyrdom"), and paradoxically, self-punishment produces the very desires it is meant to repress: as Anthony whips himself in atonement for his visions of wrath and pride, he stimulates feelings of lust: "Such agony! Such bliss! It's like being kissed! I'm melting to the marrow! I could die!"; immediately afterward, the Queen of Sheba appears. Again Flaubert is careful to articulate the relationship between privation and desire, here by having Hilarion analyze Anthony: "Hypocrite, who buries himself in solitude to better enjoy the excesses of envy."

Whereas the temptations of the flesh that characterize especially the first two sections of the text are rather transparent manifestations of Anthony's basic desires, the appearance of Hilarion in the third section seems to complicate matters by introducing the saint's fears and doubts rather than outright wishes. It is soon clear, however, that his former disciple merely reflects Anthony's overwhelming desire for knowledge. Indeed, Hilarion, who "knows everything," speaks of "our thirst for truth" and asks Anthony, "Do you desire to know . . .?" Hilarion tempts Anthony with knowledge, like the snake in Eden or Mephistopheles in Goethe's *Faust*. In Flaubert's text, however, it is clear that Hilarion is merely Anthony's alter ego, since Hilarion says, "I never left you" and since his voice is later characterized as "an echo of his thought—an answer to his memory." Hilarion simply says what Anthony wants to hear, because in Flaubert's work the devil is no more than the saint's inner voice. As Hilarion denigrates Anthony's rivals, for example, the future saint cannot help but smile, and as the doubt sown by Hilarion grows, Anthony's faith wavers and his inhibitions topple, thus laying bare the desires that they formerly held in check.

Even the parade of heretics and idols who contradict Anthony's beliefs in sections 4 and 5 can be read as projections or desires on his part when seen from the preceding perspectives. Most obviously, the proliferation of creeds reflects Anthony's desire to know everything, even at the risk of weakening his own beliefs. Moreover, despite his seeming disagreement and disgust with the various heretics and idols, Anthony often identifies with certain speakers, most openly with Apollonius: "That one's worth all of Hell." Flaubert further suggests this process of identification through the characters' use of a recurrent speech pattern, involving the repetition of the subject pronoun "I" with a list of verbs reflecting the speaker's past accomplishments. This similar way of speaking links Anthony with the Queen of Sheba, Simon, Apollonius, the Buddha, Hercules, and the God of the Ancient Testament. Thus although Anthony may disagree with the substance of the heretics' and idols' beliefs, the process of identification serves to elevate him to their level of fame and power. Furthermore, the contradictions among their beliefs, readily apparent to Anthony and to the reader, create a sense of irony that weakens each of them and thus thrusts Anthony into the position of dominance that his pride would have him occupy. Finally, by contradicting each other, the various doctrines tend to cancel each other out and, by extension, weaken all belief systems, including Anthony's ascetic Christianity, which is further imperiled by the frequent parallels with other doctrines pointed out by Hilarion: "Don't you find that they have . . . sometimes . . . certain similarities with the truth!" By "relativizing" all belief systems, Hilarion, Anthony's inner voice, causes them to weaken, totter, and finally disappear, along with the repressive obstacles and taboos that they had erected and that prevented Anthony from fulfilling his desires, both of the flesh and of the spirit. Indeed, as Anthony comes to perceive the parallels between himself and the so-called heretics, he experiences a new sense of freedom, and the barriers built by his beliefs begin to tumble:

> It's towards God that they are trying to direct themselves by all these paths! By what right can I curse them, as I stumble along on my own? When they disappeared, I was perhaps about to learn even more. It was spinning too fast; I didn't have the time to answer. Now, it's as if there were more space and more light in my mind. I am calm. I feel capable . . .[4]

Later, as he observes the Greek gods on Olympus, he experiences a similar freedom: "Ah! my chest is opening up. A joy I didn't know is descending to the depths of my soul! How beautiful it is! how beautiful!" The joy is that of freedom from restraint, which opens the floodgates of repressed desires. The disappearance of the gods near the end of section 5 is not so much a defeat of ancient deities by the Christian God but the defeat of all gods at the hands of Satan, the figure of knowledge, pride, and desire that ends the section.

The two final sections of *Saint Anthony* may initially appear too speculative, too metaphysical to reflect the type of sensual and spiritual wish fulfillment represented thus far. However, in the numerous pairs of conflicting concepts introduced by the devil—infinity and nothingness, matter and form, death and debauchery, immobility (the Sphinx) and change (the Chimera)—also lurk the multifarious forms of desire.

The flight into the heavens on the devil's wings, for example, recalls the Queen of Sheba's bird, who "flies like desire." This Faustian thirst for knowledge, along with the sense of dominance it implies, is represented throughout the text by an elevated viewpoint and leads here to a feeling of freedom in Anthony akin to that he experienced in understanding the heretics and in seeing the gods: "Ah! how freely I'm breathing! The immaculate air fills my soul! No more weight! no more suffering!"

Moreover, one element of each pair of concepts is easily read in terms of desire: Debauchery is no more than a form of lust and refers to herself as "your eyes' desire"; the notion of infinity clearly reflects the extent of

Anthony's desire to know "all or nothing," the pride that drives him, and the "joy of discovering the world"; and form and immobility, which impose order on matter and change, are among the creative artist's foremost goals, a notion Flaubert expresses throughout his correspondence.

But what of nothingness, death, change, and matter, which would seem to negate their counterparts? To what extent do these opposites of various desires themselves constitute forms of desire? Again, Flaubert provides some subtle, surprising, but clear answers. Death, in which one gives up the sometimes painful struggle and will to live, to be conscious, is painted as "consolation, rest, forgetfulness, everlasting peace." Indeed, from the beginning of the book, self-destruction is linked to the temptation of martyrdom and thus pride, about which Anthony muses: "if I were to desire it . . ." The figure of Death herself suggests that Anthony's suicide would be the ultimate form of pride, allowing him to rival God: "To do a thing that makes you God's equal; imagine that! He created you; you are going to destroy his work, you, by your courage, freely." The Chimera, who embodies change and instability, is nonetheless a figure of fantasy, fulfilling "eternal follies, projected felicities, future plans, dreams of glory, vows of love," in short, desires. Matter, connoting formlessness and mindlessness, is nonetheless seen by Anthony as "happiness, happiness . . . the desire to fly . . . flowing like water" and constitutes his ultimate temptation, expressed in his final spoken words: "to be matter!"

Most of all, each element of a pair is seen to reflect the desire for its opposite, as if neither component can exist without its counterpoint and counterpart. Infinity resembles nothingness because of their shared quality, vastness. Matter and form are interdependent elements of creation, as we shall further examine at the end of this chapter. Death and debauchery are opposites, yet each necessarily implies the other, since there can be no death without life, nor life without death: "—You destroy, for my renewals! —You engender, for my destructions!" The Sphinx and the Chimera, while arguing and contradicting each other, also desire each other: "—O Fantasy, carry me off on your wings, to alleviate my sadness! —O Unknown, I am in love with your eyes!"

Desire, as charted by Flaubert, must seek its opposite in order to sustain itself. Self-contradiction is a condition of self-perpetuation, negation a mainstay of existence, because desire must always destroy itself in order, paradoxically yet precisely, to remain unattainable. Hence, a key to sexuality is abstinence, and the ultimate form of sexual desire, illustrated several times in the text, is castration, which allows the object of desire to remain unrealizable and thus forever desirable.[5] Wish fulfillment is itself a contradiction, since a wish is precisely that which is not fulfilled, that which dies when fulfilled. Since it operates in the realm of the imagination, desire disappears on contact with reality. Desire attained must thus negate its object to perpetuate itself, since desire implies an absence or a lack. If nature abhors a vacuum, desire must continually create one in order to continue its very flow, its perpetual pursuit. Desire thus implies continual renewal or the transformation from one form to another, as embodied by Simon, the Buddha, and Jupiter, who assume different guises, by the Queen of Sheba and Helen, who become many different women, and especially by the protean Hilarion, a figure who is the epitome of desire's elusiveness.

Just as the psychic mechanisms of disguise, identification, and symbolism enable desire to avert the barriers and taboos of repression in order to seek fulfillment, so do the processes of substitution, displacement, and transformation enable desire to avoid fulfillment and thus perpetuate and renew itself. These are, indeed, the very mechanisms and processes of the dream work, studied by Freud several years after the publication of *The Temptation of Saint Anthony.* No wonder that Freud so liked the text and described it as highlighting the "real riddles of life."[6]

Thus despite their diversity, Anthony's visions can all be read as forms of his desires that stem from his psyche, the workings and patterns of which lend centrality and coherence to this apparently amorphous text.

Kaleidoscopic Forms

In addition to the ordering principles produced by the recurrence throughout the text of elements from Anthony's past, his readings from the Bible, and the images of his desires, another source of his visions, which textually precedes both his Biblical readings and his recollections of the past, can be found in the initial description of the setting. The objects of the decor are rediscovered throughout the text—not only in the setting, in which one might expect to find them, but in the visions and dialogues, in which they add another dimension to a psychological reading, based as it is on recurrence. These elements of the setting continuously reform to produce new images, whose parts are similar but whose specific nature changes and assumes a different meaning according to the new combination, much like a kaleidoscope, which causes the same multicolored beads to form new patterns with each twist of the tube.

This perpetual transmutation of forms matches the elusive nature of desire described earlier, but, especially, it sheds light on unresolved issues, such as the metaphysical question of the relationship between form and matter and, indeed, the intriguing problems encountered in reading Flaubert. The reappearance of the elements of the setting reinforces the principle of inner association as a key to reading Flaubert's works, while the changes they undergo show how transformation is a notion essential to understanding the text's metacritical message: that literary form stems from matter, that it emerges from within the text and perpetuates itself by transfiguration and renewal.

The reader/spectator is immediately struck by the setting's painterly presentation, with its frequent notations of spatial positions and relationships, its nuanced descriptions of color and light, and its precise designation of shapes and contours. These visual elements no doubt recall Flaubert's debt to Breughel's *Temptation of Saint Anthony,* except that, unlike Breughel's painting, remarkable for its profusion of figures, Flaubert's setting is stark and reduced to the bare essentials.

Set "high" on a mountain top, "on a platform, rounded like a half-moon," is the hermit's cabin, flanked by a "long cross" and a "twisted old palm tree leaning over the abyss," with the Nile "like a lake" below. In the distance can be seen waves of sand "like beaches" and mountains "like a wall." As the "sun sinks," its "rays of flame" hit the clouds, "arranged like the tufts of a gigantic mane," lending the scene a "hardness of bronze" capped by a vibration of light in a "golden powder." Despite the striking visuality of the scene, the curiously evocative adjectives "high," "long," "old," and "twisted," coupled with the numerous similes and metaphors (moon, lake, wall, flame, mane, bronze, and powder), lend an imaginative, even psychological dimension to the setting, which is complemented by the precariously positioned "palm tree leaning over the abyss," much like Herod, in the beginning of *Herodias,* set to confront his inner self.

All of these initial details recur repeatedly throughout the text, not only in later descriptions of the actual setting but in the dialogues and in the imaginary settings Anthony encounters. The cross, for example, reappears some 22 times, not surprising perhaps since it symbolizes the beleaguered faith of this future saint. But the cross also undergoes a series of transformations: it grows and takes other forms, such as the constellation the Southern Cross and Anthony's "crossed arms," an image that recalls the "arms of the cross," which transmutate into a symbol whose meaning is quite different from that of the pure, religious cross that spawns it: "Then the two shadows formed behind him by the arms of the cross project themselves forward. They become like two large horns: Anthony cries out: Help, my God!" Generated by the cross, the horns themselves become a dominant hallucinatory motif in setting and dialogue alike, recurring more than 16 times; they are attached to a variety of animals, culminating with a unicorn, and gods, especially the devil, alias Hilarion: "Anthony, with arms outstretched, leans on the two horns of the Devil."

Similarly, the tree reappears some 20 times, not only in the form of palms, pines, cedars, and sycamores but also as the tree of evil, the tree of knowledge, and a mysterious specimen in which many trees merge into a single one. Again, like the cross, the tree takes on a form with quite different implications: "At the same time, the objects transform themselves. At the edge of the cliff, the old palm tree with its tuft of yellow leaves, becomes the torso of a woman leaning over the abyss, and whose long hair is swaying." The "tuft" harks back to the clouds in the initial setting, and the female figure recalls Ammonaria, whose torso and long hair also appear to Anthony:

> In the middle of a doorway, in full sunlight, a naked woman was attached to a column, two soldiers whipping her with lashes; with each blow her entire body was twisting. She turned around, mouth open;—and, across the crowd, through the long hair covering her face, I thought I recognized Ammonaria.[7]

Here the word "twisting" strengthens the link between the woman and the "twisted" tree, while the "column" engenders yet another motif, which recurs some 14 times and is often associated with women ("I could have been tied to the column next to yours"; "She is sobbing, her head leaning on a column") as well as with trees ("The columns sway like the trunks of trees"; "a forest of columns").

It is not only the objects of the initial setting that recur repeatedly but also the similes attached to them. The "flames," whose status was purely metaphorical in the initial description, infiltrate the text on all levels—dialogue, plot, and theme: a flame or fire accompanies numerous characters, from the gymnosophist and Simon to Anthony's mother and the Chimera, ultimately attaining a spiritual status. The "mane" of the clouds recurs only a few times, but it engenders images of lions, which appear some 16 times, usually threatening Christians and thereby underscoring the central theme of martyrdom, but also transmuting into various mythological beasts composed of a lion and several other forms, such as the Myrmecoleo, the Griffon, and the Sphinx. The moon appears some 16 times, as does the sun, both often taking the form of gods and ultimately becoming symbols of the sexes, the moon representing the female, the sun the male, the two forming a couple, as they do in *Salammbô*.

Moreover, there are many instances in which the various threads stemming from the initial setting are interwoven in new patterns in subsequent passages. A naked woman holding three flames leans on a lion who wanders among columns that sway like tree trunks; the Buddha speaks of lions, suns, and flames; the sun and the moon appear alongside a god with bulls' horns in the midst of forests of columns; a half-lion and a horned rabbit have flaming eyes that pierce the trees in the final pages of the text.

Thus the tendrils that stem from the initial description of the setting stretch throughout the text, intertwining to create an organic structure, much like the branches of the multiple trees that form a single trunk constitute a "monstrous framework," in which reside numerous animals, along with a solitary man, the image of Anthony himself. Moreover, the elements of the initial setting not only recur, they reform and recombine to produce new images and meanings in a text that seems to generate itself, to renew itself by the transformation of its basic matter into myriad forms. One might well argue that the relationship of form to matter is the central question in *Saint Anthony,* expressed not only as a metaphysical issue involving the essence of life but as a metacritical issue involving the essence of the text.

The word "form" recurs no fewer than 35 times and itself reforms into words like "platform" and, of course, "transform," the latter a key concept in reading this dynamic text, as the occurrence of such similar terms as "transfigure" and "metamorphosis" suggests.

Philosophically or theologically speaking, as Flaubert describes it through the dialogues and debates in *Saint Anthony,* form is an intermediary between infinity and nothingness on the one hand, and between thought and matter on the other. Form is that which crystallizes a thought by giving it a material presence, thereby rescuing matter from chaos at the same time. According to Anthony's formulation of the process, forms (or figures) manifest themselves in matter through specific images, but the forms persist in a more general and ethereal state. Moreover, Hilarion explains that as thoughts evolve over time and forms fade, similar thoughts take on different forms, which generate particular images as they pass from one culture to another. This evolution explains the relativism of belief systems demonstrated in *Saint Anthony,* that is, why ceremonies and creeds remain remarkably similar despite vast differences in time and space. Similarly, all deities, whose existence merely marked the attempt, perhaps in vain, to give form to the subtle thoughts or desires of a given moment, are destined to disappear, but they also continue to survive in other eras and cultures through new forms.

Of course, much the same can be said of literary form, which itself represents the artist's attempt to crystallize a thought, to impose order on the chaos of earthly experience, to translate subject "matter" into image, thought, and theme. However, if we transpose Hilarion's metaphysical judgment into this literary framework, we come to realize that "forms fade; and they must progress through metamorphoses." Since thoughts evolve, literature cannot rely on old forms to translate them but must conceive of innovative forms, of texts that are, like *Saint Anthony,* neither novel nor play but a new, hybrid literary genre. Furthermore, form itself, by its very architectural and static nature, arrests change and thus spells the death of narrative, much as a lesson learned negates the experience that engendered it. Thus the elements of the text must themselves evolve and transform, much as we have seen the objects of the setting undergo metamorphoses throughout *Saint Anthony*.

Just as the philosophical debate in *Saint Anthony* underlies a literary discussion, Flaubert's depictions of the universe often bear an uncanny similarity to descriptions of the literary text. When, for example, Anthony observes celestial bodies and perceives "the intersection of their lines, the complexity of their directions," he could just as well be alluding to the network of associations spawned by the setting. Again, in pointing to the stars, the devil notes that "they attract each other at the same time that they repel each other. The action of each one results from the others and contributes to them,—without means of any auxiliary, by the force of law, the sole virtue of order," reminding us of the "internal force" of inner associations that hold together Flaubert's hypothetical "book about nothing."[8] Indeed, since Flaubert once described the literary text in terms of the universe ("as the earth, without being supported, maintains itself in the air"), it is difficult to read this description of the universe without relating it to the literary text. Finally, Anthony's own description of the world as a self-sustaining entity whose parts can nonetheless be modified to affect its overall order reminds us of the very principle of transformation that we have been examining:

> For the world,—as a philosopher explained it to me,—forms a whole whose parts all influence each other reciprocally, like the organs of a single body. It's a matter of knowing the natural attractions and repulsions of things, then putting them into play. . . . One could thus modify what appears to be immutable order?[9]

For Flaubert, the text is a universe in which he holds the position of God, invisible and silent but more than willing to tinker with the principles of order.

To avoid the twin temptations, in philosophy or in literature, of accepting the formless or of imposing an inherited form, like a cookie cutter, on the subtleties of thought and the vastness of matter, forms must stem from matter itself and evolve constantly in order to be viable representations of the flexible, fluid forces of a given moment. Form, for Flaubert, is not what is identical and immutable but what persists despite difference and change, like the geometrical forms that emerge from the particular objects of a landscape, or the resemblances that stem from the different family portraits in a gallery, or the meaning that derives from the various stages in an individual's thought and life.

In *Saint Anthony,* the form of the cross persists behind the images it engenders of the devil's horns and thus resists dissolution into matter by emerging, in the final passage of the text, in the figure of Jesus Christ; the meaning and formal mechanism of this miracle is confirmed by Anthony's final gesture, making the sign of the cross. Indeed, the appearance of a final and finalizing image at the end of *Saint Anthony,* much like the parrot in *A Simple Heart,* the leper/Christ figure in *Saint Julian,* and even the blind man in *Madame Bovary,* reaffirms Flaubert's faith in form—however transient, however kaleidoscopic—despite the temptation of matter and the awesome burden of translating the infinite.

Chapter Seven

Bouvard and Pécuchet: Learning Life's Lessons

That *Bouvard and Pécuchet* was unfinished at the time of Flaubert's death in 1880 alone makes it a highly problematic novel. Additionally, the novel features two characters who are caricaturally simplistic yet compellingly sympathetic, a plot that is episodic, subject matter that is encyclopedic, and Flaubert's usual dispassionate and thus uninformative narrator, all of which makes for an immensely ambiguous work. As Bouvard and Pécuchet, two retired copyists, delve relentlessly into various domains of science, realms of art, and other areas of human endeavor ranging from politics and religion to education and love, scavenging scraps of undigested ideas and tidbits of half-baked notions in the process, the reader experiences a sort of intellectual indigestion. Confronted by a confusing menu of modern knowledge not unlike the catalog of ancient lore that characterizes *The Temptation of Saint Anthony,* the reader struggles to forge an interpretation by processing a monumental amount of information, first by wrestling with the novel's composition and structuring principles, then by attempting to grasp its elusive meanings.[1]

The text that Flaubert left, which represents nearly all of the first part of the novel, by far the most substantial of the two projected parts, is comprised of 10 chapters; each has its own distinct subject matter yet displays discernible parallels to the other chapters, all of which appear to revolve around the nature, possibilities, and limits of learning.

Yearning for Learning: Chapter 1

The opening chapter begins in 90-degree heat on the deserted Boulevard Bourdon, typical of empty summer streets in Paris (from which the lucky have fled to the countryside); two men, coming from opposite directions, sit down on the same bench at the same time and begin a conversation that will last a lifetime. Bouvard is big, casual, and outgoing; Pécuchet is smaller, more serious, and reserved; both, they discover, are copyists. Their mutual attraction, which the narrator likens to love at first sight, seems to stem from an overall feeling of dissatisfaction with life in Paris and from each character's intuition that the other possesses what he lacks and desires: "while listening to the other each one rediscovered forgotten parts of himself." In short, they are alter egos, whose meeting is akin to self-discovery and whose presence opens the possibilities for learning about life and about one's self. As they visit antique stores, museums, and libraries or take long walks in the nearby countryside, exchanging ideas on all manner of subjects (themes that will come to characterize the remainder of the novel), they reinforce each other and begin to recover their lost self-esteem. Subsequently, each becomes increasingly dissatisfied with his present work and surroundings. When Bouvard unexpectedly inherits a small fortune from his "uncle" (in reality his natural father), the two copyists make plans to move to the countryside after Pécuchet's retirement, two years hence. After months of looking, they settle on a farm in the Calvados region of Normandy (Flaubert's native region), and in early 1841, they set out for their new home in Chavignolles. During the trip, Bouvard takes the wrong coach, and Pécuchet, accompanying their belongings in the moving van (which breaks an axle, thereby shattering the china), gets lost, a series of misadventures that prefigures the novel's main course of action. When they finally settle into their new beds, they fall asleep, snoring in the moonlight and dreaming of the ideal country life they will lead.

Learning from Books: Chapters 2 to 5

In chapter 2, the reader is presented with the setting—the house with its divided garden, and the nearby farm, run rather poorly by Master Gouy and his wife—and introduced to the cast of characters: Germaine, the old servant; Monsieur Vaucorbeil, the doctor; the Count de Faverges, a former member of Parliament; Monsieur Foureau, the mayor; Monsieur Marescot, the lawyer; Abbé Jeufroy, the priest; and Madame Bordin, a widow of means. Most important, the chapter introduces the first field of knowledge to be examined in the novel: agriculture. Stimulated by a visit to the Count de Faverges's utopian estate, Bouvard and Pécuchet vow to transform their own farm by making themselves proficient in agronomy. Choosing to disregard the practical advice of the locals, the pair instead goes to every country fair and reads the classic studies on the subject. Through a combination of misunderstood readings, mismanaged personnel, and natural disasters, Bouvard fails at farming, just as Pécuchet goofs at gardening. Repeated descriptions of ordinary inadequacies are punctuated by scenes of monumental catastrophe, such as when the haystacks catch fire through spontaneous combustion and when the trellises supporting the fruit trees collapse onto the flower beds during a storm. Faced with failure in agronomy and arboriculture (not to mention severe financial losses), the two would-be rustics come across a book entitled *The Garden Architect* (*L'Architecte des jardins*) and decide to transform their garden into an artistic marvel. The book describes gardens by categories that range from the romantic and exotic to the majestic and mysterious and suggests appropriate artifacts to achieve them; Bouvard and Pécuchet are so impressed with what they read that they decide to combine the various styles. Thus they fill their garden with objects as disparate as an Etruscan tomb, a Chinese pagoda, a fish pond, a maze, a burned cabin, and a felled tree, which they complement by sculpting the yews into all manner of forms, the most striking of which is a peacock, and by decorating the gate with 500 pipe bowls of various shapes. Their pride is such that "like all artists they needed applause," so they invite the village notables to a grand dinner to unveil their work of art, during which appears a mysterious tramp, the former carpenter Gorju, to whom Bouvard gives a glass of wine. The dinner proves as "tasteless" as the garden, which draws laughter and criticism from the villagers, thus leading the would-be garden architects to a vow of seclusion and revenge. To pass the time, they turn to making preserves and alcohols (including the soon-to-be-famous liqueur "Bouvarine"). Their efforts produce the already predictable series of failures culminating in a major disaster, here the explosion of the still, which leads Bouvard and Pécuchet to the conclusion that they must learn about chemistry.

Chapter 3 begins with the exploration of chemistry, then details the other domains of the natural sciences to which our heroes are led. When chemistry proves too abstract, a visit to Doctor Vaucorbeil's study inspires the pair to turn to anatomy, even to purchase a life-size (if not lifelike) dummy on which to practice that the local citizenry first takes for a corpse. Anatomy soon leads to physiology, which entails further experiments, culminating in an episode in which Pécuchet, having climbed onto the scales to measure natural weight loss, and Bouvard, sitting in a bathtub to measure how body temperature affects water temperature, are held at bay for several hours by a stray dog. Eventually soothing the animal, they then attempt to perform an experiment, magnetizing steel pins by sticking them into the dog's back; this does little to please the poor creature, which runs away in pain. These failures notwithstanding, the intrepid researchers move on to study diet and even medicine, and when they practice some innovative cures, a few of which manage to succeed, they have a run-in with the good doctor. When they begin to take every minor ailment that befalls them as a symptom of one disease or another, they abandon medicine, only to be inspired by the night sky to study astronomy, which leads them to reflections on the relativity and arbitrariness of existence. Their interest in natural phenomena leads them first to animal husbandry and then to the more predictable domain of geology, which occupies them for much of the chapter. Their various journeys to collect samples end inevitably in mishap, as they are arrested in one case and panic in another, due to reflections on the possible cataclysmic events marking the end of the earth. Nonetheless, their discoveries lead them to challenge Abbé Jeufroy about biblical accounts of creation, and another scene of public encounter, attended by the Count de Faverges along with several new characters—Girbal, the tax collector; Captain Heurtaux, a landowner; Beljambe, the innkeeper; and Langlois, the grocer—leads again to criticism and laughter at Bouvard and Pécuchet's expense. As the chapter ends, Gorju, the former tramp, reappears, looking years younger and almost fashionable, this time offering them a drink. The pair accepts Gorju's invitation to his modest home, where they then bargain with him for a Renaissance chest—decorated with a grotesque mixture of scenes from Greek and Roman mythology and from the Bible, including one in which Adam and Eve pose indecently—and for his servant girl, Mélie, with whom they are fascinated and who joins their household to help the aging Germaine.

Although Gorju is slow to repair the chest, its purchase has nudged Bouvard and Pécuchet in another direction: "six months later, they had become archaeologists; and their house looked like a museum." The fourth chapter thus revolves around what we call today the social sciences, and the novel's main compositional patterns begin to emerge. Their museum, like their garden, is a helter-skelter collection of heteroclite objects that include a Gallo-Roman sarcophagus, a hearth plate that depicts a monk fondling a shepherdess, and a grotesque statue of an inebriated-looking Saint Peter, with gaping mouth and turned-up nose, who holds an apple-green key to paradise as he sits on a butter jar, covered by a canopy with two cupids. Again, the explorers' interests lead them to still other areas of inquiry; they move from archaeology to architecture and then to antiques, all of which can be understood only by studying history, whose dates can be remembered only through mnemonic devices (like seeing their house as a series of century symbols) and whose significance can be discovered only by studying philosophy. Philosophy's contradictions can be resolved only if Bouvard and Pécuchet write a history of their own, which they eventually choose to do, producing a study of the life of the Duc d'Angoulême, a rather insignificant figure given to inane sayings. Again, the pair's readings and excursions are interspersed with encounters with the villagers—Madame Bordin, Marescot, Faverges, Abbé Jeufroy, Foureau—although here the interaction takes place in individual visits rather than in a single large scene. Misunderstanding and misadventure prevail once again, as in the scene in which Bouvard and Pécuchet clandestinely unearth from the churchyard what they take to be a celtic druid's sacrificial basin and what the priest, who observed them in the act, believes to be a baptismal font; the priest demands that they return the object, in exchange for which he gives them a soup tureen, which Marescot declares to be worthless, prompting Pécuchet to destroy it, only to doubt later the lawyer's credibility. Near the end of the chapter, as in the two previous ones, Gorju appears, claiming that the chest has been demolished by a stray cow and blaming a nearly empty bottle of Calvados on Germaine, who is then fired despite the social scientists' lingering doubts; their hesitations then lead them to abandon history because it doesn't take into account psychology or imagination, and turn instead toward literature.

Chapter 5 details Bouvard and Pécuchet's opinions of literary works and theories, beginning with the historical novels of the era preceding Flaubert's, often called the romantic period. Initially enraptured by the British novelist Sir Walter Scott, they come to find him too repetitious, and one or the other judges the French novelists Alexander Dumas to be too inaccurate, George Sand too didactic, and Honoré de Balzac, despite his powers of observation and imagination, too documentary. As for the theater, they first tackle the tragedies of Racine and Voltaire before moving on to the comedies of Molière, the bourgeois dramas of Diderot, and the romantic plays of Victor Hugo. Again yielding to the need for an audience, they read to Madame Bordin, as Mélie and Gorju listen in, from Racine's *Phèdre,* Molière's *Tartuffe,* and Victor Hugo's *Hernani.* Bouvard gets so carried away declaiming to Madame Bordin that he later makes advances (quickly repelled), leading the narrator to a rare direct comment that "art, in certain circumstances, shakes up mediocre minds, and worlds can be revealed by the heaviest-handed of interpreters." Generally the villagers disparage their neighbors' artistic efforts, which makes them all the more determined to pursue their new direction and write a play, the difficulties of which lead them to examine different types of inspiration, rules, audiences, critics, and grammarians and eventually to conclude that "syntax is a fantasy and grammar an illusion." When past experience and personal preference fail to produce the text ("Pécuchet was for sentiment and ideas, Bouvard for image and color"), they turn in desperation to theorists, quickly realizing that "all the makers of rhetorics, poetics and aesthetics seem to be imbeciles." The chapter ends with another gathering during which Madame Bordin, Marescot, Vaucorbeil, and the Count de Faverges proclaim that the only goal of art is morality and that the public must censor offensive works; Bouvard and Pécuchet, on the other hand, defend the right of art to represent any subject, however reprehensible.

Learning from Experience: Chapters 6 and 7

The discussion of art at the end of the previous chapter provides a fitting prelude to the subject of politics, which dominates chapter 6. This chapter, which opens with the news from Paris of the Revolution of 1848 and the founding of the Second Republic, thus inaugurates interesting intertextual intersections with part 3 of *Sentimental Education,* in which Flaubert depicts the same historical events in Paris, and with the scene in *Madame Bovary* that describes the country fair ("*comices agricoles*"), paralleled here by the villagers gathering to plant liberty trees. Attending this religiously tinged ceremony is the entire cast of characters, along with several new ones: Petit, the schoolmaster; Coulon, the justice of the peace; and Plaquevent, the rural constable. Many of the citizens seek to join the rejuvenated yet perpetually inept National Guard, and as political arguments abound, several of the notables are determined to run for office, including Gorju, now one of the leaders of the workers (who believe themselves enfranchised by the new government), the Count de Faverges, representing the old guard, the mayor, Foureau, and even Bouvard and Pécuchet, all of whom bad-mouth one another and thus open the way for an outsider to prevail. Gorju and the workers, many unemployed, become progressively disenchanted, demanding work, and when the June counterrevolt fails, Gorju among others is arrested for seditious speech. In the presidential elections, all of Chavignolles votes for Bonaparte and becomes reactionary to the point of cutting down the liberty trees, which prompts Bouvard and Pécuchet to study such political issues as voting rights and the "divine right" of the monarchy.

Only they, along with Petit, remain progressive, but even the radical schoolmaster, in fear for his job, is coerced by Abbé Jeufroy into reintroducing prayer and catechism lessons into the classroom. As the foundling and foundering republic begins to sink, the soon-to-be-reelected Count de Faverges holds a banquet for the village notables, at which all hail the return to "law and order" despite the protests of Bouvard and Pécuchet, who leave the dinner disillusioned and determined to study political science. As they pass from Thomas Aquinas to Jean-Jacques Rousseau, from the utopists Fourier and Saint-Simon to the socialists Louis Blanc and Proudhon, Bouvard and Pécuchet disagree more and more vehemently with each other but later reconcile in their goal of studying economics. When they learn in December 1851 that Bonaparte has abolished the republic and intends to declare himself emperor, their disgust with politics is complete: "Bouvard mused: 'Heh, Progress, what a joke!' He added: 'And Politics, beautiful filth!' " The chapter ends with Gorju's return from prison and Pécuchet ogling Mélie as she draws water from the well.

As the end of the previous chapter suggests, the focal point of chapter 7, the shortest in the novel, is women. Flaubert sets the stage by describing the monotony and boredom of country life:

> Sad days began.
>
> They no longer studied for fear of disappointment, the residents of Chavignolles stayed clear of them, the newspapers they tolerated taught them nothing, and their solitude was profound, their idleness complete.[2]

As Bouvard and Pécuchet become more and more annoyed with each other, they grow farther apart, leading them to seek companionship elsewhere. When Pécuchet overhears Gorju's mistress, Madame Castillon, begging him to continue their affair, his own dormant passions are awakened, and he becomes obsessed with Mélie. He provokes Germaine in order to fire her, and the path now clear, he finally loses his virginity, in his late sixties, on a woodpile in the basement, not suspecting that Mélie is already quite experienced. At the same time, with equal secrecy, Bouvard has been assiduously courting Madame Bordin, who finally agrees to marry him if he will grant her but one favor, to be revealed when they sign the marriage contract several days later. When he finds out that she wants his farm as a dowry, he storms out of the lawyer's office and returns to confide in Pécuchet, who reveals to him in turn that he has contracted venereal disease from Mélie. Their discouragement about women is as complete as their disappointment with their studies and their neighbors, and embracing each other tenderly, they swear again to live in isolation, devoted only to each other, having learned the value of friendship. Following Pécuchet's cure, much to the dismay of Germaine, rehired to replace the fired Mélie, they both take up hydrotherapy.

Learning from Beyond: Chapters 8 and 9

After a brief stint with gymnastics and other forms of physical exercise, Bouvard and Pécuchet turn to spiritualism, the unifying principle for chapter 8. A séance that assembles many of the main characters convinces the previously skeptical duo that there are forces and phenomena that lie beyond the senses, and their study of magnetism and mesmerism leads them to faith healing, which again brings them into the public eye. Their healing of several people and a flatulent cow leads to a certain renown and renewed rivalry with the doctor, and in order to silence him (as well as to show off their newfound prowess), they invite the village notables to a public séance. As several of their subjects, holding cords attached to a magnetized pear tree, undergo mass hypnosis and exhibit various types of trances and cures, the public remains generally unimpressed until one of the entranced subjects is asked to evoke a vision of what the doctor's wife is doing at home. When the prediction is soon confirmed, the public is dumbfounded; no one laughs this time, but the priest warns Bouvard and Pécuchet not to continue with practices banished by the church, a warning that serves only to spur them on to further studies. They then move on from spiritualism and Swedenborgianism to magic and necromancy before attempting to summon the departed spirit of Bouvard's father in a ceremony involving a candle in a skull. They experience a vague presence and hear a cry, which turns out to be from Germaine, who fainted while observing them and who then leaves their service immediately, her gossip turning the villagers even more against them. To replace her they engage the hideously deformed and idiotic Marcel, who convinces them that in the area are hidden lost gold ingots, which they attempt to uncover by using a divining rod. Pécuchet lapses into more and more frequent trances, which turn out to be caused by self-hypnosis induced by the reflection of his cap's visor. To better understand the problematic relationship between spirit and matter, soul and body, they begin studying the great philosophers, from Plato and Aristotle to Locke and Spinoza, from Descartes and Leibniz to

Kant and Hegel, Bouvard leaning toward materialism, Pécuchet toward idealism. As they pass through metaphysics, epistemology, and ethics to logic and language, disagreeing vehemently with each other, they initially feel elevated intellectually but begin to find their surroundings hostile (they destroy the statue of Saint Peter after repeatedly bumping into it) and eventually become prisoners of their own abstractions, their attraction to meditation rendering them unable to "cultivate their garden."[3] As arguments and proofs continue to cancel each other out, they become increasingly skeptical of all truth, and their profound doubt reinforces their sense of isolation and pessimism: "Thus a pitiful faculty developed in their minds, that of seeing stupidity and no longer tolerating it." In a final large gathering (the third in this chapter) the would-be philosophers further alienate the villagers by defending a convict, Touache, on the grounds that free will doesn't exist. When, during a walk, they observe a dog's carcass, they are overwhelmed by the idea of death, and concluding that "anything was better than this monotonous, absurd, and hopeless existence," their thoughts turn to suicide, which they attempt, on the evening of December 24, by hanging themselves, only to be stopped by the thought that they haven't done their wills and by the perception of lights in the distance as the villagers file toward midnight mass. Their revived sense of curiosity, a propelling force throughout the novel, pushes them to join in the ceremony, and as the host is raised, accompanied by the tinkling of a bell, the bleating of a lamb, and a choir of voices, they "felt like a new dawn was rising in their souls."[4]

Chapter 9 thus deals with religion, and our heroes soon undertake pious readings, Bouvard remaining somewhat skeptical but Pécuchet determined to discover faith, avoid vice, and practice virtue. Encouraged by the vendor of pious objects, Gouttman, they soon exchange their museum pieces for an equally heterogeneous collection of such religious objects as holy portraits, statues, and a cradle; Pécuchet in particular regrets the smashed statue of Saint Peter. They undertake a pilgrimage to the shrine of Our Lady of Deliverance, and even the reluctant Bouvard is moved by allusions to ideal womanhood incarnate in the Virgin Mary. As they return to the inn they run into Gouttman in the company of none other than Bouvard's old Parisian pal Barberou, now a wine merchant, who vows to bring them a book that tells the real truth about religion. As financial troubles mount, they finally sell their farm to the persistent Madame Bordin in exchange for an annual income and eventually agree to take holy communion, along with the rest of the villagers, who begin to look on them somewhat favorably once again. As Pécuchet turns to reading the mystics and Bouvard takes up the book sent by Barberou, they have more and more questions to raise with Abbé Jeufroy. Their vehement discussions are depicted in a series of dialogues interspersed throughout the chapter, on subjects that include the scriptures, other religions, martyrs, and miracles. One memorable discussion takes place during a driving downpour, others occur at the abbé's house, and still others at the Count de Faverges's chateau, to which Bouvard and Pécuchet are now invited several times a week. It is there that the reader encounters the count's daughter, Mlle Yolande, her future husband, the Baron of Mahurot, their companion, Madame Noares, a religious fanatic who has taken a liking to Pécuchet, and Victor and Victorine, two waifs whom she convinces the count to take under his wing because their mother is dead and their father, later revealed to be the convict Touache, is in prison. The count's coterie clearly sees religion primarily as a mainstay of social order, and Bouvard and Pécuchet, currently content with social climbing, bite their tongues until a final fateful gathering during which they proclaim marriage to be a civil affair, not a religious sacrament, defend polygamy, and even vow to become Buddhists, which does not fail to get them dismissed from the gathering, permanently one suspects. On their way home they run into Gorju, now fully shaven and in the count's employ, as well as Victor and Victorine, whose poor behavior has led to their being shipped off to a reform school and the convent, respectively. Partly out of genuine sympathy for the children and partly to spite the count, Bouvard and Pécuchet, on the spur of the moment and with the mayor's consent, decide to take the abandoned children into their care.

Learning from Teaching: Chapter 10

The central theme of chapter 10, as the reader might predict, is education. After reading a number of books on the subject, the two educators decide on an experimental, natural method, based on experience more than abstraction, that follows especially the precepts Rousseau illustrates in his novel *Emile*. They begin with French, sprinkling instruction with on-the-spot lessons and educational games, and ponder the possibilities of teaching their pupils foreign languages, taking care not to limit the girl to a traditional role—"they are usually brought up as veritable idiots, their whole intellectual baggage being limited to mystical nonsense"—a reminder perhaps of Emma's convent education in

Madame Bovary. The pupils' initial failures reveal, they feel, the need to assess their aptitudes, so the educators turn to phrenology, the study of cranial form, which they practice throughout the area. They achieve some success and renown, which leads them to further confrontations with the abbé and with the doctor, as well as with Plaquevent, whose son they judge to be unaffectionate. Their assessment then leads the constable to beat the boy, just as Gouy will later flog his horse and Victor scald the cat on the grounds that the victims are their "property," a concept and commonplace Bouvard and Pécuchet do not fail to challenge, much to the dismay of the conservative villagers. Pécuchet works with Victor and Bouvard with Victorine, but the pupils seem unmoved by all approaches and impervious to a progressive string of such subjects as arithmetic, geography, astronomy, history, drawing, and music. A visit to their old farm, now prospering under the watchful eye and steady hand of Madame Bordin, ends in disaster when Bouvard renews his advances toward the widow: both are excited by the spectacle of mating peacocks (reminiscent of the sculptured bushes), which also causes the horse to break free and knock down a clothesline full of clean laundry. Gouy's beating of the horse leads Bouvard and Pécuchet to assail Victor and Victorine with lessons of justice and ethics, which fall on deaf ears, however, because the convict's children are more prone to cruelty and vice, as Victor's scalding of the cat testifies. Similarly, a brief stint at catechism class ends when Victor beats up the lawyer's son and Victorine is later caught kissing him. Literature is ruled out because it exalts the passions; the educators can't find a way to broach the facts of life; and further lessons in physical exercise, hygiene, and diet fail as much as did those in the more traditional disciplines. When Bouvard and Pécuchet defend a poacher who is being reported by Faverges's gamekeeper, the latter reports them also, and they must appear in court, a public forum that does not fail to provoke the pair to attack the justice system and the government; their outspokenness lands them a substantial fine, although the would-be poacher is later acquitted. Such examples of injustice lead them to frequent the local café, where they hold forth on all sorts of subjects, ranging from primary education to free trade, and put forth proposals that involve a new social order and the renovation of Chavignolles, much as Baron Haussmann did for Paris—all of which ends up completely alienating the villagers. Such is their sense of isolation and consequent lack of gratitude that they refuse to reply to simple requests for information from Pécuchet's Parisian pal Dumouchel, now married, who has been supplying them with all manner of information and items for years. When Victorine is discovered sleeping with a hunchbacked traveling tailor and Victor is caught harboring stolen money, their disillusionment with educational theories and their determination to get rid of the children is complete, but their faith in learning and teaching does not waiver: they concoct a new project, involving adult instruction, which they intend to present to the entire village at the café in a monumental gathering scene that would have come near the end of part 1 of the novel had Flaubert lived to write it.

Flaubert's notes make it possible nonetheless to reconstruct the lecture scene with some accuracy and to conjecture about the remainder of the novel with some confidence. Pécuchet's speech was to be pedantic, focusing on the stupidity of the government and the Church; Bouvard's, more familiar, would have advocated female emancipation and criminal rehabilitation. In Flaubert's notes, Foureau, the mayor, is able to disrupt the meeting by reading an old petition from Bouvard, requesting that a brothel be established in Chavignolles, and he and Pécuchet return home, as the villagers conspire against them. The following day, at lunch, Pécuchet launches into a pessimistic description of the future of mankind, concluding that idealism, religion, and morality will perish, America will conquer the world, vulgarity will prevail, and resources will run out. Bouvard takes a different view, based on the scientific progress of mankind, which, he predicts, will bring fascinating inventions and profound changes in literature and in life. He has hardly finished when the police arrive to arrest them for offenses against religion and public order (not unlike the arguments raised by the government years earlier against *Madame Bovary*). The coincidental visits of their former Parisian friends Dumouchel and his new wife and later Barberou are paralleled by the arrival of most of the villagers, drawn by news of their impending arrest. Many seek vengeance: Gorju demands an allowance for the pregnant Mélie, and others "defend" Bouvard and Pécuchet in insulting terms, claiming that they are mere bunglers and are not to be taken seriously. The warrant for arrest turns out to be no more than a warning, but Bouvard and Pécuchet must give up Victor and Victorine, who display complete indifference, causing their two mentors to weep; as everyone leaves they are depressed, dispossessed, and in disgrace. It was at this moment of absolute failure and emptiness that Flaubert was to have them reveal simultaneously to each other a secret idea, the same one, that each has been harboring: to become copyists as before. They were to have Gorju construct a double-sided desk, and in the final words of the outline, "they set about it."

Just what they were to copy, that is, the subject matter for part 2 of the novel, is unfortunately less clear from Flaubert's notes, which has led scholars to three different sets of conjectures. The proximity of the *Dictionary of Inherited Ideas* (*Dictionnaire des idées reçues*) on Flaubert's desk when he died has caused some to conclude that it would have constituted the second part of the novel, and indeed it is often published with *Bouvard and Pécuchet*.[5] Others, however, contend that Flaubert often used *The Dictionary* as a source for stupid bourgeois clichés to attribute to the characters in many of his novels and may thus have been merely consulting it at the time of his death. They further argue that Bouvard and Pécuchet would not have been able to compose such a work, noting that they were merely meant to copy, not to compose. Another theory, based on manuscripts now housed in Rouen, is that Bouvard and Pécuchet were to copy all sorts of documents haphazardly, including a letter from the lawyer that alluded to them as two harmless imbeciles; this solution, however, by its very dependence on disorder, would seem to impose insoluble composition problems. A final solution involves their copying a *Sottisier* (an album of "stupid sayings"), a collection of quotations gleaned from their readings that would contain the contradictions, absurdities, tautologies, anachronisms, and clichés they had noticed in their readings and often mentioned during their arguments. This solution seems true at once to the task indicated, which involves copying, not composing; to the characters, who have shown themselves capable of seizing the errors; to the dictates of the novel, which involves some organizing principle; to Flaubert's expressed intention to portray "these two guys who copy a sort of critical and farcical encyclopedia"; and to the author's obsession with the stupidities found in the written works he was obliged to read in order to compose the novel. But what meaning are we meant to derive from such an ending, not to mention from the completed part of the text in its present form?

The Limits of Learning/Learning One's Limits

As usual with Flaubert, one must begin to seek meaning not in the phenomena themselves but in the relationships among them, that is, in the work's structure. We have observed that, despite its encyclopedic and episodic nature, the novel yields clear patterns, which point to a vision of human experience not unlike that painted in Flaubert's other works. Each episode, whether a segment of a chapter or an entire chapter, begins with a problem or a project, which Bouvard and Pécuchet attempt to solve or carry out by first reading books, whose lessons they then try to apply to reality either by experiments (which invariably fail) or in excursions (which inevitably end in mishap). Their studies often lead to a collection (garden, library, museum) of grotesque objects (the chest, the statue), whose heteroclite nature is matched by the hodgepodge organization of the subject matter, not only on the level of the chapter but also on that of the sentence, whose syntax often amounts to a list of objects so disparate as to produce an ironically comic effect.[6] The protagonists' discoveries usually culminate in public displays or gatherings that result either directly in failure and ridicule or else in seeming successes that end up producing conflict, usually with the doctor (science), the abbé (religion), the count (politics), or the mayor (public order). Either path thus leads to a desire for vengeance and a sense of isolation that drive them back into their equally chaotic household, where scenes involving Germaine, Mélie, Marcel, and Gorju often bring a chapter to its merciful end, while suggesting what will occur in the following one. This simplified pattern of desire, failure, and discouragement gains in intensity as the novel progresses, as does a sense of disintegration and arbitrariness that leads to the vision of human experience as "monotonous, absurd, and hopeless" that nearly drives Bouvard and Pécuchet to suicide, a vision and temptation similar to those we have encountered with Emma, Frédéric, Saint Anthony, and Saint Julian.

Yet despite their similarities to earlier characters, Bouvard and Pécuchet are different from Flaubert's other "dreamers." Their visions and the readings that fuel them are less an attempt to escape from reality than an effort to deal with the problems reality raises; their failures are less a result of the conflict between vision and reality than of the horrible people and events that reality puts in their path; it is not their warped vision that distorts reality; reality is incomprehensible in its own right. They are also resilient and irrepressible in their determination to continue to learn in order to improve reality. Thus, despite their limits (and perhaps because of them), Bouvard and Pécuchet are in some ways more sympathetic and less irritating than their predecessors; of course, they also have each other.

Indeed, the relationship between the two protagonists forms the novel's main structuring principle. From the outset Flaubert creates a pattern based on contrast followed by consensus or, put another way, of antithesis followed by synthesis. The two characters' first encounter, for example, is described as follows:

> Two men appeared.
>
> One was coming from the Bastille, the other from the Jardin des Plantes. The taller one, clothed in linen, was walking with his hat back on his head, his vest unbuttoned and his tie in hand. The shorter one, whose body disappeared in a chestnut coat, had his head lowered under a hat with a pointed visor.
>
> When they arrived in the middle of the boulevard, they sat down, at the same moment, on the same bench.[7]

Even before we learn which titular character is which, the *B* in Bastille points to Bouvard and the *P* in Plantes to Pécuchet, their order of presentation thus matching that of the title. The very syntax of the first sentence in paragraph two is antithetical ("One . . . the other"), as is the paragraph structure ("The taller one . . . The shorter one"), which suits their different natures, presented typically by Flaubert's choice of detail rather than by the narrator's commentary: Bouvard is dressed more casually, Pécuchet with more constraint.[8] They are stereotyped from the outset as the proverbial "odd couple," and their actions are often as contentious as those of Oscar and Felix, as farcical as those of Laurel and Hardy, and as hopeless as those of Vladimir and Estragon in Samuel Beckett's *Waiting for Godot*. Their differences are transcended, however, in the final paragraph, when they sit at the "same time" in the "same spot" and moments later discover that *both* have written their names in their hats and that *both* are copyists. The final sentence of the first chapter reveals this same structure of antithesis and synthesis: "*Bouvard* on his back, mouth open, bareheaded; *Pécuchet* on his right side, his knees tucked into his stomach, covered in a cotton nightcap, and *both* of them were snoring in the moonlight, which was entering through the windows" (our emphasis). This pattern of difference followed by similarity or even identity is so prevalent and thus predictable as to become comic. Moreover, the pattern often determines the ordering of paragraphs (one for Bouvard, the following for Pécuchet, the third for both) and of entire chapters: Bouvard is materialistic; Pécuchet idealistic; both become skeptics, reaching the conclusion that the very plausibility of their conflicting positions points to their mutual cancellation and thus to the folly of all philosophical speculation. Furthermore, the pattern is concretized in the text by two objects, both of which appear in chapter 8: the seesaw that the two gymnasts use to hoist each other alternately and the grocer's scales whose "oscillation between two weights that seem equal represents the workings of our mind as it deliberates." These objects thus become emblematic of the compositional principle and indeed the mental process of extremes reaching equilibrium that Flaubert has applied to the text. More than a mere organizing device, however, the pattern itself underscores meaning, since it suggests the limits of any one position, the desirability of harmonizing or balancing positions, and the value of friendship.

Yet another structuring principle, more subtle and more speculative, is suggested in the novel's first sentence by Flaubert's choice of setting: the Boulevard Bourdon.[9] Not only does the word *Bou*l*e*v*ard* phonetically contain the character's name, the beginning of which also appears in *Bou*rdon along with an echo of Madame *Bordin,* his future object of desire, but the meaning of the word *bourdon* is highly suggestive. Although the boulevard, constructed in 1806, was named for one of Napoleon's officers, the word *bourdon* also has multiple meanings, denoting at once a bumblebee, a pilgrim's staff, a typographical omission, and a great bell, the latter two meanings particularly applicable to the novel. Certainly the novel is full of bells—the church bell that tolls for both religious and public events (like the burning haystacks), the school bell that Bouvard and Pécuchet use (with little success) to call Victor and Victorine to their studies, the ringing of which ought to produce order. Of particular note in the novel, however, is the recurrence of the related word "*bourdonnement,*" which denotes a drone or buzzing noise, that is, an irritating sound without order or meaning. When Bouvard is confronted with the idea of a geological cataclysm, for example, "his temples were buzzing" ("*ses tempes bourdonnaient*"), and he begins to experience vertigo. When Pécuchet tries to read aloud from a Racine play, "from the first sentence his voice got lost in a sort of drone ('*bourdonnement*'). It was monotonous and, although strong, indistinct." When Germaine hears the two would-be magicians walking around during the night, "she confused the sound of their footsteps with the buzzing ('*bourdonnement*') in her ears and the imaginary voices that she heard coming out of the walls." When Bouvard and Pécuchet, already dumped to the depths of depression by their study of philosophy, spot a dog's carcass, they are struck by "the buzzing ('*bourdonnement*') of the flies, in this intolerable odor, ferocious and almost devouring." The sound, an unintelligible noise suggesting an omission of meaning, thus surges repeatedly as a reminder of the limits of learning; it is associated with catastrophe, boredom, hallucination, and death; it is the sound of the absurd ringing in the vast reaches of the meaningless universe, the opposite of the reassuring order of the bell that suggests the quest for knowledge and truth propelling Bouvard and Pécuchet. The drone is the noise in the system, the fly in the ointment, the catch in the clause, the insurmountable obstacle raised before us that reminds us of our limits. But does its prevalence imply the futility of all learning, doomed as it is to impasse?

Flaubert certainly sets out to satirize not only the learners, Bouvard and Pécuchet, whose repeated mistakes approach the farcical, but, it would appear, all of learning, since no domain remains unscathed in its inability to solve the problems that society, the universe, nature, and human nature heap onto humankind. But we must remember that in order to satirize Bouvard and Pécuchet, Flaubert himself had to duplicate their readings and, moreover, exceed them, since he frequently has the narrator point out where they go wrong. Moreover, as modern readers making our way through this vast encyclopedia of futile fact and opinion, we may well recall our liberal-arts education, with a smorgasbord of courses, each offering a partial glimpse of the seemingly endless reaches of knowledge that stretch tantalizingly before us and that we can now contemplate daily in our own rooms as we explore in bewildered awe the infinite informational expanses of the Internet. Indeed, as critics attempting to write about Flaubert, contemplating the mountain of books and articles that we must consult and that grows faster than our ability to climb it, we quickly come to realize the relevance of Flaubert's satire of the learning enterprise. But does this mean that we should abandon the effort, give in to the absurdity of the task? Does Bouvard and Pécuchet's decision to become copyists constitute a defeat? In our judgment, not at all; their decision marks, rather, an affirmation of the learning process regardless of the product, regardless of its inability to change the world. For "copying" we should read studying or reading without regard to result like Bouvard and Pécuchet, cultivating one's garden like Candide, pushing the rock back up to the summit like Sisyphus, keeping the faith like Saint Anthony, continuing to write until collapse like Flaubert. Only the fool would abandon the quest for knowledge; only the bourgeois, subject of both the *Dictionary of Inherited Ideas* and the *Sottisier,* would claim that all is knowable and that he knows it all. Some of us are content to specialize, to master a small segment of the vast field of human knowledge, now occupying, we are told, a place called cyberspace. Others, like Bouvard and Pécuchet, who refuse to give up but continue to copy, or Saint Anthony, who renews his struggle against temptation with each new dawn, or Flaubert, noted for the variety of his works, the vastness of his vision, and the depth of his devotion to art, attempt to learn their limits by coming to grips with the limits of learning.

Chapter Eight
Conclusion: Why Read Flaubert?

In a book whose focus has been on the reader's reactions and role in the literary process as well as on the new ways of reading Flaubert inaugurated, it is perhaps now time to ask the inevitable question of why Flaubert is so widely read, even today.

Certainly, like all great novelists, from Cervantes and Mark Twain to Dickens and Dostoyevsky, Flaubert's works constitute a gallery of unforgettable portraits: the scheming dreamer Emma, the pretentious bourgeois Homais, the sun- and moon-crossed lovers Mâtho and Salammbô, the irritatingly indecisive Frédéric, the haunted hunters Anthony and Julian, the simple-hearted saint Félicité, the sympathetic bunglers Bouvard and Pécuchet.

Moreover, when superimposed, the central characters form a composite portrait that amounts to Flaubert's image of humankind: a solitary individual, fraught with inadequacies (Félicité), beset by inner visions (Julian), and embroiled in contradictions (Herod), who is embedded in a society hostile to the individual and governed by rigid roles and restraints (Emma) that are reinforced by conventional codes and clichés (Homais), all of which culminates in inertia (Frédéric) and death (Mâtho and Salammbô). Beyond the reaches of bourgeois society lies a universe of disintegration and decay whose infinite bounds are incomprehensible and meaningless (Anthony). This vision of human experience is expressed in any number of passages in each of the works, such as the following from *Bouvard and Pécuchet,* which captures our two heroes' feelings as they attempt to comprehend philosophy:

> It seemed to them like they were in a balloon, at night, in a glacial cold, carried off on an endless course, toward a bottomless abyss, and with nothing around them but the unseizable, the immobile, the eternal. It was too much.[1]

The central character in each of Flaubert's works could well have experienced (if not expressed) such a feeling; each could be a passenger on this absurd balloon ride. Yet of these troubled travelers, only Emma abandons ship; all of the others struggle to stay afloat. Moreover, each would inflate the balloon to drift even higher, toward an ideal man (Emma), woman (Frédéric), or notion (Salammbô, Anthony). Their persistent, perilous voyages enable Flaubert to explore many of the survival mechanisms clung to by humankind: dreaming and communication (in *Madame Bovary*), motivation and meaning (in *Salammbô*), education and memory (in *Sentimental Education*), form and faith (in *Saint Anthony*), sacrifice and sainthood (in *Three Tales*), learning and friendship (in *Bouvard and Pécuchet*).

What is unique in Flaubert and paralleled perhaps only by Proust among the great French novelists is the extent to which all of these issues, the major ones that characterize human existence, are linked to art, to the literary mode in which they are represented.[2] Certainly several of Flaubert's novels contain opinions about art, some misguided, like the discussion of novels between Emma and Léon; others overstated, like the pompous pronouncements of Pellerin; still others a mixture of idiocy and insight, like those contained in the lengthy chapter (5) of *Bouvard and Pécuchet* that details the pair's literary studies.

Other opinions, while seemingly directed at different topics, are remarkably relevant to literature, such as the comparison of human language to a cracked kettle in *Madame Bovary* or the description in *Saint Anthony* of the universe as a self-contained system, which mirrors Flaubert's conception of the text and is repeated in a similar passage in *Bouvard and Pécuchet:*

> The person who could embrace, at the same time, all substance and all thought would see no contingency, nothing accidental, only a geometric series of terms, linked to each other by necessary laws.
>
> "Ah! that would be beautiful!" said Pécuchet.[3]

This geometric series recalls, of course, the networks of inner associations that we have described in each of Flaubert's works, particularly *Three Tales, Madame Bovary,* and *The Temptation of Saint Anthony*.

Yet another technique typical of Flaubert's artistry and preoccupation with art is the creation of an emblematic object that serves to summarize the entire work. The three tiers on Emma's wedding cake prefigure the three stages of her life, the three parts of the novel, beginning with the convent, then moving to marriage and finally to adultery. The parrot that Félicité "sees" in her last moments has come to symbolize all of the people, events, and values in her life and thus serves to crystallize the entire narrative.

In several cases, objects are emblematic of the very literary mechanisms embodied in the text: Salammbô's veil echoes the masking of meaning that serves as the novel's central theme and indeed mirrors the reader's struggle in attempting to interpret the text; the grocer's scales reflect the process of two extremes reaching equilibrium that is the very compositional principle in *Bouvard and Pécuchet;* finally, the stained-glass window, revealed to be the source of Saint Julian's tale, becomes an emblem of the literary process, which transforms the contingencies of human existence into a permanent, ordered objet d'art that we then strive to decipher.

The initiated reader who unearths such finds and reconstructs the networks of associations that invest them with meaning joins Flaubert in rising above the fray, in wresting meaning from chaos, in forging permanence out of disintegration, in experiencing the twin mechanisms of discovery and recollection that constitute the pleasure of the text. In the final analysis, it is this pleasure that explains why we read Flaubert and the truly great writers who, like him, persist with the struggle despite the fateful and ultimately fatal ironies of the human condition.

For Flaubert, literature is less a reflection or even a rejection of reality than a reaction or response to it, an act of defiance and faith, of sacrifice and redemption, whose persistence encourages us to carry on, whatever form our own quest may take.

Notes and References

Preface

1. Shortly after the publication of Stratton Buck's *Gustave Flaubert* (New York: Twayne Publishers, 1966), the appearance of two books, both in English, helped to map (and to a degree divide) the landscape of Flaubert studies, both here and abroad: Victor Brombert's *The Novels of Flaubert: A Study of Themes and Techniques* (Princeton: Princeton University Press, 1966) shows how technique reinforces theme and reflects the author's temperament, thus implying coherence as a defining characteristic of Flaubert's works; Jonathan Culler's *Flaubert: The Uses of Uncertainty* (Ithaca: Cornell University Press, 1974) stresses the gaps, discontinuities, and uncertainties with which Flaubert thwarts the reader. Thus centennial conferences on Flaubert in 1980, such as the one at the University of Wisconsin (proceedings published in *Nineteenth-Century French Studies* 12:3 [Spring 1984], ed. Lorin Uffenbeck), were often characterized by rivalry (for the most part good-natured) between two camps: the partisans of coherence and the proponents of uncertainty. As befits an introductory book and our own eclectic stance, we straddle both positions, appreciating at once the subtleties of deconstructive analysis and the solidity of the structured approach, though we lean, as our study cannot fail to reveal, toward the latter. More recent general books on Flaubert of particular interest to the English-speaking reader include Harold Bloom, ed., *Gustave Flaubert* (New York: Chelsea House, 1989); Michal Peled Ginsburg, *Flaubert Writing: A Study in Narrative Strategies* (Stanford: Stanford University Press, 1986); Stirling Haig, *Flaubert and the Gift of Speech: Dialogue and Discourse in Four "Modern" Novels* (Cambridge, England: Cambridge University Press, 1986); Robert Griffin, *Rape of the Lock: Flaubert's Mythic Realism* (Lexington, KY: French Forum, 1988); Laurence Porter, ed., *Critical Essays on Gustave Flaubert* (Boston: Hall, 1986); Vaheed Ramazani, *The Free Indirect Mode: Flaubert and the Practice of Irony* (Charlottesville: University Press of Virginia, 1988); Naomi Schor and Henry Majewski, eds., *Flaubert and Postmodernism* (Lincoln: University of Nebraska Press, 1984); and William VanderWolk, *Flaubert Remembers: Memory and the Creative Experience* (New York: Peter Lang, 1990).

Most of these and other general books on Flaubert, in English and in French, are described briefly in our annotated bibliography. Books and articles on specific works are cited in the appropriate chapter.

Among the most interesting general articles in English on the question of reading and writing in Flaubert are Victor Brombert, "Flaubert and the Temptation of the Subject," *Nineteenth-Century French Studies (NCFS)* 12:3 (Spring 1984): 280–96; Graham Falconer, "Introduction," *NCFS* 12:3 (Spring

1984): 271–79; Eugene Gray, "Flaubert's Esthetics and the Problem of Knowledge," *NCFS* 4 (1976): 295–302; Marshall Olds, "Flaubert's Dis/En Closures," *French Forum* 13:1 (January 1988): 57–68; Dennis Porter, "Flaubert and the Difficulty of Reading," *NCFS* 12:3 (Spring 1984): 366–78; Christopher Prendergast, "Flaubert: Writing and Negativity," *Novel* 8 (1975): 197–213; and Michael Riffaterre, "Flaubert's Presuppositions," *Diacritics* 11:4 (Winter 1981): 2–11.

2. For two interesting but opposing views on Flaubert's theories as expressed in his correspondence, see P. M. Wetherill, *Flaubert et la création littéraire* (Paris: Nizet, 1964), which stresses contradictions, and Claire-Lise Tondeur, *Gustave Flaubert, critique: Thèmes et structures* (Amsterdam: John Benjamins, 1984), which emphasizes coherence.

3. Flaubert to Louise Colet, 16 January 1852, *Correspondance*, vol. II (Paris: Conard, 1926–33), 346. References to Flaubert's correspondence, unless otherwise indicated, are to *Correspondance* (Paris: Conard, 1926–33), 9 vols. and *Supplément* (Paris: Conard, 1954), 4 vols., hereafter *Correspondance* and *Supplément*.

4. For longer excerpts examined in terms of style we give the French text in an endnote. The best study of Flaubert's style is still Albert Thibaudet's *Flaubert* (Paris: Gallimard, 1935), especially chapter 10, "Le Style de Flaubert" (205–64); many examples of subtle textual analysis may also be found in Brombert, *The Novels of Flaubert: A Study of Themes and Techniques,* and Culler, *Flaubert: The Uses of Uncertainty*. In our study, we concentrate as much on the broad aspects of style (voice, viewpoint, semantics, figuration, and structure) as on the material quality of language (grammar, syntax, sound, and rhythm).

5. Flaubert to Mlle Leroyer de Chantepie, 19 February 1857, *Correspondance,* vol. IV, 164.

6. Flaubert to Louise Colet, 16 January 1852, *Correspondance*, vol. II, 345.

Chapter One

1. Important biographical studies of Flaubert include Benjamin F. Bart, *Flaubert* (Syracuse: Syracuse University Press, 1967); Herbert R. Lottman, *Flaubert: A Biography* (Boston: Little Brown & Co., 1989); Enid Starkie, *Flaubert: The Making of the Master* (New York: Atheneum, 1967), *Flaubert the Master: A Critical and Biographical Study (1856–1880)* (London: Widenfeld & Nicolson, 1971); and Henri Troyat, *Flaubert* (Paris: Flammarion, 1988), trans. Joan Pinkham (New York: Viking, 1992).

2. See especially Jean-Paul Sartre's "psychobiography" *L'Idiot de la famille: Gustave Flaubert de 1821 à 1857* (Paris: Gallimard, 1971–73).

3. On the subject of Flaubert's early works, none of which was published in his lifetime, see, in addition to Sartre (cited in note 2), Jean Bruneau, *Les Débuts littéraires de Gustave Flaubert* (Paris: Colin, 1962); Jonathan Culler,

"The Rites of Youth," in *Flaubert: The Uses of Uncertainty* (Ithaca: Cornell University Press, 1974); Marie Diamond, *Flaubert: The Problem of Aesthetic Discontinuity* (Port Washington, NY: Kennikat Press, 1975); Eric L. Gans, *The Discovery of Illusion: Flaubert's Early Works, 1835–1837* (Berkeley: University of California Press, 1971); Michal Peled Ginsburg, "The Early Works," in *Flaubert Writing: A Study in Narrative Strategies* (Stanford: Stanford University Press, 1986); and Timothy Unwin, *L'Oeuvre de jeunesse de Gustave Flaubert* (Amsterdam: Rodopi, 1991).

Chapter Two

1. Overall studies of *Three Tales* include Aimée Israël-Pelletier, *Flaubert's Straight and Suspect Saints: The Unity of "Trois contes"* (Amsterdam: Benjamins, 1991), and Alan Raitt, *Trois contes* (London: Grant and Cutler, 1991). Articles on the same subject include Marc Bertrand, "Parole et silence dans les *Trois contes* de Flaubert," *Stanford French Review* 1 (1977): 191–203; Raymonde Debray-Genette, "Profane, Sacred: Disorder of Utterance in *Trois contes,*" in Schor and Majewski, eds., *Flaubert and Postmodernism* (Lincoln: University of Nebraska Press, 1984): 13–29; Raymonde Debray-Genette, "Du mode narratif dans les *Trois contes,*" *Littérature* 2 (1971): 39–70; Karen Erickson, "Prophetic Utterance and Irony in *Trois contes,*" in Barbara Cooper and Mary Donaldson-Evans, eds., *Modernity and Revolution in Late Nineteenth-Century France* (Newark: University of Delaware Press, 1992): 65–73; Michael Issacharoff, "*Trois contes* et le problème de la non-linéarité," *Littérature* 15 (1974): 27–40; Frederic Jameson, "Flaubert's Libidinal Historicism: *Trois contes,*" in Schor and Majewski, eds., *Flaubert and Postmodernism*, 76–83; Rachel Killick, " 'The Power and the Glory'? Discourses of Authority and Tricks of Speech in *Trois contes,*" *The Modern Language Review* 88:2 (April 1993): 307–20; Ann Murphy, "The Order of Speech in Flaubert's *Trois contes,*" *The French Review* 65:3 (February 1992): 402–14; Per Nykrog, " 'Les Trois contes' dans l'évolution de la structure thématique chez Flaubert," *Romantisme* 6 (1973): 55–66; John O'Connor, "*Trois contes* and the Figure of the Double Cone," *PMLA* 95 (1980): 812–26; Ian Reid, "The Death of the Implied Author? Voice, Sequence, and Control in Flaubert's *Trois contes,*" *Australian Journal of French Studies* 23:2 (May-August 1986): 195–211; Susan Selvin, "Spatial Form in Flaubert's *Trois contes,*" *Romanic Review* 74:2 (March 1983): 202–20; and Frederic Shepler, "La Mort et la rédemption dans les *Trois contes* de Flaubert," *Neophilologus* 56 (1972): 407–16.

2. Studies of "A Simple Heart" include Julian Barnes's witty novel *Flaubert's Parrot* (New York: Vintage Books, 1984) and numerous articles, among them Philippe Bonnefils, "Exposition d'un perroquet," *Revue des Sciences Humaines* 181 (1981): 59–78; Ross Chambers, "Simplicité de coeur et duplicité textuelle: Etude d'*Un Coeur simple,*" *Modern Language Notes* 96:4 (May 1981): 771–91; Raymonde Debray-Genette, "Les figures du récit dans *Un Coeur sim-*

ple," *Poétique* 3 (1970): 348–64; Carol DeDobay-Rifelj, "Doors, Walls, and Barriers in Flaubert's *Un Coeur simple,*" *Studies in Short Fiction* 11 (1974): 291–95; Stirling Haig, "Parrot and Parody: Flaubert," in Emanuel Mickel, ed., *The Shaping of Text: Style, Imagery, and Structure in French Literature: Essays in Honor of John Porter Houston* (Lewisburg, PA: Bucknell University Press, 1993): 105–12; Ingrid Stipa, "Desire, Repetition and the Imaginary in Flaubert's *Un Coeur simple,*" *Studies in Short Fiction* 31:4 (Fall 1994): 617–26; and Nathaniel Wing, "Reading Simplicity: Flaubert's 'Un Coeur simple,' " *NCFS* 21:1–2 (Fall-Winter 1992–93): 88–101.

3. "Félicité se pencha pour la voir; et, avec l'imagination que donnent les vraies tendresses, il lui sembla qu'elle était elle-même cette enfant; sa figure devenait la sienne, sa robe l'habillait, son coeur lui battait dans la poitrine; au moment d'ouvrir la bouche, en fermant les paupières, elle manqua s'évanouir." (part 3)

4. "Une vapeur d'azur monta dans la chambre de Félicité. Elle avança les narines, en la humant avec une sensualité mystique; puis ferma les paupières. Ses lèvres souriaient. Les mouvements de son coeur se ralentirent un à un, plus vagues chaque fois, plus doux, comme une fontaine s'épuise, comme un écho disparaît; et, quand elle exhala son dernier souffle, elle crut voir, dans les cieux entr'ouverts, un perroquet gigantesque, planant au-dessus de sa tête." (part 5)

5. See especially Juliette Frølich, "Battement d'un simple coeur: Stéréographie et sonorisation dans *Un Coeur simple* de Flaubert," *Littérature* 46 (May 1982): 28–40.

6. Studies on "Saint Julian" include Benjamin Bart and Robert Cook, *The Legendary Sources of Flaubert's "Saint Julien"* (Toronto: University of Toronto Press, 1977), and William Berg, Michel Grimaud, and George Moskos, *Saint/Oedipus: Psychocritical Approaches to Flaubert's Art* (Ithaca: Cornell University Press, 1982), as well as many articles on sources and several on art and psychology, including Jean Bellemin-Noël, "Gustave, Poulou, Julien et nous autres," *La Revue des Lettres Modernes* 1165–72 (1994): 3–20; Shoshana Felman, "Flaubert's Signature: *The Legend of Saint Julian the Hospitable,*" in Schor and Majewski, eds., *Flaubert and Postmodernism,* 46–75; and Jane Marston, "Narration as Subject in Flaubert's 'La Légende de Saint Julien l'Hospitalier,' " *NCFS* 14:3–4 (Spring-Summer 1986): 341–45.

7. Published originally in Latin as *Legenda Aurea* by Jacobus Voraginus, the text is titled *La Légende dorée* in French.

8. Much of the discussion of "Saint Julian" is borrowed from Berg's earlier work on the tale in *Saint/Oedipus: Psychocritical Approaches to Flaubert's Art* (Ithaca: Cornell University Press, 1982), 13–67.

9. From Sigmund Freud, *Interpretation of Dreams,* vol. 4 of *The Standard Edition of the Complete Psychological Works of Sigmund Freud,* trans. James Strachey et al. (London: Hogarth Press, 1953–74), 160.

10. See Freud, *The Ego and the Id,* in vol. 19, *ibid.,* 32.

11. On the ending of "Saint Julian," see especially Felman and Marston (as cited in note 6).

12. Studies on "Hérodias" include Raymonde Debray-Genette, "Représentation d'*Hérodias,*" in Claudine Gothot-Mersch, ed., *La Production du sens chez Flaubert* (Paris: 10/18, 1975), 328–57; Juliette Frølich, "La Voix de Saint Jean: Magie d'un discours: lecture d'un épisode de 'Hérodias,' " *La Revue des Lettres Modernes* 865–72 (1988): 87–103; Gérard Genette, "Demotivation in 'Hérodias,' " in Schor and Majewski, eds., *Flaubert and Postmodernism,* 193–201; R. B. Leal, "Spaciality and Structure in Flaubert's 'Hérodias,' " *The Modern Language Review* 80:4 (October 1985): 810–16; Shelley Purcell, " 'Hérodias': A Key to Thematic Progression in *Trois contes,*" *Romanic Review* 80:4 (November 1989): 541–47; François Rastier, "Thématique et génétique: L'Exemple d'Hérodias,' " *Poétique* 23:90 (April 1992): 205–28; Jane Robertson, "The Structure of 'Hérodias,' " *French Studies* 36:2 (April 1982): 171–82; and M. Tillett, "An Approach to 'Hérodias,' " *French Studies* 21 (1967): 24–31.

13. See Mark, 6:22–28.

14. Indeed, there are several textual links between Salome and the horses, who, like her, have "child-like eyes": their movements are "supple," hers are "elastic"; they are "light like birds," she is "lighter than a butterfly."

15. See John, 3:30.

Chapter Three

1. For a fascinating discussion of the ideological implications of the novel's style in relation to the trial, see Dominick LaCapra, *"Madame Bovary" on Trial* (Ithaca: Cornell University Press, 1982). Other books on *Madame Bovary* include Benjamin Bart, ed., *"Madame Bovary" and the Critics: A Collection of Essays* (New York: New York University Press, 1966); Harold Bloom, ed., *Gustave Flaubert's "Madame Bovary"* (New York: Chelsea House, 1988); Ion Collas, *"Madame Bovary": A Psychoanalytic Study* (Geneva: Droz, 1986); Eric Gans, *"Madame Bovary": The End of Romance* (Boston: Twayne Publishers, 1989); Stephen Heath, *Madame Bovary* (Cambridge, England: Cambridge University Press, 1992); Louise Kaplan, *Female Perversions: The Temptations of Emma Bovary* (New York: Doubleday, 1992); Anna Lambros, *Culture and the Literary Text: The Case of Flaubert's "Madame Bovary"* (New York: Peter Lang, 1995); Alain de Lattre, *La Bêtise d'Emma Bovary* (Paris: Corti, 1981); Rosemary Lloyd, *Madame Bovary* (New York: Routledge, Chapman and Hall, 1989); Margaret Lowe, *Toward the Real Flaubert: A Study of "Madame Bovary"* (Oxford: Clarendon, 1984); Laurence Porter and Eugene Gray, eds., *Approaches to Teaching Flaubert's "Madame Bovary"* (New York: MLA, 1995); Patricia Reynaud, *Fiction et Faillite: Economie et métaphores dans "Madame Bovary"* (New York: Peter Lang, 1994); Mario Vargas-Llosa, *The Perpetual Orgy: Flaubert and "Madame Bovary,"* trans. Helen Lane (New York: Farrar Strauss Giroux, 1986); and André Vial, *Le Dictionnaire de Flaubert: Le Rire d'Emma Bovary* (Paris: Nizet, 1974).

Among the many general articles on *Madame Bovary,* the following are of particular interest: Graham Falconer, "Création et conservation du sens dans *Madame Bovary,*" in Claudine Gothot-Mersch, ed., *La Production du sens chez Flaubert*, 395–429; Claudine Gothot-Mersch, "La Description des visages dans *Madame Bovary,*" *Littérature* 15 (October 1974): 17–26; Dennis Porter, "*Madame Bovary* and the Question of Pleasure," in Schor and Majewski, eds., *Flaubert and Postmodernism*, 116–38; Michael Riffaterre, "Relevance of Theory/ Theory of Relevance," *The Yale Journal of Criticism* 1:2 (Spring 1988): 45–64; Lawrence Rothfield, "From Semiotic to Discursive Intertextuality: The Case of *Madame Bovary,*" *Novel* 19 (1985): 57–81; Jean Rousset, "*Madame Bovary* or the Book about Nothing," in Raymond Giraud, ed., *Flaubert: A Collection of Critical Essays* (Englewood Cliffs, NJ: Prentice-Hall, 1964), 112–31; Naomi Schor, "Details and Decadence: End-Troping in *Madame Bovary,*" *Sub-Stance* 26 (1980): 27–35; and Claire-Lise Tondeur, "Le Désir, la fluidité et la dissolution," *Neophilologus* 73:4 (October 1989): 512–21.

2. Albert Camus, *Le Mythe de Sisyphe* (Paris: Gallimard, Collection Idées, 1942), 18, 48.

3. On the question of irony in Flaubert, see especially Vaheed Ramazani, *The Free Indirect Mode: Flaubert and the Poetics of Irony* (Charlottesville: University Press of Virginia, 1988); Jonathan Culler, *Flaubert: The Uses of Uncertainty,* 185–207; Pierre Campion, "Le Piège de l'ironie dans le système narratif de *Madame Bovary,*" *Revue d'Histoire Littéraire de la France* 92:5 (September-October 1992): 863–74; Sherry Dranch, "Flaubert: Portraits d'un ironiste," *NCFS* 11: 1–2 (Fall-Winter 1982–83): 106–16; Rainer Warning, "Reading Irony in Flaubert," *Style* 19:3 (Fall 1985): 304–16; and Henry Weinberg, "Irony and 'Style indirect libre' in *Madame Bovary,*" *Canadian Review of Comparative Literature/Revue Canadienne de Littérature Comparée* 8:1 (Winter 1981): 1–9.

4. For studies on the beginning of *Madame Bovary,* including Charles's hat, see Culler, *Flaubert: The Uses of Uncertainty,* 91–112; LaCapra, *"Madame Bovary" on Trial,* 150–55; and Eric Gans, *"Madame Bovary": The End of Romance,* 61–66; for articles on the same subject, see Didier Philippot, "La Casquette de Charles Bovary ou le chef-d'oeuvre inconnu de l'autolâtrie bourgeoise," *Les Lettres Romanes* 48:3–4 (1994): 219–36; Alan Raitt, " 'Nous étions à l'étude . . . ,' " *La Revue des Lettres Modernes* 777–81 (1986): 161–92; Jean Ricardou, "Belligérance du texte," in Claudine Gothot-Mersch, ed., *La Production du sens chez Flaubert,* 85–103; and John Williams, "The Disappearing First-Person Narrator in *Madame Bovary,*" *The Language Quarterly* 23:3–4 (Spring-Summer 1985): 31–32.

5. On the use of italics in Flaubert see Claude Duchet, "Discours social et texte, italique dans *Madame Bovary,*" in Michael Issacharoff, ed., *Langages de Flaubert. Actes du Colloque de London (Canada)* (Paris: Minard, 1976), 143–60, and "Signifiance et in-signifiance: le discours italique dans *Madame Bovary,*" in Claudine Gothot-Mersch, ed., *La Production du sens chez Flaubert,* 358–94; Henry Weinberg, "The Function of Italics in *Madame Bovary,*" *NCFS* 3 (1975):

97–100, and "Foci of Convergence in *Madame Bovary*," *Language and Style* 16:4 (Fall 1983), 468–77. On the question of "charivari" see especially Jean-Marie Privat, *Bovary. Charivari: Essai d'Ethno-critique* (Paris: CNRS, 1994).

6. "En face, au-delà des toits, le grand ciel pur s'étendait, avec le soleil rouge se couchant. Qu'il devait faire bon là-bas! Quelle fraîcheur sous la hêtrée? Et il ouvrait les narines pour aspirer les bonnes odeurs de la campagne, qui ne venaient pas jusqu'à lui." (part 1, chapter 1)

7. For discussions of Flaubert's use of free indirect discourse, see Stirling Haig, *Flaubert and the Gift of Speech,* and Vaheed Ramazani, *The Free Indirect Mode: Flaubert and the Poetics of Irony*.

8. In fact, both the cupid and the swing recur during Emma's affair with Léon in part 3 of the novel. For discussions of the wedding cake, see Culler, *Flaubert: The Uses of Uncertainty,* 171–73, Joyce Lowrie, "Let Them Eat Cake: The Irony of la pièce montée in *Madame Bovary,*" *Romanic Review* 82:4 (November 1990): 425–37, and Jean Ricardou, "DE NATURA ficTIONis," in Ricardou, *Pour une théorie du nouveau roman* (Paris: Seuil, 1971), 33–38.

9. "Il fallait qu'elle pût retirer des choses une sorte de profit personnel; et elle rejetait comme inutile tout ce qui ne contribuait pas à la consommation immédiate de son coeur,—étant de tempérament plus sentimentale qu'artiste, cherchant des émotions et non des paysages." (part 1, chapter 6)

10. "Ce n'étaient qu'amours, amants, amantes, dames persécutées s'évanouissant dans des pavillons solitaires, postillons qu'on tue à tous les relais, chevaux qu'on crève à toutes les pages, forêts sombres, troubles du coeur, serments, sanglots, larmes et baisers, nacelles au clair de lune, rossignols dans les bosquets, *messieurs* braves comme des lions, doux comme des agneaux, vertueux comme on ne l'est pas, toujours bien mis, et qui pleurent comme des urnes. Pendant six mois, à quinze ans, Emma se graissa donc les mains à cette poussière des vieux cabinets de lecture. Avec Walter Scott, plus tard, elle s'éprit de choses historiques, rêva bahuts, salle des gardes et ménestrels. Elle aurait voulu vivre dans quelque vieux manoir, comme ces châtelaines au long corsage qui, sous le trèfle des ogives, passaient leurs jours, le coude sur la pierre et le menton dans la main, à regarder venir du fond de la campagne un cavalier à plume blanche qui galope sur un cheval noir." (part 1, chapter 6)

11. The term *bovarysme* was coined by Jules de Gaultier in *Le Bovarysme: La Psychologie dans l'oeuvre de Flaubert* (Paris: Cerf, 1892).

12. "il n'y a peut-être pas dans tout Flaubert une seule belle métaphore," in Marcel Proust, "A propos du style de Flaubert," *Nouvelle Revue Française* (January 1920): rep. Raymonde Debray-Genette, ed., *Flaubert* (Paris: Marcel Didier, 1970), 47.

13. "Ils commencèrent lentement, puis allèrent plus vite. Ils tournaient: tout tournait autour d'eux, les lampes, les meubles, les lambris, et le parquet, comme un disque sur un pivot. En passant auprès des portes, la robe d'Emma, par le bas, s'ériflait au pantalon; leurs jambes entraient l'une dans l'autre; il baissait ses regards vers elle, elle levait les siens vers lui; une torpeur la prenait,

elle s'arrêta. Ils repartirent; et, d'un mouvement plus rapide, le Vicomte, l'entraînant, disparut avec elle jusqu'au bout de la galerie, où, haletante, elle faillit tomber, et, un instant, s'appuya la tête sur sa poitrine. Et puis, tournant toujours, mais plus doucement, il la reconduisit à sa place; elle se renversa contre la muraille et mit la main devant ses yeux." (part 1, chapter 8). For an excellent discussion of this passage, see Gans,*"Madame Bovary": The End of Romance,* 86–88.

14. "Mais c'était surtout aux heures des repas qu'elle n'en pouvait plus, dans cette petite salle au rez-de-chaussée, avec le poêle qui fumait, la porte qui criait, les murs qui suintaient; les pavés humides; toute l'amertume de l'existence lui semblait servie sur son assiette, et à la fumée du bouilli, il montait du fond de son âme comme d'autres bouffées d'affadissement." (part 1, chapter 9)

15. Erich Auerbach, *Mimesis: The Representation of Reality in Western Literature*, trans. Willard Trask (New York: Doubleday, 1957), 427–28.

16. "Dans l'après-midi, quelquefois, une tête d'homme apparaissait derrière les vitres de la salle, tête hâlée, à favoris noirs, et qui souriait lentement d'un large sourire doux à dents blanches. Une valse aussitôt commençait, et, sur l'orgue, dans un petit salon, des danseurs hauts comme le doigt, femmes en turban rose, Tyroliens en jaquette, singes en habit noir, messieurs en culotte courte, tournaient, tournaient entre les fauteuils, les canapés, les consoles, se répétant dans les morceaux de miroir que raccordait à leurs angles un filet de papier doré. L'homme faisait aller sa manivelle, regardant à droite, à gauche et vers les fenêtres. De temps à autre, tout en lançant contre la borne un long jet de salive brune, il soulevait du genou son instrument, dont la bretelle dure lui fatiguait l'épaule." (part 1, chapter 9)

17. "Un jour qu'en prévision de son départ elle faisait des rangements dans un tiroir, elle se piqua les doigts à quelque chose. C'était un fil de fer de son bouquet de mariage. Les boutons d'oranger étaient jaunes de poussière, et les rubans de satin, à liséré d'argent, s'effilochaient par le bord. Elle le jeta dans le feu. Il s'enflamma plus vite qu'une paille sèche. Puis ce fut comme un buisson rouge sur les cendres, et qui se rongeait lentement. Elle le regarda brûler. Les petites baies de carton éclataient, les fils d'archal se tordaient, le galon se fondait; et les corolles de papier, racornies, se balançant le long de la plaque comme des papillons noirs, enfin s'envolèrent par la cheminée.

"Quand on partit de Tostes, au mois de mars, madame Bovary était enceinte." (part 1, chapter 9)

18. For interesting discussions of Flaubert's presentation of Yonville, see Culler, *Flaubert: The Uses of Uncertainty,* 75–77, as well as James Hamilton, "The Ideology of Place: Flaubert's Depiction of Yonville-l'Abbaye," *The French Review* 65:2 (December 1991): 206–15.

19. On Flaubert's use of parentheses, see Robert Morrissey, "Breaking In (Flaubert in Parentheses)," *Sub-Stance* 56 (1988): 49–62.

20. For more on the *Dictionary of Inherited Ideas,* see our discussion of *Bouvard and Pécuchet* in chapter 7.

21. "Un homme, au moins, est libre; il peut parcourir les passions et les pays, traverser les obstacles, mordre aux bonheurs les plus lointains. Mais une femme est empêchée continuellement. Inerte et flexible à la fois, elle a contre elle les mollesses de la chair avec les dépendances de la loi. Sa volonté, comme le voile de son chapeau retenu par un cordon, palpite à tous les vents, il y a toujours quelque désir qui entraîne, quelque convenance qui retient." (part 2, chapter 3)

For discussions of gender in *Madame Bovary,* in addition to Louise Kaplan, *Female Perversions: The Temptations of Emma Bovary* (New York: Doubleday, 1992), and Lucette Czyba, *Mythes et idéologie de la femme dans les romans de Gustave Flaubert* (Lyon: Presses Universitaires de Lyon, 1983), see Diana Festa-McCormick, "Emma Bovary's Masculinization: Convention of Clothes and Morality of Conventions," *Women and Literature* 1 (1980): 223–35; Naomi Schor, "For a Restricted Thematics: Writing, Speech, and Difference in *Madame Bovary,*" in Hester Eisenstein and Alice Jardine, eds., *The Future of Difference* (Boston: Hall, 1980), 167–92; and Tony Williams, "Gender Stereotypes in *Madame Bovary,*" *Forum for Modern Language Studies* 28:2 (April 1992): 130–39.

22. "il lui sembla qu'elle tournait encore dans la valse, sous le feu des lustres, au bras du vicomte, et que Léon n'était pas loin, qui allait venir . . . et cependant elle sentait toujours la tête de Rodolphe à côté d'elle. La douceur de cette sensation pénétrait ainsi ses désirs d'autrefois, et comme des grains de sable sous un coup de vent, ils tourbillonnaient dans la bouffée subtile du parfum qui se répandait sur son âme." (part 2, chapter 8)

23. For studies of consciousness in Flaubert, see especially the "phenomenological" studies of Georges Poulet, *Etudes sur le temps humain* (Paris: Plon, 1950) and *Métamorphoses du cercle* (Paris: Plon, 1961), and Jean-Pierre Richard, *Littérature et sensation* (Paris: Seuil, 1954).

24. "Elle s'était appuyée contre l'embrasure de la mansarde et elle relisait la lettre avec des ricanements de colère. Mais plus elle y fixait d'attention, plus ses idées se confondaient. Elle le revoyait, elle l'entendait, elle l'entourait de ses deux bras; et des battements de coeur, qui la frappaient sous la poitrine comme à grands coups de bélier, s'accéléraient l'un après l'autre, à intermittences inégales. Elle jetait les yeux autour d'elle avec l'envie que la terre croulât. Pourquoi n'en pas finir? Qui la retenait donc? Elle était libre. Et elle s'avança." (part 2, chapter 13)

25. For discussions of the cab scene, see especially Culler, *Flaubert: The Uses of Uncertainty,* 121–22, Sartre, *L'Idiot de la famille*, 1278–85, and LaCapra, *"Madame Bovary" on Trial,* 161–65.

26. "Elle se déshabillait brutalement, arrachant le lacet mince de son corset, qui sifflait autour de ses hanches comme une couleuvre qui glisse. Elle allait sur la pointe de ses pieds nus regarder encore une fois si la porte était fermée, puis elle faisait d'un seul geste tomber ensemble tous ses vêtements;—et, pâle, sans parler, sérieuse, elle s'abattait contre sa poitrine, avec un long frisson." (part 3, chapter 6)

27. "Elle resta perdue de stupeur, et n'ayant plus conscience d'elle-même que par le battement de ses artères, qu'elle croyait entendre s'échapper comme une assourdissante musique qui emplissait la campagne. Le sol, sous ses pieds, était plus mou qu'une onde, et les sillons lui parurent d'immenses vagues brunes, qui déferlaient. Tout ce qu'il y avait dans sa tête de réminiscences, d'idées, s'échappait à la fois, d'un seul bond, comme les mille pièces d'un feu d'artifice. Elle vit son père, le cabinet de Lheureux, leur chambre là-bas, un autre paysage. La folie la prenait . . .

"Il lui sembla tout à coup que des globules couleur de feu éclataient dans l'air comme des balles fulminantes en s'aplatissant, et tournaient, tournaient, pour aller se fondre dans la neige, entre les branches des arbres. Au milieu de chacun d'eux, la figure de Rodolphe apparaissait. Ils se multiplièrent, et ils se rapprochaient, la pénétraient . . ." (part 3, chapter 8). See Gans, *"Madame Bovary": The End of Romance,* 119–22, for an excellent analysis of this passage.

28. In fact, the sound "tour" recurs throughout the novel, in instances as disparate as Binet's lathe (*tour*) and the whirlwind (*tourbillon*) of Emma's consciousness, and its circularity is matched semantically by "roue" (wheel), which is found in Rouault and in Rouen, among other examples.

29. "Il y avait dans la côte un pauvre diable vagabondant avec son bâton, tout au milieu des diligences. Un amas de guenilles lui recouvrait les épaules, et un vieux castor défoncé, s'arrondissant en cuvette, lui cachait la figure; mais, quand il le retirait, il découvrait, à la place des paupières, deux orbites béantes tout ensanglantées. La chair s'effiloquait par lambeaux rouges; et il en coulait des liquides qui se figeaient en gales vertes jusqu'au nez, dont les narines noires reniflaient convulsivement. Pour vous parler, il se renversait la tête avec un rire idiot;—alors ses prunelles bleuâtres, roulant d'un mouvement continue, allaient se cogner, vers les tempes, sur le bord de la plaie vive.

> "Il chantait une petite chanson en suivant les voitures:
> Souvent la chaleur d'un beau jour
> Fait rêver fillette à l'amour.
> "Et il y avait dans tout le reste des oiseaux, du soleil et du feuillage.
> (part 3, chapter 5)

The blind beggar has caused a lot of ink to flow; in addition to Brombert, *The Novels of Flaubert: A Study of Themes and Techniques,* 74–75, see Max Aprile, "L'Aveugle et sa signification dans *Madame Bovary,*" *Revue d'Histoire Littéraire de la France* 76 (1976): 385–92; Sheila Bell, " 'Un Pauvre Diable': The Blind Beggar in *Madame Bovary,* in Robert Gibson, ed., *Studies in French Fiction in Honour of Vivienne Milne* (London: Grant and Cutler, 1988), 25–41; Mary Donaldson-Evans, "A Pox on Love: Diagnosing *Madame Bovary*'s Blind Beggar," *Symposium* 44:1 (Spring 1990): 15–27; Murray Sachs, "The Role of the

Blind Beggar in *Madame Bovary,*" *Symposium* 22 (1968): 72–80; P. M. Wetherill, "*Madame Bovary*'s Blind Man: Symbolism in Flaubert," *Romanic Review* 61 (1970): 35–42; D. Anthony Williams, "Une Chanson de Rétif et sa reécriture par Flaubert," *Revue d'Histoire Littéraire de la France* 91:2 (March-April 1991): 239–42; and Michael Williams, "The Hound of Fate in *Madame Bovary,*" *College Literature* 14:1 (Winter 1987): 54–61.

30. For studies on Emma's death, see Sarah Goodwin, "Emma Bovary's Dance of Death," *Novel* 19:3 (Spring 1986): 197–215; Lauren Pinzka, "Death/Desire in *Madame Bovary,*" *Iris* 3:2 (Winter 1987): 26–41; and Yvonne Rollins, "Vertiges et vestiges de la danse macabre dans l'oeuvre de Flaubert," *NCFS* 16:3–4 (Spring-Summer 1988): 329–43.

31. For discussions of fatality, see Brombert, *The Novels of Flaubert: A Study of Themes and Techniques,* 53–54, and Culler, *Flaubert: The Uses of Uncertainty,* 143–47. Opinions on Charles vary from seeing him as the epitome of the grotesque, as in Michèle Breut, *Le Haut et le bas: Essai sur le grotesque dans "Madame Bovary"* (Amsterdam: Rodopi, 1994), to finding him sympathetic, as in Marc Girard, *La Passion de Charles Bovary* (Paris: Imago, 1995).

32. "comme si la plénitude de l'âme ne débordait pas quelquefois par les métaphores les plus vides, puisque personne, jamais, ne peut donner l'exacte mesure de ses besoins, ni de ses conceptions ni de ses douleurs, et que la parole humaine est comme un chaudron fêlé où nous battons des mélodies à faire danser les ours, quand on voudrait attendrir les étoiles." (part 2, chapter 12)

33. Flaubert to Louise Colet, 18 December 1853, *Correspondance*, vol. III, 401.

34. In his correspondence, Flaubert himself used the comparison of the artist's lot to that of Sisyphus: "What a rock of Sisyphus to roll is style, and especially prose. *It's never finished.*" Flaubert to Louise Colet, 7 October 1853, *Correspondance,* vol. III, 362.

Chapter Four

1. General studies of *Salammbô* include Martine Frier-Wantiez, *Sémiotique du fantastique: Analyse textuelle de "Salammbô"* (Bern: Peter Lang, 1979), and Anne Green, *Flaubert and the Historical Novel: "Salammbô" Reassessed* (Cambridge: Cambridge University Press, 1982), along with many articles, including Jeanne Bem, "Modernité de *Salammbô,*" *Littérature* 40 (1980): 18–31; Richard Berrong, "*Salammbô*: A Myth of the Origin of Language," *Modern Language Studies* 15:4 (Fall 1985): 261–69; Patrick Brady, "Archetypes and the Historical Novel: The Case of *Salammbô,*" *Stanford French Review* 1 (1977): 313–24; B. Jay, "Anti-History and the Method of *Salammbô,*" *Romanic Review* 63 (1972): 20–33; Georg Lukács, "*Salammbô,*" in Raymond Giraud, ed., *Flaubert: A Collection of Critical Essays* (Englewood Cliffs, NJ: Prentice-Hall, 1964), 141–53; Jacques Neefs, "*Salammbô*: Textes critiques," *Littérature* 15 (1974): 52–64; and Jean Rousset, "Positions, distances, perspectives dans *Salammbô,*" *Poétique* 6 (1971): 145–54.

2. For a discussion of "otherness" see Lawrence Schehr, "*Salammbô* as the Novel of Alterity," *NCFS* 17:3–4 (Spring-Summer 1989): 326–41; for problematical meaning see Michal Peled Ginsburg, "*Salammbô,*" in her *Flaubert Writing: A Study in Narrative Strategies* (Stanford: Stanford University Press, 1986), 108–31, and the studies cited in note 6.

3. For excellent readings of the novel's beginning, see Brombert, *The Novels of Flaubert: A Study of Themes and Techniques,* 98–102, and Culler, *Flaubert: The Uses of Uncertainty,* 213–16.

4. "D'abord on leur servit des oiseaux à la sauce verte, dans des assiettes d'argile rouge rehaussée de dessins noirs, puis toutes les espèces de coquillages que l'on ramasse sur les côtes puniques, des bouillies de froment, de fève et d'orge, et des escargots au cumin, sur des plats d'ambre jaune.

"Ensuite les tables furent couvertes de viandes: antilopes avec leurs cornes, paons avec leurs plumes, moutons entiers cuits au vin doux, gigots de chamelles et de buffles, hérissons au garum, cigales frites et loirs confits. Dans des gamelles en bois de Tamrapanni flottaient, au milieu du safran, de grands morceaux de graisse. Tout débordait de saumure, de truffes et d'assa foetida. Les pyramides de fruits s'éboulaient sur les gâteaux de miel, et l'on n'avait pas oublié quelques-uns de ces petits chiens à gros ventre et à soies roses que l'on engraissait avec du marc d'olives, mets carthaginois en abomination aux autres peuples." (chapter 1)

5. "Ils se demandaient ce qu'elle pouvait leur dire avec les gestes effrayants dont elle accompagnait son discours . . . ils tâchaient de saisir ces vagues histoires qui se balançaient devant leur imagination, à travers l'obscurité des théogonies, comme des fantômes dans des nuages." (chapter 1)

6. On the veil and its relationship to meaning, see Veronica Forrest-Thomson, "The Rituel of Reading *Salammbô,*" *Modern Language Review* 67 (October 1972): 787–98; Sima Godfrey, "The Fabrication of *Salammbô,*" *MLN* 95 (1980): 1005–16; Carol Mossman, "*Salammbô:* Seeing the Moon through the Veil," *Neophilologus* 73:1 (January 1989): 36–45; and Jacques Neefs, "Le Parcours du Zaïmph," in Claudine Gauthot-Mersch, ed., *La Production du sens chez Flaubert*, 227–52.

7. "Malédiction sur toi qui as dérobé Tanit! Haine, vengeance, massacre et douleur! Que Gurzil, dieu des batailles, te déchire! que Matisman, dieu des morts, t'étouffe! et que l'Autre—celui qu'il ne faut pas nommer—te brûle!" (chapter 5)

8. "Alors on amena un taureau blanc avec une brebis noire, symbole du jour et symbole de la nuit. On les égorgea au bord d'une fosse. Quand elle fut pleine de sang, ils y plongèrent leurs bras. Puis Narr'Havas étala sa main sur la poitrine de Mâtho, et Mâtho la sienne sur la poitrine de Narr'Havas. Ils répétèrent ce stigmate sur la toile de leurs tentes." (chapter 6)

For discussions of violence in the novel, see Brombert, *The Novels of Flaubert: A Study of Themes and Techniques,* 96–97, along with Marc Bizer,

"Polybe et la rhétorique de la violence," *Revue d'Histoire Littéraire de la France* 95:6 (November-December 1995): 974–88; David Danaher, "Effacement of the Author and the Function of Sadism in Flaubert's *Salammbô*," *Symposium* 46:1 (Spring 1992): 3–23; Bernard Masson, "*Salammbô* ou la barbarie à visage humain," *Revue d'Histoire Littéraire de la France* 81:4–5 (1981): 585–96; and Andrew McKenna, "Flaubert's Freudian Thing: Violence and Representation in *Salammbô*," *Stanford French Review* 12:2–3 (Fall-Winter 1988): 305–25.

9. "Les Barbares enfoncèrent leurs lignes; ils les égorgeaient à plein glaive; ils trébuchaient sur les moribonds et les cadavres, tout aveuglés par le sang qui leur jaillissait au visage. Ce tas de piques, de casques, de cuirasses, d'épées et de membres confondus tournait sur soi-même, s'élargissant et se serrant avec des contractions élastiques . . . enfin la litière du Suffète (sa grande litière à pendeloques de cristal), que l'on apercevait depuis le commencement, balancée dans les soldats comme une barque sur les flots, tout à coup sombra. Il était mort sans doute?" (chapter 6)

10. Free indirect discourse involves interrupting the narrator's voice with expressions of the characters, indicated here by the question mark. For a further explanation of the technique see our chapter 3.

11. "Et de ses lèvres violacées s'échappait une haleine plus nauséabonde que l'exhalaison d'un cadavre. Deux charbons semblaient brûler à la place de ses yeux, qui n'avaient plus de sourcils; un amas de peau rugueuse lui pendait sur le front; ses deux oreilles, en s'écartant de sa tête, commençaient à grandir, et les rides profondes qui formaient des demi-cercles autour de ses narines, lui donnaient un aspect étrange et effrayant, l'air d'une bête farouche." (chapter 6)

12. "Afin de mieux leur résister les Barbares se ruèrent, en foule compacte; les éléphants se jetèrent au milieu, impétueusement. . . . Avec leurs trompes, ils étouffaient les hommes, ou bien les arrachant du sol, par-dessus leur tête il les livraient aux soldats dans les tours; avec leurs défenses, ils les éventraient, les lançaient en l'air, et de longues entrailles pendaient à leurs crocs d'ivoire comme des paquets de cordages à des mâts." (chapter 8)

13. "Une épouvante indéterminée la retenait; elle avait peur de Moloch, peur de Mâtho. Cet homme à taille de géant, et qui était maître du zaïmph, dominait la Rabbetna autant que le Baal et lui apparaissait entouré des mêmes fulgurations; puis l'âme des Dieux, quelquefois, visitait le corps des hommes. Schahabarim, en parlant de celui-là, ne disait-il pas qu'elle devait vaincre Moloch? Ils étaient mêlés l'un à l'autre; elle les confondait; tous les deux la poursuivaient." (chapter 10)

14. "il serrait contre elle ses noirs anneaux tigrés de plaques d'or. Salammbô haletait sous ce poids trop lourd, ses reins pliaient, elle se sentait mourir; et du bout de sa queue il lui battait la cuisse tout doucement; puis la musique se taisant, il retomba." (chapter 10)

15. "Salammbô était envahie par une mollesse où elle perdait toute conscience d'elle-même. Quelque chose à la fois d'intime et de supérieur, un ordre

des Dieux la forçait à s'y abandonner. . . . Mâtho lui saisit les talons, la chaînette d'or éclata, et les deux bouts, en s'envolant, frappèrent la toile comme deux vipères rebondissantes. Le zaïmph tomba, l'enveloppant . . .

—'Moloch, tu me brûles!' et les baisers du soldat, plus dévorateurs que des flammes, la parcouraient; elle était comme enlevée d'un ouragan, prise dans la force du soleil." (chapter 11)

16. Hannibal (247–183 B.C.) is no doubt the most recognizable Carthaginian personage. As general during the Second Punic War with Rome, he penetrated well into Italy (after a surprise maneuver crossing the Alps) before finally being defeated in North Africa.

17. On the ending see Peter Starr, "*Salammbô:* The Politics of an Ending," *French Forum* 10:1 (January 1985): 40–56.

18. Regarding the structure, see A. Busst, "On the Structure of *Salammbô,*" *French Studies* 44:3 (July 1990): 289–99, and Jacques Neefs, "Le Parcours du Zaïmph."

19. On style and artistry in *Salammbô,* see especially Brombert, *The Novels of Flaubert: A Study of Themes and Techniques,* 102–13, Dennis Porter, "Aestheticism versus the novel: The Example of *Salammbô,*" *Novel* 4 (1971): 101–6, and Marilyn Rose, "Decadent Prose: The Example of *Salammbô,*" *NCFS* 3 (1975): 213–23.

Chapter Five

1. Books on *Sentimental Education* include Maurice Agulhon et al., *Histoire et langage dans "L'Education sentimentale"* (Paris: SEDES, 1981); Jeanne Bem, *Clefs pour "L'Education sentimentale"* (Tubingen: Place, 1981); Pierre Cogny, *"L'Education sentimentale" de Flaubert: Le Monde en creux* (Paris: Larousse, 1975); Peter Cortland, *The Sentimental Adventure: An Examination of Flaubert's "Education sentimentale"* (The Hague: Mouton, 1967); René Dumesnil, *"L'Education sentimentale" de Gustave Flaubert* (1869) (Paris: Nizet, 1963); Jean-Pierre Duquette, *Flaubert ou l'architecture du vide: Une lecture de l'"Education sentimentale"* (Montreal: Presses de l'Université de Montréal, 1972); William Paulson, *"Sentimental Education": The Complexity of Disenchantment* (New York: Twayne Publishers, 1992); Alan Raitt, *L'Education sentimentale* (Paris: Imprimerie Nationale, 1979); and David Williams, *The Hidden Life at Its Source: A Study of Flaubert's "L'Education sentimentale"* (Hull, England: Hull University Press, 1987).

Several general articles on the novel concern the problems of reading: Peter Brooks, "Retrospective Lust, or Flaubert's Perversities," in his *Reading for the Plot: Design and Intention in Narrative* (New York: Vintage, 1984), 171–215; Graham Falconer, "Reading *L'Education sentimentale:* Belief and Disbelief," *NCFS* 12:3 (1984): 329–43; Julia Ingram, "The Aesthetics of Fragmentation: *L'Education sentimentale,*" *NCFS* 18:1–2 (Fall-Winter 1989–90): 112–32; Dorothy Kelly, "Oscillation and Its Effects: Flaubert's *L'Education sen-*

timentale," *Romanic Review* 80:2 (March 1989): 207–17; Dominick LaCapra, "Collapsing Spheres in Flaubert's *Sentimental Education,*" in his *History, Politics and the Novel* (Ithaca: Cornell University Press, 1987): 83–110; Henri Mitterand, "Sémiologie flaubertienne: le Club de l'Intelligence," *La Revue des Lettres Modernes* 703–6 (1984): 61–77; Michel Raimond, "Le réalisme subjectif dans *L'Education sentimentale,*" *Cahiers de l'Association Internationale des Etudes Françaises* 23 (1971): 299–310; Ruth Ronen, "Political Coherence in Literary Prose," *Style* 20:1 (Spring 1985): 66–74; and Hayden White, "The Problem of Style in Realistic Representation: Marx and Flaubert," in Harold Bloom, ed., *Gustave Flaubert* (New York: Chelsea House, 1989), 91–109.

On the journey, see especially Brombert, *The Novels of Flaubert: A Study of Themes and Techniques,* 140–46. In his uniformly excellent book, the chapter on *Sentimental Education* is perhaps the strongest.

2. In his excellent reading of the novel's beginning, William Paulson shows how Flaubert's style captures the impersonal, mechanical processes of the early industrial age (*Sentimental Education: The Complexity of Disenchantment* [New York: Twayne Publishers, 1992], 25).

3. "Un jeune homme de dix-huit ans, à longs cheveux et qui tenait un album sous son bras, restait auprès du gouvernail, immobile. A travers le brouillard, il contemplait des clochers, des édifices dont il ne savait pas les noms; puis il embrassa, dans un dernier coup d'oeil, l'île Saint-Louis, la Cité, Notre-Dame; et bientôt, Paris disparaissant, il poussa un grand soupir." (part 1, chapter 1)

4. See, for example, our discussions of Flaubert's *Dictionary of Inherited Ideas* in chapters 3 (*Madame Bovary*) and 7 (*Bouvard and Pécuchet*).

5. In addition to Sartre, *L'Idiot de la famille*, and Marthe Robert, *En haine du roman: Etude sur Flaubert* (Paris: Balland, 1982), for further discussions of the psychological dimensions of Frédéric's family configuration see Jeanne Bem, "Sur le sens d'un discours circulaire," *Littérature* 15 (October 1974): 95–109; Michel Brix, "Portrait d'un jeune homme 'entortillé par sa maman': Le Personnage de Frédéric Moreau dans *L'Education sentimentale,*" *Les Lettres Romanes* 44:4 (November 1990): 297–313; Arthur Mitzman, "Flaubert's Escape from the Family Romance," in Henk Hillenaar and Walter Schonau, eds., *Fathers and Mothers in Literature* (Amsterdam: Rodopi, 1994): 103–12; and Naomi Segal, "The Sick Son: A Motif in Stendhal and Flaubert," *Romance Studies* 19 (Winter 1991): 7–19.

6. "Derrière les Tuileries, le ciel prenait la teinte des ardoises. Les arbres du jardin formaient deux masses énormes, violacées par le sommet. Les becs de gaz s'allumaient; et la Seine, verdâtre dans toute son étendue, se déchirait en moires d'argent contre les piles des ponts." (part 1, chapter 3)

7. The exclamation mark points to an example of free indirect discourse, in which Frédéric's expressions are mixed in with the narrator's voice. See our discussion in chapter 3 (*Madame Bovary*) as well as Paulson's linking of its use to social clichés in chapter 7 of *The Complexities of Disenchantment*.

8. The scene of the masked ball is discussed in detail by Culler, *Flaubert: The Uses of Uncertainty,* 93–99, as well as by Robert Benet, "Clé de lecture pour *L'Education sentimentale:* Le Bal masqué chez Rosanette," *L'Information Littéraire* 45:3 (1993): 13–22, and Margaret Scanlan, "Le Bal masqué in Flaubert's *L'Education sentimentale,*" *International Fiction Review* 8:2 (Summer 1981): 137–40.

9. "Une autre soif lui était venue, celle des femmes, du luxe et de tout ce que comporte l'existence parisienne. Il se sentait quelque peu étourdi, comme un homme qui descend d'un vaisseau; et, dans l'hallucination du premier sommeil, il voyait passer et repasser continuellement les épaules de la Poissarde, les reins de la Débardeuse, les mollets de la Polonaise, la chevelure de la Sauvagesse. Puis deux grands yeux noirs, qui n'étaient pas dans le bal, parurent; et légers comme des papillons, ardents comme des torches, ils allaient, venaient, vibraient, montaient dans la corniche, descendaient jusqu'à sa bouche. Frédéric s'acharnait à reconnaître ces yeux sans y parvenir. Mais déjà le rêve l'avait pris; il lui semblait qu'il était attelé près d'Arnoux, au timon d'un fiacre, et que la Maréchale, à califourchon sur lui, l'éventrait avec ses éperons d'or." (part 2, chapter 1)

10. "La fréquentation de ces deux femmes faisait dans sa vie comme deux musiques: l'une folâtre, emportée, divertissante, l'autre grave et presque religieuse; et, vibrant à la fois, elles augmentaient toujours, et peu à peu se mêlaient; car, si Mme Arnoux venait à l'effleurer du doigt seulement, l'image de l'autre, tout de suite, se présentait à son désir, parce qu'il avait, de ce côté-là, une chance moins lointaine; et, dans la compagnie de Rosanette, quand il lui arrivait d'avoir le coeur ému, il se rappelait immédiatement son grand amour." (part 2, chapter 2)

11. For superb discussions of the effects of Flaubert's style (particularly applicable to *Sentimental Education*), see Brombert, *The Novels of Flaubert: A Study of Themes and Techniques,* 161–84, Culler, *Flaubert: The Uses of Uncertainty,* 202–7, Gérard Genette, "Silences de Flaubert," in his *Figures* (Paris: Seuil, 1966), 223–43, and Albert Thibaudet, *Gustave Flaubert,* 205–64.

12. For a discussion of the same technique of juxtaposed speeches in the country fair episode from *Madame Bovary,* see chapter 3.

13. "Les résidences royales ont en elles une mélancolie particulière, qui tient sans doute à leurs dimensions trop considérables pour le petit nombre de leurs hôtes, au silence qu'on est surpris d'y trouver après tant de fanfares, à leur luxe immobile prouvant par sa vieillesse la fugacité des dynasties, l'éternelle misère de tout; et cette exhalaison des siècles, engourdissante et funèbre comme un parfum de momie, se fait sentir même aux têtes naïves. Rosanette bâillait démesurément. Ils s'en retournèrent à l'hôtel." (part 3, chapter 1)

14. "La lumière, à de certaines places éclairant la lisière du bois, laissait les fonds dans l'ombre; ou bien, atténuée sur les premiers plans par une sorte de crépuscule, elle étalait dans les lointains des vapeurs violettes, une clarté blanche. Au milieu du jour, le soleil, tombant d'aplomb sur les larges verdures,

les éclaboussait, suspendait des gouttes argentines à la pointe des branches, rayait le gazon de traînées d'émeraudes, jetait des taches d'or sur les couches de feuilles mortes; en se renversant la tête, on apercevait le ciel, entre les cimes des arbres. Quelques-uns, d'une altitude démésurée, avaient des airs de patriarches et d'empereurs, ou, se touchant par le bout, formaient avec leurs longs fûts comme des arcs de triomphe; d'autres, poussés dès le bas obliquement, semblaient des colonnes près de tomber." (part 3, chapter 1) The description of the Fontainebleau forest has been discussed by Thibaudet, *Gustave Flaubert,* 234–38, Brombert, *The Novels of Flaubert: A Study of Themes and Techniques,* 177–78, and Culler, *Flaubert: The Uses of Uncertainty,* 100–10; comparing the three treatments gives the reader the opportunity to appreciate their excellence and the differences among them. See also Eric LeCalvez, "Génétique et hypotextes descriptifs: La Forêt de Fontainebleau dans *L'Education sentimentale,*" *Neophilologus* 78:2 (April 1994): 219–32.

15. Among the numerous discussions of the representation of history in *Sentimental Education* are Pierre Campion, "Roman et histoire dans *L'Education sentimentale,*" *Poétique* 22:85 (February 1991): 35–52; Philippe Desan, "From History to Fiction: A Reading of Flaubert's *L'Education sentimentale,*" *Pacific Coast Philology* 18:1–2 (November 1983): 108–13; Eugenio Donato, "Flaubert and the Question of History: Notes for a Critical Anthology," *MLN* 91 (1976): 850–70; Graham Falconer, "Le Statut de l'histoire dans *l'Education sentimentale,*" in G. Harris and P. Wetherill, eds., *Littérature et révolutions en France* (Amsterdam: Rodopi, 1990), 106–20; Lynne Layton, "Narcissism and History: Flaubert's *Sentimental Education,*" in Lynne Layton and Barbara Schapiro, eds., *Narcissism and the Text: Studies in Literature and Pyschology of Self* (New York: New York University Press, 1986); P. Niang, "L'Insertion de l'histoire dans *L'Education sentimentale* de Gustave Flaubert," in Harris and Wetherill, eds., *Littérature et révolutions en France,* 77–105; Albert Sonnenfeld, "*L'Education sentimentale*: Un siècle d'actualité," *French Review* 44 (1970): 299–309; William VanderWolk, "History and the Redemptive Power of Memory in Flaubert's *L'Education sentimentale,*" *L'Esprit Créateur* 27:2 (Summer 1987): 74–81; Jean Vidalenc, "Gustave Flaubert, historien de la révolution de 1848," *Europe* 485–87 (1969), 51–71; and P. Wetherill, "Flaubert and Revolution," in David Bevan, ed., *Literature and Revolution* (Amsterdam: Rodopi, 1989), 19–33.

16. On the significance of the Sénécal/Dussardier pairing, see Paulson, *The Complexities of Disenchantment,* 105–12 and 128–30, Robert Denommé, "From Innocence to Experience: A Retrospective View of Dussardier in *L'Education sentimentale,*" *NCFS* 18:3–4 (Spring-Summer 1990): 424–36, and Chantal de Grandpré, "Sénécal et Dussardier: La République en effigie," *French Review* 64:4 (March 1991): 621–31.

17. For discussions of the jewel box, see Stirling Haig, "Madame Arnoux's Coffret: A Monumental Case," *Romanic Review* 75:4 (November 1984): 469–82, and Georges Zaragoza, "Le coffret de Madame Arnoux ou

l'achèvement d'une éducation," *Revue d'Histoire Littéraire de la France* 89:4 (July-August 1989): 674–88.

18. "il exécrait Mme Dambreuse parce qu'il avait manqué, à cause d'elle, commettre une bassesse. Il en oubliait la Maréchale, ne s'inquiétait même pas de Mme Arnoux, ne songeant qu'à lui, à lui seul, perdu dans les décombres de ses rêves, malade, plein de douleur et de découragement; et, en haine du milieu factice où il avait tant souffert, il souhaita la fraîcheur de l'herbe, le repos de la province, une vie somnolente passée à l'ombre du toit natal avec des coeurs ingénus." (part 3, chapter 5)

19. "Il voyagea.

"Il connut la mélancolie des paquebots, les froids réveils sous la tente, l'étourdissement des paysages et des ruines, l'amertume des sympathies interrompues.

"Il revint.

"Il fréquenta le monde, et il eut d'autres amours encore. Mais le souvenir continuel du premier les lui rendait insipides; et puis la véhémence du désir, la fleur même de la sensation était perdue. Ses ambitions d'esprit avaient également diminué. Des années passèrent; et il supportait le désoeuvrement de son intelligence et l'inertie de son coeur." (part 3, chapter 6)

20. A Bildungsroman is a novel of education, in which the protagonist learns a lesson. See, for example, Meili Steele, "*L'Education sentimentale* and the Bildungsroman: Reading Frédéric Moreau," *Romanic Review* 78:1 (January 1987): 84–101.

21. On the significance of this episode and the ending of the novel, see Brombert, *The Novels of Flaubert: A Study of Themes and Techniques,* 150–56, Culler, *Flaubert: The Uses of Uncertainty,* 152–56, and Diana Festa-Peyre, "Aging by Default: Frédéric Moreau and His Times in Flaubert's *Sentimental Education,*" *Symposium* 47:3 (Fall 1993): 201–18.

22. "Or, un dimanche, pendant qu'on était aux vêpres, Frédéric et Deslauriers, s'étant fait préalablement friser, cueillirent des fleurs dans le jardin de Mme Moreau, puis sortirent par la porte des champs, et, après un grand détour dans les vignes, revinrent par la Pêcherie et se glissèrent chez la Turque, en tenant toujours leurs gros bouquets.

"Frédéric présenta le sien, comme un amoureux à sa fiancée. Mais la chaleur qu'il faisait, l'appréhension de l'inconnu, une espèce de remords, et jusqu'au plaisir de voir, d'un seul coup d'oeil, tant de femmes à sa disposition, l'émurent tellement, qu'il devint très pâle et restait sans avancer, sans rien dire. Toutes riaient, joyeuses de son embarras; croyant qu'on s'en moquait, il s'enfuit; et, comme Frédéric avait l'argent, Deslauriers fut bien obligé de le suivre.

"On les vit sortir. Cela fit une histoire qui n'était pas oubliée trois ans après.

"Ils se la contèrent prolixement, chacun complétant les souvenirs de l'autre; et, quand ils eurent fini:

"—C'est là ce que nous avons eu de meilleur! dit Frédéric.

"—Oui, peut-être bien? c'est là ce que nous avons eu de meilleur! dit Deslauriers." (part 3,chapter 7)

This passage has, of course, been the subject of a great number of commentaries, among which are those of Brombert, *The Novels of Flaubert: A Study of Themes and Techniques,* 125–28, Paulson, *The Complexities of Disenchantment,* 135–36, and Gans, "*Education sentimentale*: The Hero as Storyteller," *MLN* 89 (1974): 614–25.

Chapter Six

1. Studies of *The Temptation* include Jeanne Bem, *Désir et savoir dans l'oeuvre de Flaubert: Etude de "La Tentation de Saint Antoine"* (Paris: Payot, 1979), as well as numerous articles, among them Charles Bernheimer, "*Etre la matière!* Origin and Difference in Flaubert's *La Tentation de Saint Antoine,*" *Novel* 10 (1976): 65–78; Dominique Cardin, "Le Principe des métamorphoses: Essai sur la dernière version de *La Tentation de Saint Antoine* de Flaubert," *Dalhousie French Studies* 18 (Fall 1994): 99–109; Robert Griffin, "The Transfiguration of Matter," *French Studies* 44:1 (January 1990): 18–33; Marshall Olds, "Hallucination and Point of View in *La Tentation de Saint Antoine,*" *NCFS* 17:1–2 (Fall-Winter 1988–89): 170–85; Peter Starr, "Science and Confusion: On Flaubert's *Temptation,*" *MLN* 99 (December 1984): 1072–93; and Yves Thomas, "Luxe et désert dans *La Tentation de Saint Antoine,*" *Les Lettres Romanes* 44:3 (August 1990): 181–92.

2. Michel Foucault, "La Bibliothèque fantastique," in Raymonde Debray-Genette, ed., *Flaubert* (Paris: Marcel Didier, 1970), 171–90 (text quoted here 185–86). For further discussions of ordering in *Saint Anthony,* see Jeanne Bem, *Desir et savoir,* 241–45; Michel Butor, "La Spirale des sept péchés," *Critique* 26 (1970): 387–412; and R. Leal, "The Unity of Flaubert's *Tentation de Saint Antoine,*" *The Modern Language Review* 85:2 (April 1990): 330–40.

3. On the role of memory as an organizing principle, see Michal Peled Ginsburg, *Flaubert Writing: A Study in Narrative Strategies* (Stanford: Stanford University Press, 1986), 67–76; Marie Diamond, *Flaubert: The Problem of Aesthetic Discontinuity* (Port Washington, NY: Kennikat Press, 1975), 122–27; and Renate Blumenfeld-Kosinski, "La structure dynamique de *La Tentation de Saint Antoine* de Flaubert: Une Mémoire féconde," *Romanic Review* 74:1 (January 1983): 46–53.

4. "C'est vers Dieu qu'ils prétendent se diriger par toutes ces voies! De quel droit les maudire, moi qui trébuche dans la mienne? Quand ils ont disparu, j'allais peut-être en apprendre davantage. Cela tourbillonnait trop vite; je n'avais pas le temps de répondre. A présent c'est comme s'il y avait dans mon intelligence plus d'espace et plus de lumière. Je suis tranquille. Je me sens capable . . ." (section 4)

5. For another perspective, see Pierre Danger, "Sainteté et castration dans *La Tentation de Saint Antoine,*" in Charles Carlut and Jean Seznec, eds., *Essais sur Flaubert: En l'honneur du professeur Don Demorest* (Paris: Nizet, 1979), 185–202.

6. Letter from Freud, n.d., quoted in Kitty Mrosovsky, introduction to *The Temptation of Saint Anthony,* trans. Kitty Mrosovsky (London: Penguin, 1980), 21.

7. "Au milieu du portique, en plein soleil, une femme nue était attachée contre une colonne, deux soldats la fouettant avec des lanières; à chacun des coups son corps entier se tordait. Elle s'est retournée, la bouche ouverte;—et par-dessus la foule, à travers ses longs cheveux qui lui couvraient la figure, j'ai cru reconnaître Ammonaria." (section 1)

8. See the Preface, note 6.

9. "Car le monde,—ainsi qu'un philosophe me l'a expliqué,—forme un ensemble dont toutes les parties influent les unes sur les autres, comme les organes d'un seul corps. Il s'agit de connaître les amours et les répulsions naturelles des choses, puis de les mettre en jeu. . . . On pourrait donc modifier ce qui paraît être l'ordre immuable?" (section 1)

Chapter Seven

1. General studies on *Bouvard and Pécuchet* include Pierre Cogny et al., *Flaubert et le comble de l'art: Nouvelles recherches sur "Bouvard et Pécuchet"* (Paris: SEDES, 1981), and Yvan Leclerc, *La Spirale et le monument: Essai sur "Bouvard et Pécuchet" de Gustave Flaubert* (Paris: SEDES, 1988); there are also many articles on this novel, including Dominique Barkni-Boutonnet, "Bouvard et Pécuchet: Deux particuliers," *Poétique* 21:82 (April 1990): 179–85; Charles Bernheimer, "Fetishism and Allegory in *Bouvard et Pécuchet,*" in Schor and Majewski, eds., *Flaubert and Postmodernism,* 160–76; Françoise Gaillard, "The Great Illusion of Realism, or the Real as Representation," *Poetics Today* 5:4 (1984): 753–66; Claudine Gothot-Mersch, "Le Roman interminable: Un Aspect de la structure de *Bouvard et Pécuchet,*" in Cogny et al., *Flaubert et le comble de l'art,* 9–22; John Greene, "Structure et épistémologie dans *Bouvard et Pécuchet,*" in Cogny et al., *Flaubert et le comble de l'art,* 111–128; Andrew McKenna, "Allodidacticism: Flaubert 100 Years After," in Harold Bloom, ed., *Gustave Flaubert* (New York: Chelsea House, 1989), 121–39; Jacques Neefs, "*Bouvard et Pécuchet*: The Prose of Knowledge," *Sub-Stance* 22:2–3 (1993): 154–64; Lawrence Schehr, "Flaubert entre l'indécidé et l'indécidable," *Les Lettres Romanes* 45:4 (November 1991): 293–306; Peter Starr, "The Style of (Post-) Liberal Desire: *Bouvard et Pécuchet,*" *NCFS* 18:1–2 (Fall-Winter 1989–90): 133–49; Marina Van-Zuylen, "From *Horror Vacui* to the Reader's Boredom: *Bouvard et Pécuchet* and the Art of Difficulty," *NCFS* 22:1–2 (Fall-Winter 1993–94): 112–22; Nathaniel Wing, "Detail and Narrative Dalliance in Flaubert's *Bouvard et Pécuchet,*" *French Forum* 13:1 (January 1988): 47–56; and Monique Wittig, "A propos de *Bouvard et Pécuchet,*" *Cahiers de la Compagnie Renaud-Barrault* 59 (1967): 113–22.

2. "Des jours tristes commencèrent.

"Ils n'étudiaient plus dans la peur des déceptions, les habitants de Chavignolles s'écartaient d'eux, les journaux tolérés n'apprenaient rien, et leur solitude était profonde, leur désoeuvrement complet." (chapter 7)

3. The lesson learned by the protagonists of Voltaire's philosophical tale *Candide,* implying that they should do less philosophizing and more concrete tasks.

4. For a discussion of the Christmas Eve scene, see Jacques Neefs, "La Nuit de Noël: *Bouvard et Pécuchet,*" *La Revue des Lettres Modernes* 865–72 (1988): 35–61.

5. See our discussion of *The Dictionary* in chapter 3 (*Madame Bovary*) and, especially, Culler's discussion of it in relation to bourgeois stupidity in *Flaubert: The Uses of Uncertainty,* 158–66.

6. For some interesting discussions on encyclopedism and collecting, see Leo Bersani, "Flaubert's Encyclopedism," *Novel* 21:2–3 (Winter-Spring 1988): 140–46; Eugenio Donato, "The Museum's Furnace: Notes toward a Contextual Reading of *Bouvard and Pécuchet,*" in his *The Script of Decadence: Essays on the Fictions of Flaubert and the Poetics of Romanticism* (New York: Oxford University Press, 1993), 56–79; and Normand Lalonde, "La Collection curieuse de Bouvard et Pécuchet," *Romanic Review* 83:4 (November 1992): 445–62.

7. "Deux hommes parurent.

"L'un venait de la Bastille, l'autre du Jardin des Plantes. Le plus grand, vêtu de toile, marchait le chapeau en arrière, le gilet déboutonné et sa cravate à la main. Le plus petit, dont le corps disparaissait dans une redingote marron, baissait la tête sous une casquette à visière pointue.

"Quand ils furent arrivés au milieu du boulevard, ils s'assirent, à la même minute, sur le même banc." (chapter 1)

8. On Flaubert's predilection for binary patterns, see Culler, *Flaubert: The Uses of Uncertainty,* 131–33.

9. There are several excellent readings of the novel's opening chapter, including Pierre Cogny, "La Parodie dans *Bouvard et Pécuchet:* Essai de lecture du chapitre 1," in *Flaubert et le comble de l'art,* 39–47; Georges Kliebenstein, "L'Encyclopédie minimale," *Poétique* 22:88 (November 1991): 447–61; Bernard Magné, "Boulevard écrit," *Revue Romane* 17:2 (1982): 75–88; Andrew McKenna, "Writing in the Novel: Remarks on *Bouvard et Pécuchet,*" *Language and Style* 14:2 (Spring 1981): 83–91; and Franca Quarantini, "Sur deux incipits flaubertiens," *La Revue des Lettres Modernes* 865–72 (1988): 157–81. Both Kliebenstein and McKenna talk about the significance of the word *bourdon* from perspectives that differ from each other and from ours.

Chapter Eight

1. "Il leur semblait être en ballon, la nuit, par un froid glacial, emportés d'une course sans fin, vers un abîme sans fond, et sans rien autour

d'eux que l'insaisissable, l'immobile, l'éternel. C'était trop fort. Ils y renoncèrent." (chapter 8)

2. It is interesting to note that Proust and Flaubert also top the list of French writers most studied today, each exceeding a thousand references in the MLA bibliography from 1981 to February 1996.

3. "Celui qui embrasserait, à la fois, toute l'étendue et toute la pensée n'y verrait aucune contingence, rien d'accidentel, mais une suite géométrique de termes, liés entre eux par des lois nécessaires.

" 'Ah! ce serait beau!' dit Pécuchet." (chapter 8)

Selected Bibliography

This highly selective bibliography emphasizes critical studies on Flaubert in English (unless otherwise indicated), listing mostly recent works, along with a few older "classics."

PRIMARY WORKS

Major Editions

Carnets de Travail (Work Notebooks), ed. Pierre-Marc de Biasi. Paris: Balland, 1988. Interesting collection of Flaubert's preparatory notes for the novels.

Correspondance. 9 vols. Paris: Conard, 1926–33; and *Supplément*. 4 vols. Paris: Conard, 1954. Some letters are expurgated, but this remains the standard edition until Jean Bruneau's is completed.

Correspondance, ed. Jean Bruneau. 3 vols. Paris: Gallimard, Pléiade, 1973, 1980, 1991. The best edition of Flaubert's letters up to 1868.

Oeuvres, ed. Maurice Nadeau. 18 vols. Lausanne: Rencontre, 1964–65.

Oeuvres complètes, ed. Bernard Masson. 2 vols. Paris: Editions du Seuil, 1964. Convenient but incomplete collection.

Oeuvres complètes de Gustave Flaubert. 26 vols. Paris: Conard, 1910–54. Though outdated, it remains the standard edition due to completeness.

Oeuvres complètes illustrées de Gustave Flaubert, ed. Maurice Bardèche et al. 16 vols. Paris: Club de l'Honnête Homme, 1971–76.

Translations

Bouvard and Pécuchet, trans. A. J. Krailsheimer. London: Penguin Books, 1976.

Early Works, trans. Robert Griffin. Lincoln: University of Nebraska Press, 1991. Translation of 11 shorter works, including *Diary of a Madman* and *Smarh*.

Madame Bovary, trans. Eleanor Marx Aveling, updated by Paul de Man. New York: W. W. Norton & Co., 1965. Widely used translation followed by excellent critical apparatus, including early scenarios and several classic studies of the novel.

Salammbô, trans. A. J. Krailsheimer. London: Penguin Books, 1977.

Sentimental Education, trans. Robert Baldick. London: Penguin Books, 1964.

The Dictionary of Accepted Ideas, trans. Jacques Barzun. Norfolk, CN: New Directions, 1954.

The Letters of Gustave Flaubert: 1857–1880, ed. and trans. Francis Steegmuller. Cambridge, MA: Harvard University Press, 1982.

The Temptation of Saint Anthony, trans. Kitty Mrosovsky. London: Penguin Books, 1980.

Three Tales, trans. Robert Baldick. London: Penguin Books, 1961.

Critical Studies

Books

Barnes, Julian. *Flaubert's Parrot*. New York: Vintage Books, 1984. Witty novel with revealing insights into Flaubert.

Berg, William, Michel Grimaud, and George Moskos. *Saint/Oedipus: Psychocritical Approaches to Flaubert's Art*. Ithaca: Cornell University Press, 1982. Several different psychocritical approaches discussed and applied to Flaubert's "Saint Julian."

Brombert, Victor. *The Novels of Flaubert: A Study of Themes and Techniques*. Princeton: Princeton University Press, 1966. Superb study of Flaubert's works shows how technique reinforces theme and reflects the author's temperament.

Buck, Stratton. *Gustave Flaubert*. New York: Twayne Publishers, 1966. Forerunner of the present book, Buck's solid study relates Flaubert's works to the author.

Culler, Jonathan. *Flaubert: The Uses of Uncertainty*. Ithaca: Cornell University Press, 1974. Fascinating study stresses the gaps, discontinuities, and uncertainties by which Flaubert thwarts the reader and eludes interpretation.

Debray-Genette, Raymonde. *Métamorphoses du récit: Autour de Flaubert*. Paris: Seuil, 1979. Excellent series of essays (in French) by one of France's premier Flaubert scholars.

Gans, Eric. *"Madame Bovary": The End of Romance*. Boston: Twayne Publishers, 1989. Excellent study of *Madame Bovary* based on the relationship of self and other, illustrated by insightful readings of specific passages.

Ginsburg, Michal Peled. *Flaubert Writing: A Study in Narrative Strategies.* Stanford: Stanford University Press, 1986. Perceptive study that plots the psychological patterns that determine narrative impasses and strategies.

Haig, Stirling. *Flaubert and the Gift of Speech: Dialogue and Discourse in Four "Modern" Novels*. Cambridge, England: Cambridge University Press, 1986. A subtle and insightful study of the function of dialogue in underscoring important themes and narrative techniques in four of Flaubert's novels.

Kaplan, Louise. *Female Perversions: The Temptations of Emma Bovary*. New York: Doubleday, 1992. Provocative study from a psychoanalytical perspective of gender-related issues.

LaCapra, Dominick. *"Madame Bovary" on Trial*. Ithaca: Cornell University Press, 1982. Intriguing discussion of the literary and ideological implications of the trial of *Madame Bovary*.

Paulson, William. *"Sentimental Education": The Complexity of Disenchantment*. New York: Twayne Publishers, 1992. Excellent demonstration of the importance of the social, historical, and political context for unraveling the "complexities of disenchantment" that dominate *Sentimental Education*.

Ramazani, Vaheed. *The Free Indirect Mode: Flaubert and the Practice of Irony*. Charlottesville: University Press of Virginia, 1988. Subtle study shows the connection between irony and the free indirect mode through concrete analyses of texts, especially from *Madame Bovary*.

Sherrington, R.J. *Three Novels by Flaubert: A Study of Techniques*. Oxford: Clarendon, 1970. Systematic study of viewpoint in *Madame Bovary, Salammbô,* and *Sentimental Education*.

Thibaudet, Albert. *Gustave Flaubert*. Paris: Gallimard, 1935. Best study (in French) of Flaubert's style.

Thorlby, Anthony. *Gustave Flaubert and the Art of Realism*. London: Bowes and Bowes, 1956. Short (50 pages) but sweet.

Collections of Essays

Bart, Benjamin, ed. *"Madame Bovary" and the Critics*. New York: New York University Press, 1966. Excellent collection of essays by British and American critics.

Bloom, Harold, ed. *Gustave Flaubert.* New York: Chelsea House, 1989. Good collection of modern critical views on Flaubert.

Debray-Genette, Raymonde, ed. *Flaubert*. Paris: Marcel Didier, 1970. Excellent collection of essays (in French) on Flaubert, including classic studies by Proust, Genette, Sartre, and Foucault.

Giraud, Raymond, ed. *Flaubert: A Collection of Critical Essays*. Englewood Cliffs, NJ: Prentice-Hall, 1964. Good mixture of essays, including translations of several classic French studies.

Gothot-Mersch, Claudine, ed. *La Production du sens chez Flaubert*. Paris: 10/18, 1975. Collection of papers (in French) given in 1974 at Cérisy, unified by notion of forms and production of meaning.

Porter, Laurence, ed. *Critical Essays on Gustave Flaubert*. Boston: Hall, 1986. Excellent combination of previously published classic studies and more recent essays, arranged by Flaubert's works.

Porter, Laurence, and Eugene Gray, eds. *Approaches to Teaching Flaubert's "Madame Bovary."* New York: MLA, 1995. Excellent collection of essays by leading Flaubert scholars; as fascinating for students as for teachers.

Schor, Naomi, and Henry Majewski, eds. *Flaubert and Postmodernism.* Lincoln: University of Nebraska Press, 1984. Superb collection of recent essays representing a variety of speculative approaches.

Uffenbeck, Lorin, ed. *Nineteenth-Century French Studies* 12:3 (Spring 1984). This special issue, entitled "Flaubert and the Problems of the Novel," contains an interesting combination of traditional and speculative essays.

Biographies

Bart, Benjamin. *Flaubert*. Syracuse: Syracuse University Press, 1967. A comprehensive and creative literary biography.

Bruneau, Jean, and Jean Ducourneau. *Album Flaubert*. Paris: Gallimard, Pléiade, 1972. Flaubert's life illustrated with numerous photographs and other documents.

Lottmann, Herbert. *Flaubert: A Biography*. Boston: Little, Brown, 1989. A thorough study that focuses more on Flaubert's life than on his works.

Sartre, Jean-Paul. *L'Idiot de la famille*. 3 vols. Paris: Gallimard, 1971–72. Fascinating "psychobiography" now available in English: *The Family Idiot,* trans. Carol Cosman. 5 vols. Chicago: University of Chicago Press: 1981–93.

Starkie, Enid. *Flaubert: The Making of the Master*. London: Weidenfeld and Nicolson, 1967. A perceptive study that nonetheless contains some inaccuracies.

Troyat, Henri. *Flaubert*. Paris: Flammarion, 1988. Recent biography in French, now available in English: trans. Joan Pinkham. New York: Viking, 1992.

Index

The Authors

William J. Berg and Laurey K. Martin both teach in the department of French and Italian at the University of Wisconsin–Madison. They coauthored *Emile Zola Revisited* (1992) for Twayne's World Authors Series and *Images* (1990), a cultural reader in French. Their collaborative work on Flaubert includes a study guide on *Madame Bovary* (1990) and a contribution to a recent Modern Language Association volume, *Approaches to Teaching Flaubert's "Madame Bovary"* (1995). Berg is also coauthor of *Saint/Oedipus: Psychocritical Approaches to Flaubert's Art* (1982), and he did a student edition of "A Simple Heart" in his coauthored anthology of French literature, *Poèmes, Pièces, Prose* (1973).

The Editor

David O'Connell is professor of French at Georgia State University. He received his Ph.D. in 1966 from Princeton University, where he was a National Woodrow Wilson Fellow, the Bergen Fellow in Romance Languages, and a National Woodrow Wilson Dissertation Fellow. He is the author of *The Teachings of Saint Louis: A Critical Text* (1972), *Les Propos de Saint Louis* (1974), *Louis-Ferdinand Céline* (1976), *The Instructions of Saint Louis: A Critical Text* (1979), and *Michel de Saint Pierre: A Catholic Novelist at the Crossroads* (1990). He has edited more than 60 books in the Twayne's World Authors Series.